JAMES II

JAMES II

CHRISTINE McGLADDERY

Tutor in Scottish History
University of St Andrews

JOHN DONALD PUBLISHERS LTD
EDINBURGH

To my mother, my husband Henry, and in memory of my father, A. L. McGladdery.

ISBN 0 85976 304 8

British Library Cataloguing in Publication Data
McGladdery, Christine
James II
1. Scotland. James II, King of Scotland
I. Title
941.104092

Typeset by Pioneer Associates, Perthshire
Printed and bound in Great Britain by
Billings & Sons Ltd., Worcester

Foreword

It is at once surprising and understandable that Dr McGladdery's study of James II is the first full-length biography of the king — surprising because King James was the first Stewart ruler to succeed not only in passing on a secure legacy to his son, but also in greatly enhancing the prestige of his dynasty in north-western Europe; and he therefore seems an obvious and important candidate for biographical treatment. Yet his relative neglect is understandable, as Dr McGladdery shows, because the primary sources upon which such a study must be based are woefully inadequate, with the great contemporary chronicle — Abbot Bower's *Scotichronicon* — ending in 1437, the year of James II's accession, leaving only a few series of annalistic fragments to provide pointers to the events of the reign. Nor do official records help much; no records of royal council meetings exist, and adequate information about the decisions of parliament and its committees survives only from the later fifteenth century. While some idea of royal income may be gleaned from the exchequer records, these are incomplete, and the Treasurer's accounts — with one brief exception — do not survive before 1488. In the circumstances, the potential biographer of James II might well be tempted to emulate the old Highland minister who, in the middle of a reading from the Old Testament, remarked to his congregation: 'And now, brethren, we come to a difficult passage; and having looked it boldly in the face, we will pass on.'

Dr McGladdery has indeed looked James II boldly in the face; but fortunately she has not passed on, for her subject, in spite of the difficulties, is a fascinating one. Succeeding at the age of six, James II was the fourth Stewart king, the representative of a dynasty singularly lacking in prestige at home and abroad. His three predecessors had all been removed from the kingship by palace revolutions or assassination; and there was no question that James would be old enough to rule in person for at least a decade. Furthermore, there was the overriding problem of the powerful constraints placed on monarchical power by the Scots themselves, above all an aversion to regular royal taxation. James I's recent experiment in dynamic, intensive royal government had not been a conspicuous success, and his assassination in February 1437 not only thrust his son into the kingship while still a young boy, but also condemned the Scots to a long minority dominated in its first seven years by intermittent civil war.

This very inauspicious start makes the achievement of James II all the more remarkable. From his acquisition of real authority in the autumn of 1449,

v

shortly after his marriage to Mary of Gueldres and a little before his nineteenth birthday, he would reign for less than eleven years, being killed in an accident in 1460 at the age of only 29. Yet in that short space of time James II would not only destroy the most powerful of the great late mediaeval magnate families, the Black Douglases — personally stabbing the eighth earl to death in 1452 — but would largely succeed in raising the authority and prestige of the Crown to a point where, long before the end of the reign, his position at home was unchallengeable, and he was able to channel the warlike proclivities of the Scottish nobility — its key personnel transformed by royal patronage in the mid- to late 'fifties — into war with England. His early death, at the siege of Roxburgh in August 1460, was an appropriate end for a man who had made war for most of his short life, either on his own subjects or against the English. But the necessarily unanswered question — whether James II could ever have adapted himself to the ways of peace — casts some doubt on the king's overall achievement. The contemporary chronicler's complaint that, when raiding Douglas territory in the summer of 1452, James II indiscriminately harried the lands of friend and foe alike, is suggestive; and the mild rebuke directed at King James in March 1458, at the end of the last fully documented parliament of the reign, requiring him, as all rebels had been defeated and the realm was at peace, to attend to domestic justice, perhaps indicates members of the three estates attempting — none too successfully — to put the brakes on a ruler addicted to war.

In one respect at least we know more about James II than about any of his predecessors: we know what he looked like. The contemporary portrait of the king reproduced on the dust jacket of this book, taken from the diary of Jörg von Ehingen, an Austrian visitor to James's court in the 1450s, is the first accurate likeness of any Scottish ruler. A young man looks confidently ahead of him, his hands on a dagger at his belt, the whole of the right side of his face disfigured by the livid vermilion birthmark described at length by François Villon. Yet James II would surely have been pleased that the same French poet also remembered him as a major European ruler, and that his portrait was to be found in an Austrian diary together with, among others, those of the Kings of France and England. In European terms, the Stewart dynasty had 'arrived'.

Norman Macdougall
Series Editor

Acknowledgements

In the process of writing this book, I have benefited from suggestions, discussions and advice from many people who will, I hope, accept my warmest thanks even if not expressly mentioned by name, as that would involve a companion volume!

The Conference of Scottish Medievalists has provided an invaluable opportunity to seek advice and exchange ideas, and in particular, I would like to thank Mr Bill Scott for aiding the early days of my research with a copy of his list of references for unregistered royal charters, and Dr Alan Borthwick for his additions to that list and for some very helpful discussions arising out of his research on the council and administration of James II. Dr Jenny Wormald contributed some valuable suggestions on source material and the nature of the relationship between the king and his magnates, as has Dr Steve Boardman, whose many ideas and interpretations of fifteenth-century politics and social organisation have been responsible for a number of delays and revisions! I would also like to thank Michael Brown, working on the reign of James I, for a number of very helpful suggestions concerning the transition between the reigns of James I and James II. Discussions with Dr Colin Martin have greatly extended my understanding of the siege of Roxburgh, where James II was killed, and I am very grateful to him for allowing me to reproduce in this book one of his aerial photographs of the site.

I owe a great debt of gratitude to Dr Norman Macdougall who, having supervised my PhD. thesis, found himself enduring a re-run as editor of the Stewart Dynasty series. His unfailing patience and helpful guidance have been invaluable, and I thank both Norman and Simone for years of kindness and support. The quality of patience is also one possessed by John Tuckwell of John Donald Publishers, who has kindly endured my gross under-estimate of the time it would take me to write this book.

Finally, I would like to acknowledge the tremendous moral and practical support of my mother and sisters, Sharon and Katherine, and I thank my husband Henry for his unquenchable optimism and encouragement, which included the early purchase of a word processor to ease my task. For their suggestions on ways to improve the content of the book, I thank Lyndon Hallett and Kevin Philpott, both of whom have been studiously ignored!

Christine McGladdery

Contents

Introduction:
The King with 'the fyre mark in his face'

Amongst the Stewart monarchs before 1603, James II has attracted very little attention from historians. Part of the explanation for this lies in the fact that the written sources for fifteenth century Scotland are scanty and incomplete, and those which do survive are fraught with their own intrinsic difficulties. Professor Donaldson, in his study of James II, sums up the problems;

> After the death of James I, we enter on a period when reliable narrative sources are scanty and records still inadequate. Consequently, the very course of events is at times impossible to follow; it is hard indeed to detect any pattern at all; and above all, the motives which shaped the actions and policies of both the government and its opponents are so uncertain as to be unintelligible. It is all rather like watching a play in an unknown language, and watching it, too, by a rather fitful light: that is, we see only parts of the action, and the thoughts lying behind that action are concealed from us.[1]

While there is some justification for such a pessimistic view, it is, nevertheless, possible to make some sense of the complex events of James II's minority and personal rule. It was during the reign of James II that the Stewart dynasty, the line in direct descent from the first marriage of Robert II to Elizabeth Mure, finally established itself beyond all doubt and dynastic challenge. A potentially disastrous start to the reign, followed by a major conflict with the Black Douglases, the most powerful noble family in Scotland, was converted ultimately into the consolidation of the prestige of the royal house of Stewart, both at home and abroad, and although James II was killed when he was only twenty-nine years old, he managed, during his short life, to secure an enormous increase in royal power.

James II was a striking figure, whom contemporaries described vividly with reference to a large red birth-mark which covered the left-hand side of his face. The only contemporary chronicle source for the reign, known as the Auchinleck Chronicle, describes James II 'that had the fyre mark in his face', and the French poet François Villon, wrote:

> Semblablement, le roy Scotiste
> Qui demy face ot, ce dit on,
> Vermaille comme une emastiste
> Depuis le front jusqu'au menton.[2]

1

Fascinating confirmation of this description of the king exists in the contemporary portrait of James II which survives in a diary written by Jörg von Ehingen, a former page of James II's sister Eleanor of Austria. Von Ehingen's diary is a record of his extensive travels, and he had drawings made at each court he visited which were then painted as portraits on his return home. It was late in 1458 when he travelled to Scotland and had the drawing made of James II, depicted on the cover of this book, which shows clearly the red mark on the king's face.

The appearance of James II is thus well documented, but what of his character and abilities as a king? The only recent work which deals with the reign at any great length is Dr Annie Dunlop's *Life and Times of James Kennedy, Bishop of St Andrews*, in which she describes James II as having a strong and dominating personality with 'the gift of forming and evoking warm attachments, winning the loyalty as well as extorting the obedience of his disaffected subjects, and of holding the hearts and retaining the services of men who disapproved of his actions or had suffered at his hands'.[3] However, invaluable though this book is to any student of fifteenth-century Scotland, it is not, specifically, a study of the king, but of Bishop Kennedy. Dunlop was concerned to extol the virtues of the wise Kennedy, to whom she attributed a major counselling role at the court of James II, and the king, by implication, could not go far wrong as, 'thanks to Kennedy, the crown came to be identified with the cause of the common weal (good)'.

High praise indeed, but the accuracy of such a view has been challenged strongly by recent research which has shown that the importance of Kennedy's political role was more wishful thinking than fact, and that consequently, Dunlop's remarks about James II should be treated cautiously until the rest of the evidence is considered. A more censorious note is introduced into the discussion by Dr Ranald Nicholson, who disputes Dunlop's assertion that 'subtle callousness and sustained duplicity' were foreign to the nature of James II, a comment he supports by drawing attention to the aggressive stance of James in the contemporary portrait from Von Ehingen's diary.[4]

The vagueness of recent views of James II is well illustrated by the fact that most have been formed simply by comparing him with the demerits of his father, James I, and his son, James III. Dunlop states that James II had 'greater charm of manner than James I', and Professor Donaldson assessed James as having been more scrupulous than his father (apart from the murder of Douglas) and states that he had 'at no stage conducted anything like a reign of terror and he may have been trusted as his father had never been'. Donaldson's assessment of James II in *Scottish Kings* ends with the vague assertion that there is 'ample evidence of good intentions, and some of substantial achievement'.[5]

During James II's reign, the royal house of Stewart made a number of highly advantageous foreign marriages which benefited Scotland diplomatically and economically, and there is considerable evidence to suggest that the

Scots were not simply the poor relations of Europe, attracting little interest from the larger powers. Certainly, James II did not see himself in this light, foreign policy being an area to which he devoted considerable attention when he was not preoccupied with domestic affairs.

The major occurrence in the reign was the conflict between James II and the Black Douglas family, during which the king murdered the 8th Earl of Douglas. This notorious event, the background to which will be examined in depth later, has tended to colour views of James II and give the impression that the reign was one long catalogue of violence and mayhem. As Dr Jenny Wormald has observed, 'Nothing is harder to break through than the lingering idea that Scottish lords thought only of fighting and killing people, and to suggest that it is much more likely that they were interested in many other things as well and might even have enjoyed life for some of the time'.[6]

Violence and mayhem there was, but not to the exclusion of all else, and James II certainly did not pursue a policy of attacking his nobility and reducing their power in anything approaching the manner of his father. After the Douglas problem had been laid to rest with the forfeiture of the family in 1455, the king did, in fact, set about creating earldoms for selected loyal followers and he also helped to establish the honorific dignity of lord of parliament for members of the lower nobility who had demonstrated their fidelity.

Beyond politics, enjoyment of life was certainly indulged in, and a picture emerges of James II's interests and accomplishments. He was an active and mobile king, travelling extensively throughout the realm, thus fulfilling one criterion of mediaeval kingship — being seen in the localities. His son, James III, was to be criticised severely for his failure to do this. James II was also commended for his attention to justice and he proved energetic in warlike pursuits which, by mediaeval standards, made him an admirable monarch. James presided at tournaments at Edinburgh and Stirling and at a number of organised duels, and he indulged in the sporting and leisure activities of hunting, tennis and playing cards. Courtly entertainments included travelling players performing before the king at Christmas, and James was clearly interested in music, as there are references to a guitar and a pair of organs being commissioned for the king's use.[7]

However, James II's overriding passion was for artillery, and a number of cannon were sent to the king from the Duke of Burgundy in 1457, one of which was the famous Mons Meg, now at Edinburgh castle.[8] In 1455, the siege of Threave castle in Galloway involved the use of artillery, and the Auchinleck chronicler, describing the siege of Abercorn, refers to a 'great bombard' and also to 'a gret gun the quhilk a franche man schot richt wele'. This passion for artillery was to bring the reign of James II to an abrupt end at the age of only twenty-nine in an accident described by the historian, John Major, writing in the early sixteenth century:

Hereafter did James lay siege to the castle of Roxburgh which for a long time had been held by the English in Scotland; and he was over-curious in the matter of engines of war. For a wooden ball which formed the charge of a large engine of this sort, when it was shot forth, struck the king and killed him . . . a lesson to future kings that they should not stand too close to instruments of this sort when these are in the act of being discharged.[9]

NOTES

1. Donaldson, G., *Scottish Kings*, 79.
2. Chron. Auchinleck, f. 114v; *Le Testament Villon*, edd. J. Rychner and A. Henry (Geneva, 1974) i, 46.
3. Dunlop, A. I., *The Life and Times of James Kennedy, Bishop of St Andrews*, 208.
4. Nicholson, R., *Later Middle Ages*, 348.
5. Donaldson, op. cit., 95.
6. Wormald, J., *Lords and Men*, 93.
7. *E.R.*, vi.
8. See below, ch. 8.
9. Major, J., *History*, 386.

1

1437: Assassination at Perth

On the night of 20 February 1437, James I was murdered as he prepared for bed in his rooms at the Blackfriars of Perth. This act of violence brought the six-year-old son of the king to the throne of Scotland as James II and left a faction within the political community with the problem of establishing an acceptable corps of government to see the young king through the years of his minority rule. The violence which introduced it had considerable bearing on the reign of the young king and had its origins in the personal rule of his father during the thirteen years following 1424.

James I had returned to Scotland in April 1424, after eighteen years of captivity in England, to assume the active role of king in a country which had been governed since 1406 by his uncle, Robert duke of Albany, and cousin, Murdoch, the latter from 1420, following the death of his father. James I's release from England was conditional upon the payment of a ransom totalling £40,000 in English money, at the rate of 10,000 marks per annum. Such sums could not be raised outright, therefore twenty-one hostages from the Scottish nobility were to be provided as surety, and these were to stay in England at their family's expense, to be released or exchanged in the course of the payment of the ransom. The immediate problems facing the king on his return were therefore to establish his personal authority and to secure adequate finance with which to pay the ransom and provide for the expenses of his own court. Against this background, James I acted ruthlessly and aggressively towards certain members of the nobility, particularly the Stewarts, and he must have aroused considerable resentment through his determination to impose his authority unequivocally upon a realm grown unused to firm central control.

Following the death of David II, there had been a decline in the role of central government in Scotland with the nobility enjoying considerable freedom to administer and control their own areas. The Albany Stewarts, during the years of James I's captivity in England, were happy to exercise a comparatively relaxed style of government which made few demands or exactions on the political community, a situation which has to be appreciated in order to understand the resentment caused in some quarters by James I's return in 1424. The king's concern to exert and extend his influence into all aspects of the government of his kingdom must have appeared as grossly unwelcome to those who had enjoyed the benefits of non-interference. The king was keen to establish his position and punish those who hindered him in such a way as to earn him the reputation of being acquisitive and vindictive. The Albany Stewarts were James I's primary targets after his return to Scotland. Walter Stewart was arrested at once, although the king waited for a year before launching a more concerted attack on the family. The reasons for this were probably that James had to adjust to being back in Scotland and to prepare the ground for his plans, and also that he would have been wary about proceeding too suddenly and aggressively against the family when Murdoch's brother, John, earl of Buchan, was in France with Archibald 4th Earl of Douglas and a Scottish expeditionary force. Charles VII of France had rewarded Douglas for his help against the English with the duchy of Touraine, and James may have feared the possible repercussions of an attack on the Albany Stewarts when such a powerful Scottish contingent, sympathetic to them, and having the backing of the French, was abroad and in a position to respond. This dilemma was solved at the battle of Verneuil which took place on 17 August 1424, where John earl of Buchan, Archibald earl of Douglas and Douglas's second son, Sir James, were killed.[1]

James's vindictiveness towards the Albany Stewarts was not entirely unwarranted. It does not appear that Robert duke of Albany or his son Murdoch laboured with any great enthusiasm to secure the release of James I, and this must have rankled deeply with the king who feared that the Albany faction, close blood relations to James, aspired to the kingship itself. To be fair, the Albany Stewarts could do little more to secure the king's release as long as Henry V was determined to keep him in England, but James I had grounds to feel nervous about the situation in Scotland. The Stewart dynasty was comparatively new and the position of James I could hardly be considered unassailable because of the number of descendants of Robert II by his two marriages to Elizabeth Mure and Euphemia Ross, especially as there had been some controversy about the legitimacy of Robert's first marriage, from which line James I was descended. The earldoms of Fife, Menteith and Lennox came into royal hands through the forfeiture of the Albany Stewarts in 1425, and James set to work to build up the power, position and wealth of the crown for the remainder of his reign.

One of James I's initial measures to increase the wealth of the crown was the imposition of taxation; although this was a particularly unpopular measure, its impact has been much exaggerated, as his efforts to tax met with only limited success and occurred with nothing like the regularity of English taxation which had probably impressed the king during his captivity. The problem was not that taxation was outrageously onerous, but rather that the Scots were unused to it and saw it as the thin edge of the wedge of imposition and interference from central royal government. James was aware of the unpopularity of taxation and did not push it too hard, preferring to camouflage his demands with sporadic impositions of amercements and occasional special benevolences, for example to help finance his daughter Margaret's marriage to the Dauphin of France in 1436. Such measures were no more popular than taxation because they were 'not based on consent, arbitrary in timing, amount and incidence'.[2]

A far more dangerous course of acquisition, in terms of the resentment created, was the policy of confiscation. Following the fall of the Albany Stewarts in 1425, James acquired the earldoms of Fife, Menteith and Lennox. The earldom of Buchan was seized after the death of the Earl of Buchan at the battle of Verneuil,[3] and more dubious still was the seizure of the earldom of Strathearn from Malise Graham, who was sent to England as a hostage for the king's ransom. Partial compensation for this was offered in that Graham was given the title Earl of Menteith, although he received only some of the lands of that earldom. The Dunbar family lost the earldom of March in 1435 when the king, rather belatedly, overturned the decision made by the Albany government in 1409 to restore it following a temporary period of disgrace for the Dunbars,[4] and James' seizure of the earldoms of Mar and Garioch disregarded the prior claim of the Erskines.[5]

Acquisition of lands and titles by these methods was extremely unpopular and created a deep insecurity among the political community, whose co-operation was necessary for the efficient administration of the realm. At the same time as such policies of exaction and deprivation were being carried out, the king and the court indulged in a luxurious style of living, according to the standards of fifteenth-century Scotland, and this did nothing to diffuse the growing resentment of which James appears to have been aware. In 1428 and 1435, the king required the nobility to swear oaths of fealty to the queen as a precaution against anything happening to him, in each case prior to visiting the north — the lands of the 'wild scots'. James I may be seen to have identified with the lowlands more than any of his predecessors, and he rarely ventured into the Highlands. He based himself most often in Edinburgh and Perth, with frequent visits to Stirling and Linlithgow,[6] and when he did go north, his actions were heavy-handed rather than diplomatic. In 1428, James summoned the northern magnates to Inverness where he had them arrested. Alexander lord of the Isles was taken to Perth, but he escaped and vented his fury at the king by burning Inverness. The king's reaction was to imprison the Lord of the Isles in Tantallon in an effort to break his spirit and secure his submission.[7] Other members of the nobility also suffered imprisonment at the king's hands. Gilbert Kennedy and Archibald 5th earl of Douglas were imprisoned, albeit briefly, and Sir Robert Graham, the nephew of Malise Graham, was imprisoned in 1424. Douglas, who had married Malise Graham's sister, Euphemia, was suspected of intrigue with the English to secure the release of his wife's kinsman, whom James seemed content to leave as a hostage in England, but evidence was slight and no charges were brought. It is possible that James sought only to warn Douglas against the penalties of thwarting his will, but the incident must have left Douglas, a major Scottish magnate, feeling less than fond towards his king, and this ought to be borne in mind in view of Douglas's role as Lieutenant-General following the assassination of James I.

The general rejoicing at the birth of twin sons to James I and his queen, Joan Beaufort, on 16 October 1430 must have been accompanied by a sense of relief at court that the male succession was secured. These were the only sons born to James I, although he had six daughters. In his 'Scotichronicon', Abbot Bower tells us that the first of these twin sons was called Alexander, but that he died in infancy, thus leaving the younger twin, James, to succeed. Both sons, according to Bower, were made knights at their baptism along with the son of a Roman nobleman whom he names as Stephen Porcari, and two future Black Douglas earls who were to play crucial roles in the reign of James II — William, son of Archibald 5th earl of Douglas (mistakenly styled 3rd earl by Bower), who succeeded his father as 6th earl, and William, son of James Douglas, earl of Avandale (and, briefly, 7th earl of Douglas), who succeeded his father as 8th earl. A number of other sons of Scottish nobles were made knights on this day, and Bower names John, son and heir of Simon Logan of Restalrig, the son and heir of Sir William Crichton (who became chancellor to James II) and the son and heir of Sir William Borthwick.[8]

In addition to Bower's account of the birth of the twins, which was written in 1444, the anonymous writer of the Book of Pluscarden informs us that in Edinburgh,

> seeing that they were born in the monastery of Holyrood, bonfires were lighted, flagons of wine were free to all and victuals publicly to all comers, with the sweetest harmony of all kinds of musical instruments all night long proclaiming the praise and glory of God for all his gifts and benefits.[9]

This picture of general rejoicing and devotion masked a rising tide of resentment and unease caused by the aggressiveness of the king, and this was demonstrated during the Roxburgh campaign of 1436. In contrast to his son, whose passion for artillery and warfare led him into the field on a number of occasions, James I was a relatively inexperienced military commander, but in August 1436, he led an expedition to Roxburgh with the intention of re-capturing the castle from the English. The campaign was a fiasco. The Pluscarden chronicler relates that there was 'detestable schism and most wicked division';[10] the lid seems to have lifted off the boiling pot of resentment and dissatisfaction when the nobility assembled in one place, and James was forced to abandon his plans to attack the castle. If this incident sounded warning bells, then the king failed to heed them as, in the general council assembled at Edinburgh in October, James passed measures which, rather than placating the nobility and diffusing their anger, threatened still further their individual privileges. In the area of criminal justice, ransoming or fining for theft was not to be undertaken by sheriff, baron or lord of regality — a deprivation of revenue — and special franchises of burghs or regalities were not to obstruct sheriffs and justiciars in collecting crown revenue.[11]

These were the foundations laid by James I by the Christmas of 1436 when the court established itself in Perth for the festive season. There was no popular rebellion against James I, but he had pushed far enough for a small but determined group to conclude that the only solution was his removal. Two descriptive accounts exist of the assassination of James I, one by John Shirley and the other by Piero del Monte. Shirley was an Englishman who wrote a version of events leading up to and immediately following the death of James I, several years after the event, from a Latin source which has since been lost. Piero del Monte was a Venetian sent to England by the papal curia as a collector of the papal tenth in 1435. His letter to the pope, which he wrote in London only one week after the murder, gives a version of the assassination, the source of which, del Monte claims, is a letter sent by Queen Joan to her uncle, Cardinal Beaufort.[12]

The principal actors in Shirley's account of the murder are Sir Robert Graham and Sir Robert Stewart, in league with Christopher and Thomas Chambers, two brothers named Hall and two Barclays of Tentsmuir. Shirley states that Graham, a political idealist who abhorred James' tyrannical methods, confronted the king in parliament and exhorted him to better government. In this, Graham evidently felt that he was voicing a widely held opinion, and he asked for the backing of those present for what he had to say. No support for him was forthcoming from the three estates, however, and he was exiled.[13] Shirley associates Graham and his grievances with the Stewarts of Atholl. The eldest son of Walter Stewart earl of Atholl, David, was one of the hostages sent to England in 1424 and he died, still in captivity, in 1435. The earldom of Strathearn had been conferred on Walter earl of Atholl in 1427, but only in life-rent, therefore his heir would not inherit, but it would revert to the crown when he died. As Atholl was an old man, this appears as a cynical device to camouflage James' acquisition of Strathearn,[14] but this, coupled with the death of his father, was not calculated to endear James to Atholl's grandson and heir, Sir Robert Stewart. The theory of a dynastic motive for the assassination of James I has been argued against,[15] but it is worth noting that it was not until 1430 that the queen gave birth to twin boys, only one of whom survived, and prior to that, Walter earl of Atholl was heir presumptive to the king, after James I's daughters, Margaret and Isabella.

Bower states that the king had begun a general council at Perth on 4 February 1437 (although no record of this exists), and Shirley informs us that the king and queen were staying in the Dominican friary and that Sir Robert Stewart 'did ever abide yn the kynges presence, full famulier aboute hyme at all houres and most privey above all other'.[16] Sir Robert Stewart was certainly chamberlain of the royal household at the time, and as such was responsible for the king's domestic arrangements. Shirley states that Stewart laid planks across the ditch surrounding the friary on the night of 21 February 1437 to facilitate the entry of the conspirators.

If Bower is correct that the General Council started on 4 February, it is unlikely still to have been in session, and the conspirators would have had no trouble assessing the time and place when the king was most vulnerable. The murder of the king would have caused considerable commotion, but armed assistance was slow in coming and only one man, Sir David Dunbar, brother of the Earl of March who had been dispossessed by James I, is said to have pursued the assassins when they fled from Perth north to the Atholl lands.[17] Confusion undoubtedly accounts for the slowness of the response, and the assassins must have felt that once it was accepted that the tyrant James was dead and a regency government was needed, Walter earl of Atholl would be the obvious choice to head the council. The problem posed by the murder of James I is not that anyone should want to do it — motivation abounds — but what made the conspirators imagine that they would get away with it to the extent that the political community would accept their actions. Had they anticipated a groundswell of support which would condone the murder and allow them to form a governing faction, or did these men simply not see or care beyond the removal of a man who had become so loathsome to them?

There has been a tendency to rush ahead to the crowning of James II and the execution of the conspirators as if it were a natural and untroubled progression of events following the assassination. In fact, the evidence suggests that the aftermath of the murder was a time of chaos and confusion in which the different factions struggled to gain the upper hand, and many must have waited, uncommitted but watchful, to see the outcome. Possession of the young Prince James was vital, and one of the queen's first actions after the murder of her husband must have been to head for Edinburgh and secure possession of her son. The assassination took place on 20/21 February, but the young James II was not crowned until 25 March. This delay may have been prompted by the fear of a dynastic motive for the assassination which would necessitate the removal of the young prince, but as Duncan points out, apparently this was not a motive attributed to the conspirators by contemporaries, and Bower states that the Earl of Atholl's aspiration was to 'achieve the governance of the realm . . . so that at least he himself might be considered to be a colleague of the future king'.[18] In the normal course of events, Atholl would have been the obvious choice to head a minority government as the most senior member of the nobility in line for the crown after the young king. He was not involved directly in the assassination of James I, although he admitted that he had been aware of the plot, and he must have felt that the king had made himself unpopular to such an extent that his removal would be condoned by the majority of the political community and that he would be required to help set up the minority government. This was a miscalculation. With the possession of the prince, the queen's faction managed to rally enough support to go on the offensive and round up the conspirators, although this was not accomplished immediately, but took some time and effort.

Shirley states that Sir Robert Stewart and Christopher Chambers were the first to be taken, and the severity of the punishments meted out to them (of which Shirley gives gruesome details) has been attributed to the vengeful influence of the queen. Certainly she was present when the assassins burst in to murder her husband and was herself wounded in the attack, therefore it would seem hardly surprising if her wrath were terrible. In addition, the initial executions were intended to serve as an example and a deterrent to any still wavering in their allegiance to the queen's faction. The Earl of Atholl was arrested by the Earl of Angus after the execution of his grandson, according to Shirley's account, and notwithstanding the fact that he declared that he in no way condoned or sought the death of the king, he was beheaded. It is perhaps significant that he did not suffer the horrible tortures and death of the other conspirators, and this may reflect the amount of guilt attributed to him at the time, although the queen's faction would have been reluctant to leave him alive as a focus of discontent for their rivals for power. By contrast, Sir Robert Graham and others who were held to be involved in the plot were taken to Stirling. The court was in Stirling on 3 May 1437,[19] and it is likely that the execution of Graham, who had been in captivity 'with many other traitours of his coveene',[20] occurred at this time. Shirley describes the protracted execution of Graham which was obviously intended to serve as the ultimate example for those contemplating treason and rebellion, but although all the executions are described in the space of a few pages, there is enough evidence to suggest that they took place over a period of time during which the final outcome cannot have seemed to be a foregone conclusion. According to the *Extracta*, James II was crowned by Michael Ochiltree, Bishop of Dunblane, which is a further indication of the lack of evident supremacy exercised by the queen's faction, as the Bishop of Dunblane was hardly the most influential or important of the Scottish prelates.

The earliest document of the minority, dated 7 March 1437, is a charge delivered by the government (presumably, the queen's faction) to the community of Perth to fortify the burgh as a result of the murder of James I.[21] This charge was issued from Edinburgh and indicates, at the very least, that there was concern about possible trouble from the Atholl lands to the north of Perth, and lends weight to the argument that Scone, the traditional site for Scottish coronations, was not considered safe enough for the crowning of the new king. James II was crowned at Holyrood on 25 March, and a parliament was held in Edinburgh at that time during which some of the chief conspirators were tried and executed, and some decisions would have been made concerning the administration of the realm. There is no surviving documentary evidence for the terms under which the minority government of James II was set up, and much of it has to be inferred from a later document known as the 'Appoyntement' of 1439.[22] According to this document, the queen had been recognised as custodian of her children with an allowance of 4000 marks for maintenance, and a council was appointed, the purpose of which was to assist the queen with such duties as controlling policy and patronage and making domestic appointments. The very lack of surviving evidence may be indicative of turmoil and administrative breakdown, and with the chancellor, Bishop Cameron, abroad at the time of the murder, some time would have elapsed before his return to throw in his lot with the queen's party and help in forming the minority government. There may, in fact, have been little more than an *ad hoc* arrangement made by a small group, including the queen, who had secured control of the king.

The most likely members of the initial court faction would have been those men who were at the heart of the council of James I and whose names appear on the earliest documents of the reign of James II, scant though these are. John Forrester of Corstorphine continued in the office of chamberlain. William Crichton as master of the king's household and Walter Ogilvy as treasurer. The Earl of Angus helped to round up the conspirators in the assassination and would have been an important member of the queen's faction. It is not clear exactly when Archibald 5th earl of Douglas was made lieutenant-general, but it cannot be taken for granted that it was an office he held at the outset of the minority. The Earl of Angus died in October 1437, and it may have been at this stage that Douglas was given the post of lieutenant-general. In 1430, Douglas had been temporarily imprisoned, by James I, and although he had been released and left unchallenged for the remainder of the reign, he was not particularly active at court. His uncle, James Douglas of Balvenie, had been an active supporter of James I, and with their widespread territorial possessions the Black Douglases were in a powerful position in 1437. A reference is made to Douglas being granted a payment of £60 as part of his fee in the office of King's lieutenant in the exchequer account covering the period 18 July 1437 to 16 July 1438,[23] and it is conceivable that he was granted this office after the death of Angus created a weakness in the queen's party which she sought to fill with an outwardly powerful earl who could give an aura of respectability to her bid for ultimate political control. A tradition had been established that the holders of the office of lieutenant-general were heirs to the kingship,[24] and with the death of James I and the young age of James II, Archibald 5th earl of Douglas was next in line. The establishment of Douglas in the office of lieutenant-general was not an automatic assurance of unchallenged power of policy-making resting in his hands, and the fact that a council appears to have been appointed to assist the queen may have been a reflection of the three estates' desire to retain ultimate control should the lieutenant-general appear to be abusing his office.[25] That Douglas was not an initial choice is suggested by the lack of references to him in the few remaining documents for the period, even where there are detailed witness lists. Before the death of James I, Archibald Douglas appears to have maintained a low profile and was less active at court than his uncle, James Douglas of Balvenie. By November 1437, James Douglas was styled

Earl of Avandale, a title which he may have been granted through the influence of the queen, courting Douglas support after the death of Angus. In view of later events, it would not be surprising if Balvenie were seizing the opportunities for advancement offered during the turmoil of the aftermath of James I's assassination — there is no question of his bursting from nowhere on to the political stage in 1440. In the two years during which Archibald 5th earl of Douglas held office, there is little evidence of his efficacy, and the sixteenth-century chroniclers such as Lesley and Buchanan relate a number of picturesque tales which, whatever the accuracy of their details, convey the impression of continuing faction struggles well after the crowning of the king.

NOTES

1. I am indebted to Michael Brown for pointing out the connection between Verneuil and the timing of James I's attacks on the Albany Stewarts.

2. Duncan, *James I*, 23.

3. *Scots Peerage*, i, 148, 264.

4. *A.P.S.*, ii, 23.

5. *A.B.Ill.*, iv, 165, and see p. 20 below.

6. Nicholson, *Later Middle Ages*, 314.

7. Ibid., 315.

8. Bower, W., *Scotichronicon*, ed., D. E. R. Watt, Book XVI, 263.

9. *Liber Pluscardensis*.

10. Ibid., i, 380.

11. *A.P.S.*, ii, 22–24.

12. Weiss, R., 'The Earliest Account of the Murder of James I', *E.H.R.*, vol. 52, 479–491.

13. Shirley, *Life and Death*, 50.

14. Nicholson, *Later Middle Ages*, 322.

15. Duncan, *James I*, 22.

16. Shirley, *Life and Death*, 52.

17. I am indebted to Michael Brown for his help in assessing the problems of James I's assassination, and for information he has shared with me arising from his own research into the reign of James I.

18. Bower, *Scotichronicon*.

19. *R.M.S.*, ii, no. 201 — misdated to 1439.

20. Shirley, *Life and Death*, 63.

21. *P.S.A.S.*, 33: 425.

22. See page 18.

23. *E.R.*, v, 12.

24. For a discussion of previous lieutenant-generals, see McGladdery, C. A., 'Crown-Magnate Relations in the Reign of James II of Scotland, 1437–1460' (Unpublished Ph.D thesis, University of St Andrews, 1987), 36–40.

25. General-Councils were certainly held regularly between 1438 and 1443 — at least nine, according to the records, although exactly who attended is not always recorded.

2

Confusion and Compromise, 1437–44

James I's aggressive removal of certain members of the higher nobility, particularly the Stewarts, contributed to the fact that, by the time of his assassination, their ranks had been depleted dramatically. At the start of James II's reign, once those involved in the conspiracy and murder of James I had been tracked down and executed, the only adult earls remaining in Scotland were Archibald, 5th earl of Douglas, William Douglas, earl of Angus and David Lindsay, earl of Crawford. (The earls of Sutherland and Menteith were in England as hostages for the ransom of James I.) Three adult earls in Scotland were remarkably few; at the beginning of the fourteenth century there were thirteen Scottish earldoms, with four new ones created between 1306 and 1437, when James II succeeded, and although numbers fluctuated with forfeitures and failures of lines, the average number was between eight and ten.[1] The Earl of Angus died in October 1437, leaving a son who was only eleven years old, and Archibald earl of Douglas died in 1439, leaving a son who was only fifteen. This unprecedented power vacuum in the ranks of the leaders of the traditional political community played a crucial part in the turbulence of the early years of the young king's reign.

If we cannot form a clear picture of what was taking place from official documentary evidence, then it is at least possible to draw conclusions from the evidence of unrest and dissent which appears to have characterised the early years of the minority. The removal of the energetic and authoritarian James I opened the way for the pursuit of claims which had lain suppressed but not forgotten in the minds of the aggrieved, for example, the Darnley claim to the earldom of Lennox.[2] Sir Alan Stewart, lord Darnley was in France heading the Scots mercenaries there when news of the murder of James I reached him. Darnley's mother, Elizabeth, was the younger daughter of the late Duncan earl of Lennox, but while the Albany Stewarts were in control, Darnley had little hope of realising his ambition because they also had a claim through the elder daughter, Isabella. James I had not been willing to recognise Darnley's claim, therefore his death must have appeared to Darnley as a golden opportunity to press forward with his claim to at least half of the earldom. The manner in which Darnley pursued his case is not clear, but according to the contemporary Auchinleck chronicle, on 20 September 1438, 'Allan Stewart lord Darnley was slane at polmais thorne be Sir Thomas Boyd

14

under an assouerance taken betuix tham'.[3] In the following year, on 7 July, 'schir Thomas Boyd was slane be Alexander Stewart buktuth and his sonnis and Mathow Stewart with his brother and uther syndry'.[4] It would seem that a collision of interests had occurred, as a result of Darnley's Lennox ambitions, which had involved him in a blood-feud with Boyd of Kilmarnock. No more was heard in this reign of the Darnley claim to Lennox.

This was not an isolated case, and the response of the government to disputes and claims was a statute made in general council in November 1438 which attempted to deal with the problem by revoking all alienations of lands and moveable goods in the possession of the late king at the time of his death if made without the consent of the three estates. Also, any future alienations made during the king's minority and considered to be 'in preiudice or hindering of the croune' were prohibited.[5]

The immediate political problems were compounded at this time by a severe outbreak of those twin scourges of mediaeval society, plague, followed by famine. The Auchinleck Chronicle states that the plague began in Dumfries and 'It was callit the pestilence but mercy for thar tuk it nain that ever recoverit bot thai deit within xxiiii houris'.[6] Following hard on plague and famine came civil disorder with the government attempting to deal with the problem of violent raiding and spoliation in the general councils held in November and December 1438.[7] The problem was still an issue in March 1439 when a general council held at Stirling tried to deal with the problem both of civil disorder and troublesome claimants seeking a forceful remedy for their grievances. Animosity between the Crichton and Livingston factions may have led to the ordinance passed at this general council which dealt with 'rebellys or unrewlfull menne within ony castellys or fortalicis'.[8] Crichton was established in Edinburgh castle at this time and Livingston may have felt that such an ordinance could be used against him if necessary. However, issuing ordinances was one thing and having them enforced effectively was quite another, and it was a blow to an already beleaguered government when the lieutenant-general, Archibald earl of Douglas, himself fell victim to the plague and died at Restalrig in 1439.

In the midst of all these problems which beset those trying to govern Scotland after the assassination of James I, changes had been taking place at court as political power struggles got under way, the most notable of which was the replacement of John Cameron, bishop of Glasgow, by Sir William Crichton as chancellor.[9] To understand the political manoeuvring of the minority, the position and actions of the two families of Crichton and Livingston are crucial. The rise to prominence and the subsequent vying for position of these families could have been possible only in a minority, especially when the most powerful representative of the nobility, the Earl of Douglas, had died leaving a successor who was only fourteen or fifteen years old, and had neither the maturity nor the political experience for the office of lieutenant-general.[10] The next adult male in line for the crown was Malise

Graham, earl of Menteith. He had been sent to England in the second exchange of hostages in October 1427 and was to be the longest-serving hostage, as he was not released until 1453. The denuded state of the higher nobility as outlined earlier explains the failure to appoint another lieutenant-general, but another factor was the evident willingness of Livingston and Crichton to govern without one.

Sir William Crichton had found favour at the court of James I, succeeding Walter Ogilvy in the recently created office of Master of the King's Household.[11] He had been a frequent charter witness and had also been granted the custody of Edinburgh castle which brought him a revenue of £100.[12] In addition to this, James I made Crichton sheriff of Edinburgh. Crichton continued to witness charters and hold the office of Master of the King's Household at the beginning of the reign of James II, and by 10 July 1439, he had succeeded in obtaining the office of chancellor.[13]

Sir Alexander Livingston of Callendar was a Lothian baron who had served as a hostage for James I at Durham in 1424 and was also present at the trial of the ex-governor, Murdoch, duke of Albany in the following year.[14] Beyond these references to him, however, Livingston does not seem to have been prominent under James I and the rise of the Livingstons during the minority of James II is the more remarkable for having the appearance of occurring out of the blue. Alexander Livingston was keeper of Stirling castle early in the minority of James II and the Livingston family were to base their power and influence on the holding of various offices and strongholds which they acquired systematically during the minority. It is difficult to discover the Livingstons receiving direct patronage, but they must have been encouraged in the advancement of their position. It may be that the queen was responsible for aiding the Livingstons, perhaps because she found Crichton less biddable than she had hoped for a man who had owed so much to the patronage of James I. This is certainly the impression conveyed by Lesley and Buchanan in their sixteenth-century histories, and it was their positions as keepers of Edinburgh and Stirling castles, respectively, which formed the keystone of Crichton and Livingston power in the early years of the minority and played an important role in the mutual rivalry between the two families.

A high degree of opportunism characterised the actions of a number of members of the Scottish nobility during the king's minority and the reasons for this ought to be briefly examined. The dearth of earls meant that the influential figures in both national and local politics were the lesser nobility who became known as the 'lords of parliament'. It has been assumed that James II was responsible for the creation of these lords, and he did indeed create a number of lords of parliament in 1452. However, Dr Grant has shown that there were already twenty-one lords of parliament in Scotland by that time, at least eighteen of whom appear before the end of 1445, when James II was still a minor. It is most likely that these men simply adopted the peerage title of lord, encouraged, no doubt, by the fact that Chancellor Crichton was styling himself William lord Crichton by 1439. Those who adopted the titles were active in government to the extent that they turned up at general councils or at court, where they witnessed charters, and they were the men to whom parliamentary summonses would have been sent.[15] The denuded state of the ranks of the upper nobility also encouraged the rise of the lords of parliament, as, in the absence of earls, it was the lords' importance within their own localities which gave them their political influence. The co-operation of the lords of parliament was vital to the crown, and the growth of this rank would have been encouraged by those who sought their support during the troubled years of the minority when Livingston and Crichton were vying for position.

It is on the subject of the mutual jealousy with which the Crichtons and the Livingstons regarded each other that the sixteenth-century chroniclers, when writing about the reign of James II, recount a series of picturesque stories, the most enduring being that of the queen smuggling her son out of Edinburgh castle without Crichton's knowledge and taking him to Stirling, held by Livingston, who promptly proposed to besiege Crichton in Edinburgh castle.[16] The contemporary Auchinleck Chronicle makes no mention of this, but the itinerary of the young king, calculated by dates and places of issue of royal charters and letters, shows that James II was in Edinburgh on 10 July 1439 and in Stirling one month later, on 13 August.[17] By this time, the lieutenant-general was dead and Cameron had been supplanted by Crichton as chancellor, therefore the queen may have felt isolated and considered that her interests would best be served by allying herself to Livingston. Stirling castle had been assigned to the queen as a residence and she would normally have had her children there with her unless Crichton had chosen to be obstructive, regarding the possession of the king's person as necessary to gain him a crucial advantage in the struggle against Livingston.

It is worth noting that the later chroniclers date the supposed smuggling of the young king from Edinburgh before the death of the lieutenant-general, as it was the very animosity of Douglas to both parties, according to the story, that caused Crichton and Livingston to reach a compromise and join together in defence against Douglas.[18] If the queen did experience any feelings of isolation, these are likely to have prompted her marriage to Sir James Stewart of Lorne, known as 'the Black Knight of Lorne', probably at the end of July 1439.[19] James Stewart was the younger brother of Robert Stewart, lord of Lorne, who had succeeded his father in the lordship in 1421. Of the career of his brother, James, nothing is known and he does not appear to have been active at the court of James I. However, the marriage indicates that the queen had grown dissatisfied with her alliance with the Livingstons or, at least, did not consider it to be adequate protection for her interests, and James Stewart must have been viewed as a sufficient threat to prompt Sir Alexander Livingston to react to the marriage by imprisoning the queen, her new husband and his brother.[20] The king was in Stirling at the time,[21] therefore

Livingston could be reasonably sure of the strength of his immediate position, but what exactly he hoped to gain by his action in the long term, if he was acting independently, is not clear. It is possible that Livingston had been alarmed to learn of the queen's marriage, and he may have felt that it was aimed to reduce his influence in some way. Drastic action may have seemed the only way to retain the initiative and underline his position of advantage both to Sir James Stewart, should he entertain any ideas of involving himself in government, and Chancellor Crichton. Incurring the undoubted animosity of the queen seems to have been a risk he was prepared to take, and while this may highlight the increasing weakness of the queen's faction, it may also indicate that Livingston was sufficiently secure in the knowledge that he had powerful backing for his actions. James Douglas, earl of Avandale, had been at court in Stirling on 13 August 1439, and was present on 4 September when the queen's release was negotiated.[22] It is possible that Avandale had maneouvred himself into a powerful position following the death of his nephew, the Lieutenant-General, and was concerned at the possibility of the queen rebuilding her faction and providing a block to his ambitions.

The popular reaction to the imprisonment of the queen and her husband and brother-in-law may well have been alarm at such a precipitate action, and Livingston himself must have realised that such a state of affairs could not be prolonged indefinitely and that some solution had to be found. On 4 September 1439, a general council met in Stirling at which the three estates negotiated the queen's release in terms known as the 'Appoyntement'.[23] At the same council, according to the Auchinleck Chronicle, 'Sir James was borowit (pledged security for) be the lord Gordon sir Alexander Setoun, (Alexander) lord of the Isles, Sir William of Crichton that tyme chancellor under the pane of thre thousand'.[24] The terms of the queen's release were very favourable to Livingston, who still appeared to hold the upper hand. Queen Joan was seen to declare that Livingston and his accomplices had been motivated by 'grete truth and leaute (loyalty)', and she professed to forget the 'griefe and displeasance' caused by her arrest. Also, in order to demonstrate the faith and trust she had in Livingston, she entrusted the young king to his keeping in Stirling and granted to him the 4000 marks annuity previously given to her at the start of the minority, and although she was to be allowed access to her son, her retainers were to be scrutinised and vetted by the Livingstons. Sir Alexander Livingston was obviously aware of the hollow nature of the 'Appoyntement' and realised that he must maintain a strong position or suffer for his actions. As a further attempt to insure himself, he sought the assurance of the queen and her adherents that they would never try to bring the Livingstons 'neirar the deede'.[25] A cryptic note appears in the Auchinleck Chronicle which has been taken, mistakenly, to refer to Mary of Gueldres, the queen of James II, but is, in fact, a reference to Joan Beaufort.[26] The entry is a continuation of a longer passage, the beginning of which has been lost, and reads:

. . . of the law and the kingis proffettis and of all the Realme and that the king suld come be him selfe and his and the queen be hir self and hirris bot the king suld ay remane with the queen. Bot scho suld nocht Intromet with his proffettis bot allanerlie with his person.[27]

This almost certainly forms part of the Auchinleck Chronicler's report of the events of September 1439 and reflects the political impotence of the queen at this time, but the lack of censure of the Livingstons by the general council certainly argues a measure of support from some powerful members of the political community, and Avandale would be a likely protector. The young 6th Earl of Douglas, who had succeeded his father at the age of only fifteen, appended his signet to the Appoyntement, this being the only occasion in the extant official records where he appears. The sixteenth-century chroniclers make much of his haughtiness and ambition, and it may be that James earl of Avandale saw his great-nephews as a stumbling block to his own carefully laid aspirations.

This was far from being the end of the story, and a new twist in the tale occurred very soon after the concluding of the Appoyntement with the dramatic abduction of the young king while out riding near Stirling, by Crichton with a band of armed followers, who thwarted Livingston's plans by taking James II back to Edinburgh castle before Livingston could do anything about it. This story is related by the sixteenth-century chroniclers,[28] but official records bear it out to the extent that on 18 September 1439, royal charters in the name of James II were issued in both Stirling and Edinburgh, and thereafter the court appeared to be established in Edinburgh.[29] Crichton may have been worried by the apparent strength of Livingston's position and was afraid that he would suffer unless he acted quickly to secure the king, who was the most important pawn in the minority chess game. However, this was not a clear-cut case of Livingston being ousted from government by a neat Crichton coup, as charter witness lists reveal the presence at court in Edinburgh of Alexander Livingston, which suggests, at the very least, a more amicable arrangement than the chroniclers would imply — or perhaps it was the tacit acceptance by Livingston of a *fait accompli*.[30]

The uncertainty and instability at court at this time precluded the government from taking effective measures to deal with the unrest which persisted, to some extent, in the localities. With the exception of a general council held in Stirling in August, the court remained in Edinburgh throughout 1440. In this council, the problem of law and order was recognised and an attempt made to deal with it. It was ordained that justiciars should hold ayres twice a year and the king should, where possible, be involved. With a high degree of optimism but rather less realism, it was also suggested that the king should 'ride throu oute the realme . . . quhar ony rebellione, slauchter, byrnyng, refe, forfalt or thift happynis'.[31]

On 19 August 1440, the same General Council attempted to find a temporary solution to the long-running dispute over the earldom of Mar. In 1402, Isabel countess of Mar and Garioch was widowed and childless, and her title to the earldom of Mar was coveted by Sir Alexander Stewart, the illegitimate son of Alexander Stewart, earl of Buchan, the fourth son of Robert II. According to legend, Stewart had captured Isabel and compelled her to marry him and to draw up a charter on 12 August 1404 which entailed the joint earldoms of Mar and Garioch upon himself and his own heirs, should Isabel die without bearing him a child.[32] However, Thomas Erskine, lord of that Ilk, also claimed the earldom of Mar by right of descent from Gartnait earl of Mar who had died in 1305.[33] On 20 December 1400, Thomas Erskine had made an indenture with David Lindsay, earl of Crawford, in which Crawford pledged his support for Erskine's claim to Mar.[34] Stewart's charter could not be validated without the king's ratification and this was withheld. However, on 9 December 1404, another charter was drawn up which granted Alexander Stewart a liferent of the earldom with remainder to the heirs of Isabel, and this duly received crown confirmation.[35] Despite obtaining a re-grant of the earldom of Mar on 28 May 1426 to himself, his illegitimate son, Thomas, and the heirs male of Thomas, Alexander was unable to ensure heritable possession, as his son predeceased him without issue, and upon the death of Alexander in 1435, James I claimed the earldom, as the 1426 re-grant contained the stipulation that the earldom would revert to the crown in the event of the failure of Alexander Stewart's line.[36] The earldom of Mar was annexed to the crown and Elizabeth Douglas, sister of Archibald 5th earl of Douglas, was given Garioch in life-rent.[37] Elizabeth had been married, first, to the Earl of Buchan and afterwards to Thomas Stewart, and it was on this marriage that Elizabeth's claims to Mar and Garioch were founded, albeit tenuously. However, the Lieutenant-General was her brother and this put Elizabeth and her third husband, William Sinclair earl of Orkney, in a strong position for advancing their claim.

The rival Erskine claim was based on the terms of the charter issued on 9 December 1404, which made Sir Robert Erskine (son of the Thomas Erskine of the 1400 indenture) heir of line to Isabel. Alexander Stewart died in July 1435 and on 17 November following, an indenture was made between Sir Robert Erskine, lord of that Ilk, and his son, Thomas, on one part, and Alexander Forbes, lord of that Ilk, on the other. Forbes undertook to assist Robert and Thomas in pursuit of their right to the earldoms of Mar and Garioch in return for certain specified lands.[38] The chances of Erskine persuading James I to relinquish the earldom of Mar in 1435 were virtually non-existent, but with the murder of the king in February 1437, the opportunity arose to revive the claim. On 22 April 1438, a special retour was held before Alexander Forbes, then sheriff depute of Aberdeen, which found in favour of Robert Erskine as heir to Isabel countess of Mar and Garioch 'now in the hands of lady Elizabeth, Countess of Buchan, spouse of the deceased Sir Thomas Stewart on account of conjunct infeftment thereof made by James I to Thomas and Elizabeth'.[39]

On 16 October 1438, another retour before Alexander Forbes served Erskine to the other half of the earldom of Mar as lawful heir of Countess Isabel, and in June 1439, Robert Erskine, now styling himself Earl of Mar, granted a charter to Alexander Forbes of half of the lordship of Strathdee.[40] It must have been apparent to the government that some action had to be taken to neutralise Erskine's claims, as the act of parliament passed in 1438 which prohibited the alienation of crown lands during the minority did not seem to be enough to quell Erskine's persistence; on 10 August 1440, an indenture was made at Stirling between the king and his council on one part, and Robert lord Erskine on the other, which stated that Erskine was to have the keeping of Kildrummy castle, the chief messuage of the earldom of Mar, for the duration of the king's minority. In return for this, Robert Erskine was to deliver Dumbarton castle to the crown.[41] If the members of the government involved in this indenture supposed that this arrangement would serve to shelve the dispute, they were mistaken. On 28 March 1441, a protest was made on behalf of Sir Robert Erskine 'called Earl of Mar' that a retour of the lands of Garioch had been given to the chancellor, Sir William Crichton, but that Crichton maintained 'that he did not have the retour, nor did he know where it was'.[42] Such a weak excuse did nothing to pacify Erskine, and on 2 May 1442, an instrument was drawn up narrating a decree, obtained from the lords of the king's council, to the effect that William lord Crichton, chancellor, should either grant letters of sasine in favour of Erskine of the earldom and lands of Garioch, or return his retour endorsed.[43] The principal witnesses to this instrument were the bishops of St Andrews, Glasgow and Dunblane. However, Crichton apparently remained intransigent, as Sir Robert Douglas quotes from a document, now lost, which had been in the Mar charter chest, dated 9 August 1442, which described Robert lord Erskine's protest before the king and his council in Stirling, against chancellor Crichton, that he had refused to retour him to the lordship of Garioch and give him possession of Kildrummy.[44] Consequently, Erskine seized the castle of Kildrummy by force, in retaliation for which the government seized Erskine's castle at Alloa.[45] Given Erskine's anger at the failure of Crichton to fulfil the terms of the indenture, the question arises whether or not Erskine had honoured his pledge to surrender the castle of Dumbarton to the government, and the dispute which arose in 1443 would suggest that he had not. According to the Auchinleck chronicler, on 15 July 1443, Sir Robert Semple, sheriff depute to Sir Robert Erskine, was put out of the castle of Dumbarton by Patrick Galbraith 'beand in the ower (outer) bailze havand the entre be him selfe at wallace towre and the k(ep)ing of the ower bailze'.[46] In this account, a dispute arose when Sir Robert Semple ejected Patrick Galbraith from the castle, but the latter managed to reverse the situation on the following day. The eventual outcome, on the evidence of the Exchequer Rolls, was that Robert Livingston of Callendar was given custody of the castle until 1449.[47] Patrick Galbraith's name appears on an indenture made between Robert Erskine earl of Mar and

Alexander lord Forbes in 1439.[48] The name William Semple, possibly a relative of Robert Semple, also appears, therefore it is clear that both men in the Dumbarton dispute were connected with Erskine. In an effort to wrest Dumbarton from Erskine's control, the government may have suborned Galbraith, as he was certainly rewarded out of the royal revenues for 'his services in the castle of Dumbarton' before Robert Livingston, who was one of the custumars of Edinburgh, took control.

There followed a temporary respite in the dispute with the government, and the next couple of years witnessed the various claimants to the titles and possessions of the earldoms of Mar and Garioch seeking to come to terms with one another, and to strengthen their own positions. On 26 March 1444, an indenture was made at Perth between Robert Lyle of Duchal, who claimed half of the earldom of Mar by right of his descent from a younger co-heiress of Isabel countess of Mar, and Sir Alexander Forbes.[49] By this indenture, Lyle granted to Forbes his lands of Strathdee and Kindrochit, with his part of the castle of Kindrochit, as soon as he should recover possession of half of the lands of Mar. In return, Forbes granted to Lyle heritable possession of the lands of Cluny and Whitefield in Strathearn and Angus. Forbes had already received half of the lordship of Strathdee from Robert lord Erskine in 1439, and it is clear that he was seeking to capitalise on the eagerness of the Mar claimants to court his support in his capacity as an influential member of the local nobility and an active lord of parliament. However, Forbes was aware that such agreements as had been reached in the course of the dispute would not necessarily stand unchallenged, and the indenture includes the proviso that he would regain free entry to his lands of Cluny and Whitefield 'gyffe it sale happyn in ony tyme to cum that our Soverane Lorde the Kyng recover or take the forsaide landis of Mar fra the saide Robert or fra his ayris'.[50] Robert lord Erskine also sought an agreement with Robert Lyle, and on 11 June 1444, an instrument was drawn up which sought a contract between Erskine and Lyle upon the excambion (exchange) of the lands and earldom of Garioch 'in the same form as the Earl (of Mar) made to the Countess of Orkney'.[51] There is no surviving record of a contract with the Countess of Orkney, but on 16 June, an instrument was given narrating the offer, on behalf of Robert Erskine 'earl of Mar and Garioch' to William earl of Orkney that agreements should be completed between the two earls for the excambion of the lands of Garioch and that the Earl of Mar would pay 110 marks annually to the Earl of Orkney. The latter replied that he would complete all such agreements made between them and Robert Lyle of Duchal.[52] This seems to have been as far as the claimants were able to progress at this stage and the Mar dispute settled into a period of stalemate which was not to be broken until 1448.

Confrontation between those who exercised power in the minority government and members of the nobility was not limited to the Mar dispute. The most dramatic event of the minority occurred in 1440 when Crichton and

Livingston, apparently working together, turned their attention to the young William 6th earl of Douglas, the son of the late lieutenant-general. The sixteenth-century chroniclers, Buchanan and Pitscottie, both state that William had proved haughty and ambitious, and that he was at the root of the breakdown of law and order in the country.[53] However, the boy was scarcely more than sixteen years old and there is no evidence for his involvement in government beyond the appending of his signet to the 'Appoyntement' in 1439,[54] or of his having caused problems for the government. On 24 November 1440, Earl William, his younger brother David and their close adherent, Sir Malcolm Fleming of Biggar and Cumbernauld, were entertained to dinner in Edinburgh castle, following which the two Douglases were seized and executed on the grounds of treason, although no specific charges survive and they were not forfeited.[55] Sir Malcolm Fleming was executed also, but not until the following day, presumably to allow time to form the sentence of forfeiture which was passed against him.

The motives for Crichton and Livingston taking this action remain obscure. If it was concern at the size and power of the Douglas earldom and the fear that William was a threat to their own power, then to execute him was an effective, if extreme, solution to the problem. However, his younger brother, David, was also executed and this meant that the Douglas inheritance went to the boys' great-uncle, James Douglas of Balvenie and Abercorn, who had been created Earl of Avandale in 1437 following the murder of James I.[56] Consequently, Crichton and Livingston, instead of having to deal with Douglases scarcely more than children, faced the prospect of a mature earl inheriting, if not all, then at least a large proportion of the wealth of lands and titles which formed the entailed Douglas estates. Had James Douglas chosen to revenge himself on the two perpetrators of what became known as the 'Black Dinner' for the killing of his kinsmen, then Crichton and Livingston would have faced a problem immeasurably greater than the supposed threat of an arrogant youth.

It is very unlikely that Crichton and Livingston took this action independently, and the involvement of the Earl of Avandale is suggested strongly by his subsequent actions. James, as 7th earl of Douglas, showed no inclination for revenge. Instead, he set to work to consolidate his newly elevated position, and it is worth noting that although the two boys were executed as traitors, no sentence of forfeiture was passed against them. However, Malcolm Fleming had been sentenced to forfeiture before his execution and it was the new Earl of Douglas who took it upon himself to placate Fleming's son and heir by ensuring that he was permitted to succeed to the forfeited lands, and also by giving one of his own daughters in marriage to Sir Robert Fleming.[57] That Crichton and Livingston should have aided James Douglas suggests a measure of influence which may have been at work for some time. With his stronghold of Abercorn castle by the Forth, he was a powerful magnate in the central belt of the country, and he may have exerted some control over the Livingstons, which would help to explain their advancement and their boldness in eschewing the support of the queen.

James 7th earl of Douglas wasted no time in building up the territorial power of the Douglases once more. The Dukedom of Touraine and the other lands in France which had been acquired by the 4th earl were beyond recovery because there were no male Douglas heirs in the direct line, and similarly, the lordship of Annandale had lapsed to the crown. The lordships of Galloway and Bothwell, however, were not completely beyond recovery as they had been inherited by the sister of the 6th earl, Margaret Douglas; and James realised that a marriage between her and his son and heir, William, would re-unite the lands, although this scheme was not fufilled until after the 7th earl's death.[58] James Douglas's own lands and possessions included the earldom of Avandale, lands in Banffshire, Inverness-shire, Buchan and Moray, and his castle of Abercorn on the Forth. In the short period during which he held the earldom of Douglas, he managed to secure the earldom of Moray for his third son, Archibald, although by rather dubious means. In 1429, James Dunbar, earl of Moray died leaving his two daughters, Janet and Elizabeth, as co-heiresses. The elder daughter, Janet, had married James Crichton, the eldest son of Chancellor William Crichton, and it was to the younger daughter, Elizabeth, that Archibald Douglas was married. Nevertheless, Archibald was styled Earl of Moray, and to give this move the semblance of legality, Douglas managed to secure an entail which excluded Janet Dunbar.[59]

Another area in which James earl of Douglas was able to gain influence was in the lordship of Dalkeith. On 22 May 1441, Sir James Douglas of Dalkeith had been declared incapable of discharging his duties due to mental incapacity, and letters were issued by the government placing James Gifford of Sheriffhall, Douglas of Dalkeith's brother-in-law, as custodian.[60] However, James Douglas of Dalkeith's younger brother, Henry, tried to capitalise on the situation by seeking to gain the estates himself. James earl of Douglas was Henry's father-in-law,[61] therefore he was undoubtedly more than an interested observer, especially as the lordship of Dalkeith was granted to him on 6 September 1442.[62] Douglas came into conflict with the Crichton family over the lordship of Dalkeith, the second occasion since he became earl that their interests had clashed. Douglas had crossed the chancellor's son, James Crichton, over the earldom of Moray, but on this occasion, it was the chancellor's cousin, George Crichton, who may have felt threatened by the actions of the earl of Douglas. The Crichton connection arose from the marriage of George Crichton to Janet Borthwick, the widow of Sir James Douglas of Dalkeith, and when Dalkeith's eldest son, James, had been declared insane in May 1441, Crichton undoubtedly hoped to benefit through his wife's tenure of the barony of Morton.[63] Crichton was never successful in obtaining control of Dalkeith, even after the death of the 7th earl of Douglas, as in 1444, the custody of Dalkeith passed to Patrick Cockburn, himself a Douglas adherent.

Under Douglas influence, £122 15s 5d was expended on Dalkeith in 1444–5.[64]

The extent of Douglas infiltration into all facets of Scottish political life was not confined to the secular arm. The 7th Earl sought to establish Douglas influence in the church and was aided in this by the schism which was affecting the Roman church at the time. The Scottish church exercised considerable power which was not confined to ecclesiastical matters alone; when James I returned from England in 1424 and proceeded to establish his authority, he treated the church as a department of national life which had to be well ordered and function for the good of the realm. It was vital for the church to be seen working with rather than against the monarchy, and to achieve this James had to have the co-operation of his bishops. In 1424, John Cameron was secretary to James I, shortly afterwards obtaining the post of keeper of the privy seal. When the see of Glasgow fell vacant in 1425 Cameron was elected with the king's backing and despite initial obstruction, Pope Martin V consented to the provision on 22 April 1426. The upward spiral of Cameron's career did not stop there as, by May 1427, he was formally styled chancellor. Cameron's political career was influenced by James I's relationship with the papacy, and the king lost no time in enunciating his policy in parliamentary legislation. In 1424, one act of parliament forbade churchmen to go overseas or send procurators without the express permission of the king, and another put a tax of 3s 4d on each £ worth of gold or silver exported from the realm. A parliamentary commission of 1424 forbade churchmen 'to purchess ony pensione out of ony benefice'. This extension of secular control was carried still further when an act was passed in the parliament held in March 1428 which ordained that any cleric who wished to leave the realm should first approach his bishop or the chancellor (Bishop Cameron) and 'schaw to thame gude and honest cause of his passage and mak faith to thame that he do no barratry'. No precise definition was offered for this new offence of barratry, but it signified the purchase of benefices, or pensions from benefices, at the papal curia. The matter came to a head when William Croyser, archdeacon of Teviotdale crossed swords with Cameron in a dispute over jurisdiction, and by the spring of 1429, he had brought developments in Scotland to the attention of Pope Martin V, representing, rather vindictively, that it was Cameron as chancellor, rather than James I, who was the instigator of the barratry legislation. The Pope could not ignore such a charge and it was concluded that Cameron was responsible for the act of the Scottish parliament 'against ecclesistical liberty and the rights of the Roman church' and was 'so guilty as to deserve deprivation'. In the summer of 1430, an embassy travelled to Rome from Scotland to defend Cameron and cite Croyser to appear before the Scottish parliament, but by this time Croyser was firmly established as the pope's man. This did not alter with the death of Martin V in 1430 and the election of the new pope, Eugenius IV.

These tensions continued for some years and, ultimately, were played out against the backdrop of the Little Schism. On 14 November 1431, the Council

of Basle held its first full session. The Scots were represented, albeit
unofficially, by Thomas Livingston, abbot of Dundrennan, who adhered
consistently to the conciliar movement, although James I made no official
overtures to the council until 1434. On 18 December 1433, the pope revoked
his dissolution of the Council, which led to a period of tacit peace between
the council and the papacy during which representatives could be sent
diplomatically to Basle. On 8 February 1434, Bishop Cameron was
incorporated into the Council, but unfortunately for him, so too was his
adversary, William Croyser, who lost no time in attacking the legislation
passed in Scotland which he regarded as anti-papal, but this time he extended
the attack to the king himself. Consequently, Croyser was denounced in
parliament in January 1435 and deprived of his benefices and revenues,
although the Pope continued to support him and added a demand for his
reinstatement to the call for the revocation of the objectionable barratry
legislation. King James I had been requesting that a papal legate be sent to
Scotland to discuss church reforms. This was refused, but in the autumn of
1435, Aeneas Sylvius (the future Pope Pius II) travelled to Scotland, ostensibly
to discuss the projected diplomatic alliance between Scotland and France,
but doubtless also to press the pope's demands. Bishop Cameron continued to
urge the king's request for a papal legate, but the price of this concession was
that Cameron had to act as a scapegoat. In March and April 1436, the pope
issued two bulls, one of which attacked Cameron and insisted upon the repeal
of the anti-papalist legislation, while the second demanded the reinstatement
of Croyser. In the summer of 1436, the pope finally despatched the Bishop of
Urbino to Scotland as papal nuncio, although Cameron was compelled to
remain in Rome. When the nuncio arrived in Scotland, James was able to
plead the absence of the man responsible for the controversial statutes and
both sides were able to save face in arriving at a settlement of the dispute,
with Cameron drawing the diplomatic fire. He could at least console himself
with the fact that most of that fire consisted of blanks — there was no obvious
diminution of his position either at home or at the papal court, and during this
period Cameron is referred to in papal records as 'papal assistant and
referendary'. The barratry laws remained unrepealed, but were generally
unenforced, and on 28 December 1439, Cameron was officially pardoned. In
February 1437, the situation in Scotland altered dramatically with the
assassination of James I, and Cameron returned to Scotland by the summer of
that year. He was prominent in the council formed at the beginning of the
minority of James II as he retained his post of chancellor thanks to the
support of his former patron, Archibald 5th earl of Douglas, who became
lieutenant-general. The triumvirate of Douglas, Cameron and Queen Joan did
not hold the reins of power for long. By May 1439, Cameron had been ousted
from the chancellorship by William Crichton. Douglas died the following
month and the queen was imprisoned in August after her marriage to James
Stewart of Lorne. After the sons of the lieutenant-general were executed in

1440 and the earldom of Douglas passed to their great-uncle, James earl of Avandale, Cameron's connection with the former lieutenant-general's household was sufficient to earn the hostility of the new Douglas faction. On 3 March 1441, Cameron was attacked vehemently in a petition sent to the pope in the name of James II, stating that

> John bishop of Glasgow, a son of perdition . . . is not immune from the damnable deeds of certain other traitors, his associates and adherents . . . to the prejudice of the king, then in his tenderest age, and of the kingdom. Later, he audaciously presumed to make a most treasonable conspiracy against his majesty and, with several others of the king's council, to plot to the death and to proceed in the guilty conspiracy.[65]

If the object of this attack had been to remove Cameron completely from both government and the bishopric of Glasgow, then his enemies met with only limited success. He remained as Bishop of Glasgow until his death on 24 December 1446 and he even continued to witness charters and appear in general councils, but as a major political figure, Cameron was finished, and he could no longer be regarded as an influential spokesman even for church affairs.

The man at the root of Cameron's decline was the 7th Earl of Douglas, who endeavoured to gain a foothold in church affairs by trying to have his second son, James, provided to the bishopric of Aberdeen, exploiting the schism within the church to do so. Cameron was succeeded at Glasgow by James Bruce, who had been transferred from the bishopric of Dunkeld on 3 February 1447, but he died before 4 October that year. He was succeeded in turn by William Turnbull, who achieved an influential position through constant papal and royal service. He had studied at St Andrews and Louvain, and during the Little Schism, when Pope Eugenius IV was courting support, Turnbull became papal chamberlain and was attached to the pope's household. He returned to Scotland in 1440 and was acting as keeper of the privy seal by 6 August — a position on the council second only to chancellor.

After the eclipse of Cameron there was a hiatus in Scottish ecclesiastical policy as there was a lack of firm direction. In common with James Kennedy, bishop of St Andrews, Turnbull was a consistent papalist and the ecclesiastical policy expressed in parliamentary legislation shows that this attitude was dominant in spite of sporadic opposition from secular sources — primarily the Douglases — who sought to exploit the schism for political reasons. In a meeting of the three estates in 1441, it was ordained that 'no Scot may go to Basle, adhere to the council or obey it', but this declaration did not prevent the ensuing struggle over conflicting provisions to benefices. The pope, Eugenius IV, provided Alexander Lauder to Dunkeld, Thomas Tulloch to Ross, Ingeram Lindsay to Aberdeen and John Hectoris to the Isles, and Felix (the conciliar pope) provided Thomas Livingston to Dunkeld (Eugenius had deprived him of the abbacy of Dundrennan for his consistent adherence to the Council), Andrew Munro to Ross and the sixteen-year-old James Douglas, son of the 7th earl, to Aberdeen.[66] None of the Council's appointments held, and in July 1442, a council of the Scottish church, which consisted, effectively, of the papal appointees, deprived and excommunicated those provided by Felix. This move incurred the wrath of James earl of Douglas, who had thrown in his lot firmly with the conciliarists. On 31 August 1442, the Earl of Douglas wrote to Basle and in October, William Croyser appeared there and joined with Thomas Livingston in persuading the Council to support Douglas. Scotland never adopted a policy of adherence to the conciliarists to any great extent, and the main support for the Council came from the universities. James 7th earl of Douglas died in March 1443 and his son William, who succeeded as 8th Earl, concluded that the Council was doomed to failure and, in the general council held in Stirling on 4 November 1443, it was ordained that 'ferme and fast obedience be kepit till our haly fadir the Pape Eugenne' and that 'na persone, spirituale na temporal, change the said obedience quhil the king and the realm ordane and decrete therapone'. Turnbull had taken part in the Scottish church council's decision to excommunicate all Scotsmen still supporting Basle, the first occasion that he had come into conflict with the Black Douglases, and this conflict continued when Turnbull became Bishop of Glasgow.

William, the new 8th earl of Douglas, rapidly assumed a very active role in government, and it was natural that he should turn his attention to the positions of William lord Crichton and Sir Alexander Livingston. Livingston and Crichton were still witnessing charters side by side until at least 6 August 1443, but on that date, Crichton appeared as chancellor for the last time until 1447, although the first reference to James Bruce, bishop of Dunkeld, Crichton's successor as chancellor, was not until 7 September 1444.[67] It is curious that the office of chancellor, the most important officer of state, appears to have lain vacant for the best part of a year, but there is a dearth of records and documentary evidence for this year, therefore it is impossible to form any clear impression of the functioning of the government at this time. The apparent eclipse of Crichton saw a corresponding strengthening of the Livingston position. On 16 August 1443, Sir Alexander Livingston dissociated himself by a pledged oath in the presence of Sir Robert Fleming, James Kennedy, bishop of St Andrews, John Cameron, bishop of Glasgow, James Bruce, bishop of Dunkeld and Michael Ochiltree, bishop of Dunblane, from any complicity in the murder of Malcolm Fleming.[68] In this, the Livingstons appeared to be clearing the way for an open alliance with the Douglas faction, and this in turn led to an attack on Crichton. William lord Crichton, although no longer chancellor, was still in possession of the crucial stronghold of Edinburgh castle, but rather than launch an attack on him there, which would be unlikely to meet with much success, George Crichton, William's cousin and sheriff of Linlithgow, was dealt the first blow. On 20 August 1443, only four days after Livingston's pledge, the Auchinleck chronicler writes that William earl of Douglas

> came to bernetoun (Barnton) in Lothian with ane gret ost and with him the forsaid kingis counsall beand with him and his houhald and schortlie he askit the hous on the kingis behalf and schew the kingis lettres . . . and suthlie Andrew Crichton than beand thair in captain answered sayand that the hous was in the kingis hand and Nicol of Borthwick and James of Crichton war under burrowis to the shiref Sir William Crichton and thai put in be him on the kingis behalf.[69]

Despite this plea, the Earl and his forces remained at the house for five days, after which Douglas 'schew the kingis banere' and the garrison agreed to surrender on condition that they and their goods would be spared. Following the casting down of the house of Barnton, the Douglas's next move was to have the Crichtons summoned before the king. A General Council was held in Stirling at the beginning of November 1443 'in the hender end of the quhilk counsall thai blewe out on Sir William Crichton and Sir George of Crichton'.[70] The battle lines had been drawn and Crichton retaliation was speedy, with Sir John Forrester of Corstorphine being first to feel the brunt. Sir John, who had been chamberlain to James I, was clearly associated with the Douglases at this time and he had taken part in the attack on Barnton. His own lands were situated between Barnton and Edinburgh, and it was this fact which led to the attack on Forrester property by the Crichtons as the easiest form of retaliation, although their revenge also took them further afield to damage Douglas lands and possessions. The Auchinleck chronicler writes that the Crichtons 'tuke away Sir John Forrester's gudis that is to say schepe and nolt (cattle) and syne Sir George tuke the erll of Douglas' horses and brynt his grangis of Abercorn and Strabrok and uthir five placis and brynt the samyn tyme the blak nestis (Blackness)'.[71]

There is a considerable gap in the official records from November 1443 to July 1444 which makes it impossible to trace in detail the developments in this conflict, and frustrating though this is, it does in itself show a high degree of turmoil in government with some breakdown in administration. However, as we emerge from the patchy fog of our understanding of these months, it is clear that crucial political changes had taken place at court, not least of which was the apparent consolidation of the House of Black Douglas as the controlling faction.

NOTES

1. Grant, A., 'Earls and Earldoms in Late Medieval Scotland' (c. 1310–1460), in *Essays Presented to Michael Roberts*, edd. J. Bossy and P. Jupp (Belfast, 1976).
2. Fraser, *Lennox*, i, passim.

3. Chron. Auchinleck, f. 109r.

4. Ibid. Alexander Stewart was the younger brother of Alan. The other brother was called John, therefore Matthew may have been a cousin. Fraser, *Lennox*, op. cit.

5. *A.P.S.*, ii, 31.

6. Chron. Auchinleck, f. 109v.

7. *A.P.S.*, ii, 31–2.

8. Ibid.

9. *R.M.S.*, ii, no. 201, 202.

10. *S.P.*, iii, 170.

11. *Coupar Angus Charters*, i, 68 — 28 August 1432.

12. *E.R.*, iv, 607.

13. *R.M.S.*, ii, no. 202.

14. Livingston, E. B., *The Livingstons of Callendar* (E.U.P., 1920).

15. Grant, A., 'The Development of the Scottish Peerage', passim.

16. Lesley, J., *The History of Scotland from the Death of King James in the Year 1436 to the Year 1561*. (Bannatyne Club, 1830), 13; Buchanan, G., *The History of Scotland*, transl. J. Aikman (Glasgow, 1827), vol. ii, book xi, ch. iii, f. iv.

17. *R.M.S.*, ii, no. 202, 203.

18. Lesley, *History*, op. cit; Buchanan, *History*, op. cit; Pitscottie, *Historie*, 17.

19. The Queen's arrest and imprisonment on 3 August 1439 is said to have taken place a few days after the wedding. Chron. Auchinleck, f. 109r; *E.R.*, v, 53.

20. Chron. Auchinleck, op. cit. The Auchinleck chronicler names James Stewart's brother as William, but this is clearly a mistake, as James Stewart's brothers were called Robert, Alexander and Archibald. *S.P.*, v, 3.

21. *R.M.S.*, ii, no. 204.

22. *R.M.S.*, nos. 203, 204.

23. *A.P.S.*, ii, 54.

24. Chron. Auchinleck, op. cit.

25. *A.P.S.*, op. cit.

26. Macdougall, N., 'Bishop James Kennedy of St Andrews: a reassessment of his political career', in *Church, Politics and Society*, ed. N. Macdougall (Edinburgh, 1983), 19.

27. Chron. Auchinleck, f. 121r.

28. Lesley, *History*, 16; Buchanan, *History*, f. xi.

29. *R.M.S.*, ii, no. 206, 207.

30. Ibid., no. 208 — 13 October 1439.

31. *A.P.S.*, ii, 32.

32. Crawford, *Earldom of Mar*, i, 173–6.

33. *S.P.*, v, 578–9.

34. S.R.O., GD 124/7/3.

35. Crawford, op. cit., 194–217.

36. *R.M.S.*, ii, no. 53.

37. *E.R.*, v, 55.

38. *A.B.Ill.*, 188–9; S.R.O., GD 124/1/137.

39. S.R.O., GD 124/1/138.

40. S.R.O., GD 124/1/142; RH1/2 no. 215.

41. *A.B.Ill.*, 192.

42. S.R.O., GD 124/1/149.

43. Ibid., 151.

44. Douglas, *Peerage*, 467.

45. *Spalding Misc.*, v, 262–3.

46. Chron. Auchinleck, f. 110r.

47. *E.R.*, v, 145–6.

48. *A.B.Ill.*, 189–90. Semple's name also appears on an instrument dated 11 June 1444 — S.R.O., GD 124/1/155.

49. *A.B.Ill.*, 194.

50. Ibid.

51. S.R.O., GD 124/1/155.

52. Ibid., /156.

53. Lesley, *History*, 15; Buchanan, *History*, f. xv; Pitscottie, *Historie*, 40; Chalmers of Ormond, *Ane Cronickill of the Kingis of Scotland* (Maitland Club), 1830.

54. *A.P.S.*, ii, 54.

55. Chron. Auchinleck, f. 121r.

56. *Handbook of British Chronology*, 469.

57. Fraser, *Douglas*, i, 446.

58. *Calendar of Papal Letters*, x, 130–1.

59. *A.B.Ill.*, iii, 231–2. This would not have endeared him to the Crichtons.

60. *Morton Registrum*, ii, 219.

61. Dunlop, *Kennedy*, 36.

62. Dunlop, *Kennedy*, 37.

63. Dunlop, op. cit., 59.

64. *E.R.*, v, 180–2, 146–7, 150, 180.

65. *Calendar of Scottish Supplications to Rome*, iv, series ed., I. B. Cowan (Glasgow 1983).

66. Watt, *Fasti*, 3. These provisions were made in April and May 1441.

67. S.R.O., GD 26, Sec. 3, no. 1083; *R.M.S.*, ii, no. 273.

68. *Wigtown Charters*, 29.

69. Chron. Auchinleck, f. 110v.

70. Ibid.; *A.P.S.*, ii, 33.

71. Chron. Auchinleck, op. cit.

3

The Sons of James the Gross, 1444–49

The energetic determination of James 7th earl of Douglas (known as James the Gross because he was so fat)[1] to spread the influence and control of his family was inherited wholeheartedly by his son William, who succeeded as 8th earl. William was a frequent and assiduous attender at court and witnessed more charters in the course of the reign than any other earl, even though his political career was a comparatively short one, being limited to the years 1444–1452. The pre-eminence of the Black Douglases was unmistakeable. In the parliament of June 1445, William's brothers were prominent. Archibald Douglas appeared as Earl of Moray and Hugh Douglas as Earl of Ormond (a dignity created for him out of his sister-in-law Margaret's patrimony in Aberdeen and Inverness).[2] John Douglas, the youngest brother, was infeft in Balvenie, his father's lordship in Banff. The manoeuvring which had taken place prior to the convening of the 1445 parliament has to be inferred from evidence which, though lamentably scant, provides fascinating clues.

A general council is recorded as meeting on 4 November 1443 in Stirling, and although there may have been a subsequent meeting before 1445, no record of it survives.[3] A letter from the king to Sir Alexander Home of that Ilk, dated 13 November 1444, refers to events which took place 'at the last' general council.[4] This appears to refer to a council held in 1444, possibly on or around 16 October, the king's fourteenth birthday, but for which the proceedings have been lost. From the Home letter it appears that the king's majority had been declared at the general council; the letter was an assurance to Sir Alexander Home that his land rights would be unaffected by this declaration and indicates that a general revocation was to take place sometime in the future. The political changes which took place in 1444–5 may be connected directly with the ascendancy of William earl of Douglas, and events lend weight to the view that James II's majority had been declared in an attempt to legalise the actions of the faction which controlled him. On 29 November 1444, the king himself appeared at the siege of Methven castle.[5] This castle had been granted by Robert II to his son Walter, earl of Atholl and became crown property on Atholl's attainder. It is possible that it was being held by an adherent of Sir William Crichton, but the siege was successful, the castle was taken and subsequently committed to the keeping of Alexander Livingston, second son of Sir Alexander Livingston of Callendar.[6]

A further indication that changes had taken place at court is to be found in a set of coronation oaths which purport to be those used by the parliament of 1445.[7] These oaths appear in a manuscript which belonged to Sir James Balfour of Denmilne and may be traced back to a fifteenth-century manuscript written by James Monynet in 1488. Earlier coronation oaths, including those taken in England and France, show a preoccupation with the privileges of the church and orthodox religious practice, but the 1445 oaths have a different emphasis, their overriding themes being justice and law and order — themes which were very much to the fore in 1445 when the instability at the centre of government in the early minority had led to widespread disorder, and the three estates were struggling to re-impose a measure of control.

A parliament had been held in Edinburgh at the start of the king's minority, in March 1437, when James II had been crowned,[8] but for the duration of the minority, until the king took over direct control following his marriage in 1449, all consultative and representative assemblies were general councils, with the single exception of the parliament held in Perth in 1445. On 14 June 1445, legislation was passed 'tuiching the landis quhilkis our soverane lordis fadir had in peacabill possessione the day of his deces',[9] but this was the only piece of legislation enacted at Perth, as on 28 June the parliament was continued to Edinburgh. The short stay at Perth, where the three estates had been instructed to assemble, may be explained if the coronation oaths found in Balfour's manuscript were imposed upon the king at this time, perhaps at Scone, the traditional site for the coronation of Scottish kings. The king had been only six years old at the time of his coronation at Holyrood in 1437, but in June 1445 he was almost fifteen, and better able to take oaths which could be made to mark the end of his minority, in theory if not in fact. The declaration of the king's majority by such means was undoubtedly a cynical move to strengthen the position of the faction led by the Earl of Douglas, which then had control of the king, and to lend an air of legitimacy to any attack on their political opponents.

The list of those who attended the July 1445 parliament shows a heavy Douglas influence, and the adjournment to Edinburgh was effected because of the siege of William Crichton in Edinburgh castle.[10] It would appear that negotiations had already been in progress before the arrival of the three estates, and the Edinburgh burgesses played an important part in securing a settlement.[11] In the first week of July, William Crichton surrendered on terms, although it is not clear exactly what the terms were. There was no question of Crichton being in absolute disgrace, as he was restored to government and witnessed charters on 1 and 3 July, but did not recover the office of chancellor.[12]

Douglas and his faction did not have everything their own way, as there was some resistance to the changes which had taken place at court, displacing those who felt entitled to participate directly in policy making, most notably the queen mother and James Kennedy, bishop of St Andrews. The previous year, on 17 November, they had issued letters of inhibition forbidding any payments to be made out of the revenues of Aberdeen 'to tha persownis that now has the Kyng in gouernance'.[13] On 20 November 1444, the Aberdeen magistrates declared that they would await the decision of the three estates on the matter, reflecting caution on their part and some confusion over who really exercised power at that time. Aberdeen appears to have been a storm centre during the minority of James II, and although this may be a somewhat artificial picture attributable to the tendency of Aberdeen officials to be particularly vocal in their complaints and protests, or to the accident of survival of Aberdeen burgh records, it is worth considering the conditions under which Aberdeen functioned as an indication of the general state of confusion in the country.

The burgh of Aberdeen had courted the patronage of a local nobleman, Alexander Irvine of Drum, in the hope that he would offer protection to the burgh, and in October 1440, he was invested with the title of captain and governor.[14] He held the office for two years, but the experiment does not seem to have been a successful one as, in 1442, the citizens of Aberdeen were commanded to take arms in support of the magistrates and council, the town was strengthened and fortified by the building of walls, the ports were kept shut each night, and every day, thirty men were chosen from the citizens of the town to act as an armed guard to prevent surprise.[15] This nervousness seems to have been prompted by mistrust of the local nobility, and in 1445, the Aberdeen council agreed unanimously that no lord should be chosen as captain of the burgh, and no such office was revived. In 1447, the council would not permit tacks of the town to be held by lords, and the sub-letting of fishing tacks applied to anyone 'except lordis'.[16] Disorder continued to such an extent that on 3 November 1445, the king wrote to the Bishop of Moray stating that there was to be no hosting or weapon-showing except at direct royal command and not at the command of the Bishop of Moray or the Earls of Moray and Huntly.[17] Even as late as January 1447, James II sent a letter in which he instructed Lord Keith to collect the revenues rightfully belonging to the king and stated that the Bishop of Aberdeen was to content himself with the tenth penny![18] However, it must have been virtually impossible to enforce law and order when the Earls of Ross and Crawford — justiciar and sheriff of Aberdeen respectively — violated the law themselves. Opportunism was rife.

By 1445, William earl of Douglas had managed to build up an impressive list of allies. He regarded the network of offices held by the Livingston family as potentially useful; and Douglas was prepared to work with the Livingstons, which does much to explain the eclipse of the Crichton family at this time. Sir James Hamilton of Cadzow appears to have been a staunch supporter of the Black Douglases, although his immediate connection with the family was through his marriage to Euphemia Graham, eldest daughter of Patrick Graham, earl of Strathearn, and widow of Archibald 5th earl of Douglas. This marriage must have taken place by 25 February 1441 when a dispensation in favour of James Hamilton and Euphemia Graham was issued by Pope Eugenius IV. In view of the evidence suggesting that James the Gross had been involved in the 'Black Dinner' in 1440, it seems strange that Euphemia should be content to see her husband an active supporter of the branch of the Black Douglas family which had benefited from her sons' deaths. Although her daughter, Margaret 'Fair Maid of Galloway', was married to William 8th earl of Douglas, the marriage did not take place until 1443, which may indicate that the family of the 6th Earl were dragging their feet in spite of pressure from the powerful new Douglas Earl. Hamilton's advancement took place in the minority of James II and would have owed much to Douglas influence and patronage. James Hamilton, lord of Cadzow, attained the rank of knighthood before August 1440,[19] and on 3 July 1445, he received a charter erecting all his lands and baronies into a lordship to be called the lordship of Hamilton.[20] By the same writ, issued in the June parliament of 1445, he was created a hereditary lord of parliament and took the title Lord Hamilton.[21] James Hamilton's mother was Janet Livingston, daughter of Alexander Livingston of Callendar, therefore he had strong connections with the Douglas faction during the king's minority.

The first clear connection between William 8th earl of Douglas and the Earl of Crawford (a connection which was to prove crucial later) occurs in an indenture made on 30 October 1445 between William earl of Douglas and Jean Lindsay.[22] Jean Lindsay was the daughter of David earl of Crawford and had been married to William 6th earl of Douglas, who was put to death in Edinburgh castle at the 'Black Dinner' of 1440. The terms of the indenture were that Douglas promised to assist Jean Lindsay to recover 'her terce of Anandirdale' in return for resigning all other right and claim she might have to Douglas possessions through her late husband. Annandale was unentailed and therefore lapsed to the crown rather than passing to James the Gross when he inherited the Douglas earldom as the next male in line. It appears that the 8th Earl of Douglas was seeking to neutralise any possible claims to Douglas lands or property arising from the Douglas-Lindsay marriage by offering his support in the pursuit of the recovery of Annandale, although there is no evidence of his having taken the matter further.

The Douglases were a complex family, and it is worth examining their relationship with other members of the nobility who bore their name. The Earls of Angus were the descendants of the 2nd earl of Douglas, although through an illegitimate line, and they are distinguished from the main line — the Black Douglases — by the title of Red Douglases. The rise in power and influence of the Black Douglas line led to an attempt to overshadow the Red Douglases at court. William 2nd earl of Angus did not long outlive James I, as he died in October 1437 and was succeeded by his son, James, who was only eleven years old. On 18 October 1440, James 3rd earl of Angus was betrothed to James II's sister, Joanna,[23] but in 1445, she was sent with her sister Eleanor to France, indicating that a marriage was being sought for her in Europe and that Angus was not sufficiently in favour with the ruling faction to merit a prestigious royal bride. In the July parliament of 1445, Angus was arraigned at the same time as the queen's husband, Sir James Stewart of Lorne; therefore it seems that Angus was identified firmly with the queen's party and was under attack as a consequence.[24] The queen herself may have been instrumental in securing the betrothal between James earl of Angus, who would have been thirteen years old at the time, and her daughter Joanna, but the predominant interest at court in 1445 was Black Douglas, and they would have had no desire to advance the Red Douglas Earl of Angus. In 1446, James earl of Angus died at the age of only twenty, being succeeded by his brother George, as 4th earl of Angus, who appeared at court almost immediately as a frequent charter witness.[25] It was no doubt in his mind that active participation in government and a high profile at court were needed to ensure that the Red Douglas interests were represented at a court dominated increasingly by the Black Douglases.

Opponents of the Douglases did not go unscathed; there is evidence that many suffered attacks on their property and positions. The Crichtons, as has been shown, lost influence and possessions in the struggle with the Douglases, and in 1445, James Kennedy, bishop of St Andrews, was the target for an attack. According to the Auchinleck chronicler, early in 1445, the Earl of Crawford, James Livingston, Robertson of Struan, James Hamilton of Cadzow and the Ogilvies made 'ane richt gret herschipe . . . in Fyff'.[26] The lands which were ravaged and destroyed were owned by, or under the jurisdiction of, Bishop Kennedy, and following the attack he 'cursit solempnitlie with myter and staf buke and candill contynually a zere and Interdytit all the placis quhar thir personis ware'. However, Kennedy was not entirely out of favour with the ruling faction, because on 5 February 1445, James II confirmed a charter of the privileges of St Andrews University.[27]

Opposition to the Douglases undoubtedly existed, but the fact is that the opposition faction simply was not strong enough, or well enough organised, to prevent the dominance of the Black Douglases and their allies at court. Dunbar was the final centre of resistance from which the queen, her husband James Stewart of Lorne, James earl of Angus and Adam Hepburn of Hailes defied the court faction. However, on 15 July 1445, Queen Joan died at Dunbar and Adam Hepburn 'gaf our the castell of Dunbar throu trety'.[28] The 'treaty' would have ensured that no action would be taken against the inhabitants of Dunbar, and there do not appear to have been any recriminatory measures, although on 24 November 1445, James Stewart of Lorne took out a safe-conduct to go to England, no doubt prompted by the arraignment of himself and Angus in the July parliament.[29] The Auchinleck chronicler writes that in May 1449 'Sir James Stewart the qwenes knycht was tane apon the se be the flemyngis befor the son and thair was put to deid and of thaim that come with him viii xx (eight score) of ynglismen'.[30] However, the Auchinleck chronicler's dating is contradicted by a safe-conduct issued to James Stewart to come to England as late as 17 August 1451, although as this is the last time he is mentioned seeking a safe-conduct with his sons, or appearing in the records at all, it is possible that the chronicler was relating a version which had come to him of the fate of James Stewart, but had misdated it.[31]

All was not running smoothly even within the separate court factions, and in 1446, the relationship between the Ogilvies and the Lindsays deteriorated, although the two families had been allies previously and had joined forces in the raid on Kennedy's lands in 1445. At the centre of the dispute was the justiciarship of Arbroath abbey. Alexander, master of Crawford, the eldest son of David, earl of Crawford, had been chosen for the office, but the monks of Arbroath had been unhappy about the way in which Crawford exercised his duties, feeling that he took advantage of his position and did not act in the best interests of the abbey. This may have meant that Crawford was exploiting or abusing the revenues and resources of the abbey, although no specific charges are made. The abbey responded by deposing Crawford in favour of Walter Ogilvy of Inverqharity.[32] The Master of Crawford, who had the reputation of being possessed of a fiery temperament, conceived this action as a great insult and determined to fight the decision, entrenching himself in the abbey for this purpose. By chance, Alexander, earl of Huntly, was a guest of the Ogilvies at that time and he felt obliged to join the fight with his hosts. The Auchinleck chronicler is very precise about the date of the battle which ensued, stating that it took place late on Sunday 23 January 1445 (which is 1446 by modern reckoning). The outcome of the battle was that David, earl of Crawford, who had arrived to intervene in the dispute, was mortally wounded, although the Lindsays actually won the fight and 'efter that a gret tyme held the Ogilvies at gret subjectoun and tuke thair gudis and destroyit thair placis'.[33] With the death of David, earl of Crawford, his son, Alexander, became earl, and the battle of Arbroath probably sowed the seeds of a lasting Huntly-Crawford animosity which was to surface again a few years later.

In south-east Scotland, the storm centre in the early 1440s was undoubtedly the priory of Coldingham, disputes over which continued throughout the reign and involved both ecclesiastical and secular authorities. Coldingham priory was a wealthy house and there were many who were prepared to exploit the weaknesses of its position, which was a survival from the time before the border between Scotland and England was defined. The institution of the priors of Coldingham was vested in the Bishop of St Andrews, but the actual presentation belonged to the priors of Durham, as Coldingham had been granted to the Benedictine house of St Cuthbert of Durham by the agreement of the kings of Scotland and 'divers earls of Dunbar'.[34] Severance of the English connection had been attempted, unsuccessfully, by Robert III who annexed Coldingham to the monastery of St Margaret of Dunfermline.[35] However, the rights of Durham over Coldingham had been confirmed by royal charter in 1392, an act of parliament in 1424 and litigation in Rome. Matters were further complicated as, in addition to disputes concerning the appointment of a prior of Coldingham, the office of bailie was also contested. This office conferred administrative control and temporal jurisdiction over the lands of Coldingham and was therefore a highly coveted position.

Both of these issues caused problems during the 1440s. On 6 December 1441, William Drax, prior of Coldingham, died and the Prior of Durham lost little time in presenting a Durham monk, John Oll, to the office. Dunfermline, still clinging to its claim to patronage, disputed this provision and presented William de Boys, a monk of their house. The case was referred to James Kennedy, bishop of St Andrews, who assessed the evidence and found in favour of Durham. Consequently, John Oll was invested and a precept for his induction was issued on 18 January 1442.[36] However, the problem had not been solved as the abbot of Dunfermline appealed to the Pope, asking him to confirm the rights of Dunfermline and to alienate Coldingham from Durham.[37] When the case came before the Roman court, Durham held the dual advantage of a stronger legal position and the ability to call upon considerable secular support. On 11 June 1442, Oll appeared before the king and council at Stirling (although James II was only twelve years old at the time) and presented letters from Henry VI, Cardinal Beaufort and the earls of Northumberland and Salisbury. A letter from the Prior of Durham pleaded that 'to despoil us of our right over the priory of Coldingham is expressly against the truces between the realms'.[38] The internal problems being faced by the king's council at this time resulted in an unwillingness to run the risk of open hostility with England and it was considered expedient to agree to the presentation of John Oll to the priory of Coldingham.

If agreement had been reached concerning the priory, the problem of the bailiary was not so easily dealt with. The forfeiture of the Earl of March in 1435 had left the area with no dominant and powerful magnate, therefore Coldingham became the prey of ambitious local nobles. The office of bailie of Coldingham and a tack of its lands of Aldcambus were coveted by Sir Alexander Home of that Ilk, lord of Dunglass, and also by his uncle, Sir David Home of Wedderburn, the latter receiving support from Sir Adam Hepburn of Hailes, the feudal superior of both men.[39] On 16 September 1441, John Wessingham, prior of Durham, granted the bailiary of Coldingham to Sir David Home for a period of forty years, with a promise of Aldcambus in exchange for some of his own lands. Not surprisingly, this grant was opposed by Sir Alexander Home, and in an effort to reach a compromise, the Prior of Durham and Adam Hepburn of Hailes attempted the division of the disputed possessions between the claimants, but following the induction of John Oll, Sir David and Sir Alexander appealed to Durham. After some deliberation, the council of James II and the prior of Durham reached an agreement in favour of Alexander Home, who had strengthened his own case in the meantime by obtaining letters of recommendation from James, earl of Angus, Adam Hepburn of Hailes and James Kennedy, bishop of St Andrews.[40] On 14 May 1442, Alexander Home received a patent of the bailiary for life. This was issued at Durham, and Home then proceeded to Stirling where the king and court were residing. He was admitted formally to the office on 20 May at the request of James II, James Kennedy, bishop of St Andrews and the earls of Angus, Crawford and Mar.[41]

This apparent concord did not signal an end to the problems in the south-east, as hostilities flared up once more — this time arising from a dispute over the archdeaconry of Teviotdale. This involved Patrick Home, a kinsman of Alexander Home, who had ousted William Croyser as archdeacon of Teviotdale, thereby incurring the wrath of James 7th earl of Douglas, who supported Croyser. Douglas used his position as justiciar south of the Forth to attack the decision to present Alexander Home to the bailiary of Coldingham as having been made by only a 'partiale consale' and therefore was 'of na strenth na vertu'.[42] This is illuminating in itself, as it demonstrates that Douglas's attempts to assert control at court were being thwarted by certain members of the political community; these seem to have been, principally, the Queen, Bishop Kennedy and the Earl of Angus. Such dissension provided an opportunity which was too good to miss, and David Home of Wedderburn took immediate advantage by forcibly seizing Coldingham and causing Prior Oll to flee. The forces needed to sustain this position were evidently not at David Home's disposal, and both John Oll and Alexander Home were reinstated in their respective offices, although Sir David continued to complain volubly to the Prior of Durham that Alexander Home was holding Coldingham as a fortalice from which he led raids on the lands and possessions of David Home and his family, and also on those of Adam Hepburn of Hailes.[43] The mediation of James, earl of Angus, eventually produced a settlement on 16 January 1444, by which Sir David was to recover sheep and cattle with compensation for his losses, and also five pounds Scots as half of the profits of the bailiary for the Martinmas term 1443.[44]

The solution was shortlived. Following the death of the queen in 1445, Dunbar castle had been surrendered to the Douglas-Livingston faction by its keeper, Adam Hepburn of Hailes. However, in April 1446, Sir Patrick Hepburn, Adam's son, repossessed Dunbar and captured and imprisoned John Oll, prior of Coldingham.[45] The forfeiture of the Earl of March in 1435 had brought the custody of Dunbar into the hands of Adam Hepburn of Hailes, and Patrick Hepburn must have been loath to see the loss of Hepburn influence there. The capture of John Oll may have been intended as a reprisal for the plundering raids of his ally, Alexander Home. In a letter from Coldingham written on 10 November 1446, John Oll stated that he had been held for 'a great and intolerable ransom'.[46] Shortly after this, on 30 November 1446, Archibald Dunbar, the son of the dispossessed Earl of March, captured Hailes castle, although, according to the Auchinleck chronicler, 'syne cowardlie gaf it owr to the master of Douglas sodanlie'.[47] It is not clear precisely what Archibald Dunbar hoped to gain by such a move. He may have hoped to regain Dunbar castle in exchange for Hepburn's castle of Hailes and

over-estimated the amount of support he could raise for such an action. The
government reacted swiftly by sending James Douglas, the brother of William,
earl of Douglas, to recover Hailes castle from Archibald Dunbar. Dunbar
castle, held by Patrick Hepburn, was itself put under siege by the government,
following which a settlement was reached, although the exact details are not
recorded.[48] Dunbar castle remained in crown hands and on 2 February 1449,
the Homes and the Hepburns made peace by a double marriage contract
between the heirs of both houses and a daughter of the respective families.
Ellen, the daughter of Alexander Home, was to marry Adam, son and heir of
Patrick Hepburn of Hailes, on condition that he 'has nocht the dochter of
James of Levingstoune to wyff'. Alexander Home's son, also called Alexander,
was to marry Agnes, the sister of Patrick Hepburn.[49]

Disputes which had manifested themselves at the beginning of the minority
rumbled on, and the wrangling over the earldom of Mar flared up once more
when the stalemate which had existed over Kildrummy castle since 1442 was
broken in 1448.[50] On 12 May 1447, Robert and Thomas Erskine were charged
to deliver Kildrummy castle and place it at the king's disposal during his
forthcoming trip to the north.[51] David Murray of Tullibardine and Robert
Livingston, comptroller, were to be sent ahead to make arrangements for the
king's visit, and the Erskines were to deliver the castle to these men under
pain of forfeiture, according to the terms of an 'appoyntment' made to that
effect. It is not clear exactly what this was, but Sir Robert Douglas describes
an indenture dated 20 June 1448, which was in the Mar charter chest but has
since been lost, between the king and council and Robert lord Erskine. The
terms of this indenture state that Erskine agreed to deliver the castle of
Kildrummy between that date and 3 July 1448 'to any the King should
appoint, to be kept by them till the king's majority and then to be delivered up
to either of them who should be found to have right to it, at the sight of the
three estates'.[52] In addition, Erskine was to account to the king, upon the
attainment of his majority, for his half of the earldom of Mar. In return, the
king and council agreed to return Robert lord Erskine's castle of Alloa, as
soon as Kildrummy castle was delivered. The indenture was given under the
privy seal; William Turnbull, bishop of Glasgow, James Livingston, custodian
of the king's person, Patrick lord Graham, and Andrew lord Gray bound
themselves as cautioners for king and council; and for Erskine's part, in
addition to his own seal and that of his son, Thomas, the cautioners were
Henry Douglas of Lochleven, Thomas of Wemyss and William Auchterlonie
of Kellie. Letters issued by James II from Methven on 2 June 1448 stated that
Erskine was relieved of the custody of Dumbarton castle, but Dumbarton had
been surrendered already and Robert Livingston put in possession.[53] The
letter also stated that Erskine was to be relieved of the rents and issues of
Dumbarton received from the time of entry to Martinmas 1445. However, this
ought not to be interpreted as the Erskines in disgrace, but rather as a move to

clarify and regularise the situation. On 11 September 1448, a crown charter in favour of Thomas Erskine was witnessed by three Livingstons.[54]

The king visited the north of Scotland in July 1448. The citizens of Aberdeen presented him with two tuns of Gascony wine, six lights (presumably large candles) of three stones of wax and twelve half-pounds of scorchets (sweetmeats).[55] On 24 July, James II issued a charter in Inverness, and although there is no record of his having stayed in Kildrummy, the castle was surrendered by Erskine before 21 July and Archibald Dundas, brother-in-law of Sir Alexander Livingston of Callendar, became keeper.[56] The reciprocal arrangement to surrender Alloa appears not to have materialised, and Sir Thomas Erskine made a formal protest in the general council held at Stirling on 4 April 1449, that the king and council had failed to give credence to their claims.[57] However, on 26 January 1450, in the parliament held in Edinburgh, the protest was referred to the consideration of the privy council when the king should come of age. As the king was certainly exercising royal power in his own right by this time, this was yet another example of royal procrastination, shelving the problem until the attainment of the king's perfect majority at the age of twenty-five (October 1455). The Erskines had little choice but to accept this delay, but the matter was to be resurrected later in the reign.

During the reign of James II, the royal house of Stewart followed the precedent set by the marriage alliance between James I's eldest daughter, Margaret, and Louis, dauphin of France in 1436, by seeking and obtaining a number of European marriage alliances. James II had six sisters, four of whom were married abroad in matches which conferred both diplomatic and economic advantages. Medieval Scotland has often been ignored or discounted by historians who have viewed it as a remote backwater hardly worthy of consideration in the mainstream of European affairs, and the geographic isolation of Scotland has led to the under-estimation of foreign influences at play there. However, there is ample evidence for a thriving traffic in foreign influence which took a number of forms and resulted, particularly in the towns, in an increasingly cosmopolitan society. Reputations crossed wide boundaries, as is shown in 1449 when a number of Burgundian knights visited Scotland on a chivalric mission, a detailed account of which survives in a French manuscript.[58] Jacques de Lalain was the eldest son of a Burgundian nobleman of the court of Charles the Bold, and had reputedly visited in succession the courts of France, Spain and Portugal, fighting in the lists against all challengers. The account states that Lalain had heard that there was a champion in Scotland worthy of his skill with knightly weapons, and he made arrangements to travel to Scotland to joust with him. That knight was James Douglas, brother of William earl of Douglas, who had evidently carved a reputation for himself if his renown had spread abroad. The Auchinleck chronicler recorded the visit as follows:

The zer of God 1448, the 25 day of Februar [1449 by modern reckoning], the master of Douglas, callit James, and twasom with him, that is to say, James of Douglas, brother to the larde of Lochlevyne, and the lard of Haukat (Hawkhead) focht in the barres at Strivling aganis two knychtis and ane squyar of Burgundy. And ther war thair names, Schir Jakkis de Lalane, Schir Symond de Lalane and the larde of Mongavile that was the squyar. And this was befoir King James the secund.[59]

The French manuscript by Chastellain gives a detailed account of the combat. Lalain, with the permission of his lord, the Duke of Burgundy, had issued a challenge to James Douglas, who, having convinced himself that this was motivated not by malice but in recognition of his knightly skills, accepted. After both sides had conferred, it was decided that the principal protagonists should each choose two companions who would be men of rank and known in arms. Jacques Lalain chose his uncle, Simon de Lalain, lord of Montigny, and Hervé de Meriadet. James Douglas chose the laird of Hawkhead (near Paisley) and James Douglas, brother of the laird of Lochleven. James II agreed to judge the contest and had the lists prepared at Stirling. The joust took place using lance, axe, and dagger, and was fought on foot, on the understanding that it was to be to the death, or until the king stopped it. The French account states that Jacques de Lalain fought without his vizor and with his face uncovered, which was considered a special proof of his confidence in his skill and strength. James Douglas fought in his basinet with closed vizor, and could thus be put out of breath by being thrown on the ground by his opponent, which was exactly what happened. The fight was stopped when James II threw down his truncheon, but the advantage lay with the Burgundians.[60] According to the chronicle of D'Escouchy, this visit of the Burgundian knights to Scotland was connected with the marriage of James II to Mary of Gueldres, and it was certainly in the same year. However, in his account, the French writer, Chastellain, gives no hint of this, making the visit turn entirely on de Lalain's challenge to James Douglas.

James Douglas was the twin of Archibald Douglas, and on 26 August 1447 an indenture was made to the effect that James was the elder twin.[61] This reversed an earlier understanding that Archibald earl of Moray was senior and explains why, in 1442, James the Gross should have been pressing for a church career for James.[62] James may have shown sufficient prowess in arms and chivalric pursuits to make him appear suitable for the role of Master of Douglas and heir to his elder brother William while the latter remained childless.

The foreign marriages entered into by the royal house of Stewart undoubtedly enhanced the reputation of Scotland in the courts of Europe, but the fact that those courts were happy to form such alliances, with the trouble and expense that involved, show that Scotland's rulers must already have been held in high regard. James' eldest sister Margaret had already been married to Louis, the dauphin of France, in an alliance arranged in 1436 between James I and Charles VII of France,[63] and it is this very prestigious marriage which may have prompted others to pursue Scottish marriage alliances. Similarly, there is some evidence that Douglas prestige was high on the continent. The 4th Earl of Douglas had fought and died in France and held the title Duke of Touraine, and the reputation of James Douglas, brother of the 8th Earl, in knightly skills had evidently spread abroad to the ears of the Burgundian Jacques de Lalain. In 1451, William earl of Douglas was to travel to the papal jubilee in Rome with a magnificent entourage and be 'commended by the supreme pontiff above all pilgrims', therefore the Black Douglas reputation abroad stood high.

In 1441, John, 5th duke of Brittany, sent ambassadors to Scotland to suggest his eldest son, Francis count of Montfort, as a husband for Isabella, James I's second daughter. One historian states that, during the marriage negotiations, John duke of Brittany was told that Isabella was far from being a clever conversationalist and, in fact, seemed rather simple, whereupon he ordered his ambassadors to return immediately to Scotland and conclude the alliance, declaring that a woman was clever enough when she could distinguish between her own chemise and her husband's doublet![64] A Scottish embassy had been despatched to Brittany, consisting of Sir George Crichton, William Foulis, archdeacon of St Andrews, and Sir William Monypenny, and the contract was signed on 19 July 1441. Its terms were that Isabella should receive a dowry of 100,000 saluts d'or (gold crowns) from James II, and the Duke should settle on her a jointure of £6000. Isabella sailed with an impressive train of attendants to Brittany, and was married to Duke Francis on 30 October 1442 at the castle of Aurai, two months after Francis' succession to the dukedom.

The trend towards seeking European marriage alliances continued with the marriage between James' third sister, Mary, and Wolfaert van Borsselen in 1444.[65] The importance of this marriage was the consequent strengthening of Scotland's position in the Low Countries, which were crucial trade markets but were also traditionally pro-English. Wolfaert van Borsselen's father was Henric, lord of Veere, Sandenburg, Flushing, Westkapelle, Domburg and Bronwershaven, and was admiral to Philip the Good of Burgundy. Wolfaert was heir, not only to his father, but also to his father's two wealthy and powerful cousins, and with the assured support of the Borsselen family and their vassals, the Scots could look forward not only to consolidating their position in and around Zeeland, but also to enjoying powerful and influential backing for any diplomatic alliance with Burgundy.[66]

On 14 December 1444, Princess Annabella was betrothed at Stirling to Louis, count of Geneva, who was the second son of the Duke of Savoy, and a grandson of the anti-Pope, Felix V.[67] The initiative for this alliance is alleged to have come from Savoy, and it is likely that it was an attempt to win Scottish support for the cause of the anti-Pope and the conciliar movement. Annabella was sent to Savoy, but the marriage did not take place and the betrothal was broken off formally in 1456.[68] It seems that there was pressure from Charles VII to break off the marriage contract, as relations between France and

Savoy had grown strained and the Scots were keen to maintain a good rapport with France. Princess Annabella returned to Scotland and was married subsequently to George, master of Huntly, whose attempt to marry the widowed Countess of Moray was thwarted by James II.

In 1445, the princesses Eleanor and Joanna sailed for France in the hope of securing foreign marriages with the help of their sister, the Dauphiness of France. They arrived at Tournai on 19 August to be greeted with the news that their sister, Margaret, had died three days previously.[69] However, Charles VII received the princesses at Tours on 9 September, and by 25 January 1446, they were established with their own household while negotiations for their marriages proceeded.[70] This was not wholly a disinterested act on the part of Charles VII, who appreciated that these Stewart princesses could be useful diplomatic pawns, and he was considering a marriage alliance with the Holy Roman Emperor, Frederick III, and Eleanor of Scotland in 1445. In a letter dated 27 May 1447, James II proposed his sister Eleanor as a bride for the Dauphin, a dubious and tactless suggestion considering the misery caused to Margaret by her unprepossessing and neglectful husband,[71] and, fortunately, it was not adopted. At some time before the end of August 1447, Eleanor was betrothed to Sigismund, duke of Austria.[72] Sigismund had been betrothed to Charles VII's daughter, Radegond of France, but she had died in 1445, therefore in June 1447, an Austrian embassy was sent to Charles VII to ask for the hand of Eleanor of Scotland.[73] Eleanor is said to have been married 'per verba de presenti' in the church of Beaumont near Chinon on 8 September 1448 and she left later in the year for Innsbruck.[74]

On 9 January 1448, while Eleanor's marriage was still being negotiated, James wrote to Charles VII asking for his assistance in finding a suitable bride for himself, whereupon Charles recommended the Scottish ambassadors to the court of Burgundy.[75] The marriage between Mary Stewart and Wolfaert van Borsselen had resulted in a series of embassies between Scotland and the Low Countries, and when, on 6 May 1448, James gave power to his ambassadors to arrange a marriage for him with a suitable princess of the house of Burgundy, Gueldres or Cleves, he could rely on strong diplomatic support. James was keen to ally himself in marriage with the French royal house, and had already ignored the offer of a marriage alliance with Annette of Saxony, daughter of Duke Frederick, mentioned in a letter dated 15 June 1447; but as there was no suitable kinswoman of Charles VII, James looked to the courts which enjoyed close contact with that of France. At the end of June 1446, a Scottish ambassador and his train were in the town of Arnhem, and on 5 July, a Scottish herald and an envoy from Burgundy 'came to see the maiden of Gueldres'. Such interest bore fruit, as Duke Arnold despatched a knight in his service, Otto de Puflich, to visit James II in Edinburgh in 1447. On 6 September 1448, Duke Arnold empowered Philip the Good of Burgundy to offer the hand of Mary, who was Philip's niece, and had been brought up at the court of Burgundy, to the King of Scots. The marriage contract was signed at Brussels on 1 April 1449,[76] and the marriage arrangement brought with it an alliance between Scotland and Burgundy which embraced the Duke of Brittany (married to James' sister Isabella) and the Duke of Gueldres. These signatories were bound to assist each other against aggressors; to promote each others' interests and honour and to take active part against anyone causing damage or injury, by land or sea, to the other signatories or their subjects. Negotiations or treaties with other powers were to be effected only after consultation with fellow signatories.[77]

The Treaty of Brussels, as this was known, did not include Charles VII of France, but he does not appear to have been averse to its terms. The political climate was encouraging for such a treaty, as there was an atmosphere of growing Burgundian hostility towards England and France at this time. In the winter of 1448–9, Franco-Burgundian relations improved, and on 31 December 1448, the Franco-Scottish alliance was renewed by the same ambassadors who had taken part in the negotiations for the alliance with Burgundy.[78]

Mathieu d'Escouchy describes the voyage to Scotland of Mary of Gueldres and the bridal party in June 1449.[79] Included in her train of followers and companions were the Lord of Veere and his wife, Mary, who was James II's sister, and he brought with him 'fifteen score of men in harness'. In order to take advantage of a favourable wind, they departed from Sluys at 4 a.m. on 9 June in an impressive convoy of thirteen ships, and the journey would have taken eight or nine days. On 18 June, Mary reached Leith, having first made a pilgrimage to the chapel of St Andrew on the Isle of May in the Firth of Forth.[80] The Exchequer Rolls show that Mary and her entourage rested at the convent of St Anthony at Leith, and then proceeded to Holyrood. Alexander Napier, comptroller, was allowed £9 for expenses incurred at St Anthony's convent and Holyrood, and for the hire of a boat and various other expenses connected with Mary of Gueldres.[81] Other miscellaneous payments were recorded in connection with the king's marriage and the coronation of the queen, including £12 paid to John Dempster for cloth for robes to be worn at the wedding celebrations.[82] Mary of Gueldres brought a number of her own retainers with her, and there are a few surviving references to those who remained with her. Two Dutchmen, Henry Junem and Herman were, respectively, keeper of her wardrobe and master of her stable,[83] and Henry Vanderfelde, a former tutor of the queen, received payments in 1452, as did his sons, who may have accompanied their father to Scotland in Mary of Gueldres' train in 1449.[84] On 25 June, the marriage contract was ratified under the Great Seal by the king at Stirling, and he gave his consent to a number of conditions. He was to renounce any right to the succession of the Duke and Duchess of Gueldres should they have any legitimate male heirs, and he promised to restore whatever dowry his wife should bring if she died within a year of the consummation of the marriage without bearing a child.[85] Letters had been issued by Philip duke of Burgundy, laying a subsidy of 400 livres on the town of Courtrai on 12 April 1449 'pour l'aliance qui presentement se fait avec le roi d'Escoce de nostre belle niece de Gheldres'.[86] For his part, James ratified the promise made by his ambassadors that his future wife would be awarded a portion of 10,000 gold crowns per annum from the lands of Strathearn and Atholl, the castle and seigneury of Methven and the palace and great customs of Linlithgow. Four days later, on 29 June, James gave a receipt for 10,000 gold crowns as part of the dowry payable on his marriage. Finally, on 3 July, James II and Mary of Gueldres were married at Holyrood abbey and Mary was crowned Queen of Scotland.[87]

NOTES

1. The Auchinleck chronicler states that 'James Douglas deit at the castell of abercorn to the takin thai said he had in him four stane of talch [tallow, or fat] and maire'. Chron. Auchinleck, f. 109v. Bishop Lesley states in his history that 'James Douglas . . . was ane man of gryit stature and verrey fatt'. Lesley, *History*, 16.
2. The name 'Ormond' was adopted from a hill — probably an ancient moot hill — in the estate of Ardmanach. Pinkerton, *History*, i, 198.
3. *A.P.S.*, ii, 33.
4. *H.M.C.*, Home, 85. Alexander Home's concern for his land rights is connected directly to the Coldingham dispute, discussed later in this chapter, and he had cause to fear Douglas animosity, having suffered at the hands of James 7th earl of Douglas, hence his concern if the 8th Earl were controlling the king.
5. *R.M.S.*, ii, no. 283.
6. *E.R.*, v, 201, 219, 230.
7. Lyall, R. J., 'The Medieval Scottish Coronation Service: Some Seventeenth-Century Evidence'. *Innes Review*, 28 (1977), 3–21.
8. *A.P.S.*, ii, 31.
9. Ibid.
10. William earl of Douglas, Archibald earl of Moray and Hugh earl of Ormond were present, as was David earl of Crawford. The lords spiritual were well represented with the bishops of Dunkeld, Glasgow, Brechin, Dunblane and Moray in attendance, but James Kennedy, bishop of St Andrews is noticeably absent. *A.P.S.*, ii, 59.
11. On 9 July 1445, a payment of 20s. is recorded to David Henry for going out from the castle of Edinburgh and coming to the king. *E.R.*, v, 181, 276.
12. NLS, Acc. 5976, Box 6, 10; Fraser, *Douglas*, iii, no. 413.
13. *Abdn. Counc.*, i, 399.
14. Ibid., iv, 211, 253
15. Ibid., v, 669, 663.
16. Ibid., i, 240.
17. *Moray Reg.*, 189.
18. *Abdn. Counc.*, i, 240.
19. *A.P.S.*, ii, 56.
20. *H.M.C.*, Hamilton, 15, 16.
21. *A.P.S.*, ii, 59.

22. S.R.O., Calendar of Charters, 321.

23. Fraser, *Douglas*, ii, 42.

24. *A.P.S.*, ii, 59.

25. *H.B.C.*, 467. George earl of Angus must have been seventeen or eighteen years old when he inherited the title.

26. Chron. Auchinleck, f. 111v.

27. St Andrews University Evidence, 10.

28. Chron. Auchinleck, f. 111v.

29. *Foedera*, ii, 675.

30. 'befor the son' may mean that James Stewart of Lorne was accompanied by his son, as both John and James (later earls of Buchan and Atholl) had appeared before on a number of safe-conducts.

31. *Foedera*, ii, 682.

32. *Extracta E Variis Cronicis Scocie* (Abbotsford Club, 1842), 237–44.

33. Chron. Auchinleck, f. 111v.

34. *North Durham*, app. 20, 92.

35. *Coldingham Correspondence*, 95–6, 130–2; *A.P.S.*, ii, 25.

36. *C.P.R.*, ix, 456–7; *Cold. Corr.*, 255.

37. *C.P.R.*, ix, 298–9.

38. *Cold. Corr.*, 125, 142–3.

39. Dunlop, *Kennedy*, 51.

40. *Cold. Corr.*, 120–1, 157, 123–4, 126.

41. *N.D.*, app. 99, 567. This is the only occasion in official records that Robert lord Erskine is styled Earl of Mar.

42. *Cold. Corr.*, 147–8.

43. Ibid.

44. *H.M.C.*, Milne-Home Report, 21.

45. *N.D.*, app. 22, no. 96.

46. *Cold. Corr.*, 156–7.

47. Chron. Auchinleck, f. 111r. This was James Douglas, who was to become the 9th Earl of Douglas following the murder of his brother William.

48. Patrick Cockburn earned £40 for his 'labours and expenses at the siege of the castle of Dunbar'. *E.R.*, v, 305.

49. Fraser, *Buccleuch*, ii, 39–41. It is not clear which daughter of James Livingston is referred to in this contract. It may have been Marion, who later married William 3rd lord Crichton, but no details of the earlier arrangement survive.

50. See above, p. 22.

51. *A.B.Ill.*, iv, 196.

52. Douglas, *Peerage*, 467.

53. S.R.O., GD 124/10/1.

54. S.R.O., GD 124/1/1.

55. *Abdn. Counc.*, v, 731.

56. Fraser, *Southesk*, 69; *E.R.*, v, 306.

57. *A.P.S.*, ii, 60.

58. Hume-Brown, *Early Travellers*,

59. Chron. Auchinleck, f. 113r.

60. Ibid.

61. *R.M.S.*, ii, no. 301.

62. See above, p. 28.

63. Barbé, L., *Margaret of Scotland and the Dauphin Louis* (1917), 12–31.

64. Lobineau, G. A., *Histoire de Bretagne* (Paris, 1707, reprinted 1973).

65. Dunlop, *Kennedy*, 66–7.

66. Stevenson, A. W. K., 'Trade Between Scotland and the Low Countries in the Later Middle Ages' (Unpublished Ph.D thesis, Aberdeen, 1982), 76–81.

67. Dunlop, *Kennedy*, 61.

68. Ibid., 179, 181.

69. Baxter, J. H., 'The Marriage of James II', *S.H.R.*, xxv, 69–72.

70. British Library, Additional MS. 8878.

71. Barbé, *Margaret of Scotland*, passim.

72. Baxter, op. cit; Stevenson, *Wars*, ii, 194.

73. Dunlop, op. cit., 88–9.

74. Baxter, op. cit., 71.

75. Stevenson, *Wars*, ii, 197.

76. Baxter, op. cit.

77. Stevenson, 'Trade Between Scotland and the Low Countries', 79–80.

78. The ambassadors were William lord Crichton, chancellor, John Ralston, bishop of Dunkeld, and Nicholas Otterburn, official of St Andrews and canon of Glasgow.

79. *Cronique de Mathieu d'Escouchy*, ed. G. du Fresne de Beaucourt (Paris, 1864).

80. *E.R.*, v, lxxvii.

81. *E.R.*, v, 387.

82. Ibid.

83. Ibid., 386.

84. Ibid., 500.

85. Baxter, op. cit.

86. Ibid., 72.

87. Ibid. 10,000 gold crowns = 10,000 French ecus = 5000 pounds Scots.

4

Aggression and Murder, 1449–52

Following his marriage in July, James II was soon concerned to demonstrate the fact that his minority was at an end and that he was now exercising royal power in his own right, although there was no dramatic change in court personnel immediately following the king's marriage. The men closest to the king according to the witness list on a charter dated 21 July 1449 were, William Turnbull, bishop of Glasgow, John Ralston, bishop of Dunkeld, William lord Crichton, chancellor, James Livingston, chamberlain, Master James Lindsay, provost of Lincluden, and Robert Livingston, comptroller.[1] William Turnbull, bishop of Glasgow, was a prominent figure on court witness lists and he had risen rapidly during the minority through assiduous court service. He was at court as Master William Turnbull, keeper of the privy seal, at least as early as March 1441,[2] and he held this office consistently even after his promotion to the bishopric of Dunkeld in 1447. He was translated, almost immediately, to the bishopric of Glasgow, by which time he was evidently very much a part of the king's inner council of close advisers. However, within two months of the July charter, dramatic changes had taken place at court as James II launched an attack on the Livingston family, thus bringing their ascendancy during the minority to an abrupt end.

The Livingstons appear to have had no warning of the king's intentions towards them. As late as August 1449, Sir Alexander Livingston of Callendar was nominated as an envoy to treat with English commissioners for a truce; but significantly, his name is absent from a second safe-conduct issued two months later on 16 October.[3] According to the Auchinleck chronicle:

> on the monunday the xxiii day of september James of Levingstoun was arrestit be the king and Robyn kalendar capitane of the castell of doune and David levingstoun of the grene zardis with syndry utheris and sone eftir this sir alexander levingstoun was arrestit and robyn of levingstoun of lichqw (Linlithgow) that tyme comptroller and James and his brother alexander and robyne of lithqw war put in the blakness . . .[4]

The captain of the castle of Doune was actually John Livingston, not Robin, and he may have been the brother of Alexander Livingston of Callendar.[5] David Livingston of Greenyards may have been a cousin, but this is the only occasion on which he is mentioned.[6] It is significant that James Livingston, his brother Alexander and Robert Livingston of Linlithgow (cousin of the elder

Alexander) were imprisoned in Blackness castle, the keeper of which was George Crichton, an old adversary who would have delighted in the downfall of the rival Livingstons.

The family whose rapid fall was thus engineered by James II and his supporters had achieved its pre-eminence in a remarkably short time, little more than a decade of assiduous power-seeking based on the acquisition of many of the major royal household and state offices. In the exchequer account of 26 July 1443, John de Livingston was warden of the royal mint at Stirling and he may be the same John Livingston who went on to become captain of Doune castle.[7] Robert Livingston of Callendar was captain of the castles of Dumbarton and Dunoon, and James Livingston held the offices of captain of Stirling castle and custodian of the king's person. By 1449, Alexander Livingston of Callendar was Justiciar of Scotland, and his second son Alexander of Filde was constable of Stirling castle and captain of Methven.[8] Henry Livingston held the office of comptroller between 5 July 1442 and 27 June 1444, and Robert Livingston of Linlithgow succeeded Alexander Nairn of Sandfurd in the same office between June 1447 and August 1448.[9]

The Livingstons were forfeited in the January parliament of 1450, and the younger Alexander Livingston and Robert Livingston, the comptroller, were executed. The exact charges brought against these men have not survived, but the motive appears to have been largely fiscal. Following his marriage in July, James II was confronted with the immediate financial problem of providing the new queen with a suitable tocher (marriage portion, or dower). In the marriage agreement arranged with the Duke of Burgundy, James had promised to endow Mary with an annual income of 10,000 French ecus (which was equivalent to 10,000 gold crowns or £5000 Scots), but the agreed marriage portion of the lands of Strathearn and Atholl, the castle and lordship of Methven and the palace and great customs of Linlithgow would be unlikely to yield such a sum, and the king may have feared that Mary's dowry payments would be withheld by the Duke of Burgundy as a result. The Livingston connection with the new queen's tocher was very apparent. Methven castle, of which Alexander Livingston of Filde was captain, was granted to the queen as part of her tocher in the marriage treaty ratified by James in June 1449. However, in the later ratification of the treaty made in January 1450, the castle and lordship of Methven appear to have been exchanged for the lands of Menteith. The queen was certainly seised in the lands of Menteith prior to the 1451 Exchequer account.[10] The grant to the queen of the palace and great customs of Linlithgow may also be seen to have affected Robert Livingston of Linlithgow, comptroller, as he was living in Linlithgow and controlling the revenues from the palace and its lands, therefore Robert Livingston's execution solved another of the king's financial problems, as he was in debt to Livingston for the sum of £930 Scots which he was obliged to repay out of the queen's tocher.[11]

It is possible that Robert Livingston, as comptroller, had been guilty of a serious malversation of the royal funds, and his execution was followed by a notable increase in the landed revenues of the crown. Prior to 1450, the exchequer accounts do not show significant revenues collected from the crown-held earldoms of March, Atholl, Strathearn, Menteith and Fife. As comptroller, Robert Livingston may have had ample opportunity to subvert the revenues.[12] It is not possible to prove this, as no such charge against Livingston is made in the extant records. However, the attack on Robert Livingston was not entirely a cynical device for saving money through the cancellation of debts, as in 1451 the king assigned £123 13s 7d 'to satisfy the poor creditors from whom the late Robert of Levingstoun, the king's comptroller, received goods and merchandise for the use and expenses of the king's household before his removal from office and before the entry on office of Alexander Napier'.[13]

An intriguing tailpiece to Livingston's demise occurred on 23 August 1450 when James II wrote to Henric, lord of Veere, claiming as escheat a chest of silverware which had belonged to Robert Livingston.[14] This incident should be viewed in the context of a protracted diplomatic wrangle which began when a Scottish ship, the *Copin Ring*, was wrecked at Veere and its cargo subsequently plundered. On 17 May 1450, William Turnbull, bishop of Glasgow, wrote to the lord of Veere and, with George Crichton, to the lady of Veere (James II's sister, Mary) to ask for redress. The plea was apparently unsuccessful as Turnbull repeated it on 10 July and James himself wrote on 28 August asking for restitution to be made to a deputation of Edinburgh merchants, one of whom was George Falou, who was also mentioned in the letter concerning Livingston's smuggled silverware.[15] The demands seem to have met with no response, and it has been suggested that the removal of the Scots staple from Veere to Middelburg was connected with this dispute.[16]

In addition to the fiscal motives which may be advanced for the king's attack on the Livingstons, they may also have been paying the price for their rash seizure of Queen Joan and her husband, James Stewart of Lorne, in 1439, notwithstanding their attempt to safeguard themselves from future blame in the terms of the 'Appoyntement' of that year. Such treatment of his mother may have rankled deeply with James II, and his attack on the Livingstons was all-encompassing. Although only two men were executed, the king's attack appears to have been aimed at the entire family and their adherents. The Auchinleck chronicler writes, 'all officeris that war put in be thaim [the Livingstons] war clerlie put out of all officis and all put down that thai put up . . .'[17] Into this latter category fell James Dundas of that Ilk, the brother-in-law of Alexander Livingston of Callendar, whose family was included in the disgrace of the Livingston faction. The brothers of Sir James Dundas, Archibald and Duncan, were keepers of Kildrummy and Restalrig castles respectively.[18] James Dundas was imprisoned in Dumbarton castle prior to his forfeiture and he was dead before 26 August 1452, on which date a remission was granted to the late James Dundas of that Ilk and his brother Duncan.[19] The Auchinleck chronicler, in his account of the battle of Brechin, fought in May 1452, states that 'the lard of dundas' was among those slain, and this would certainly account for his posthumous remission in August.[20] After the royal attack on the Livingstons and their adherents, the Auchinleck chronicler states that Archibald Dundas 'stuffit the towre of Dundas' and held the house against the king for several weeks, with William earl of Douglas taking charge of the siege, until the surrender of the tower at the end of April 1450.[21] Douglas had a vested interest in the fall of the tower of Dundas as, on 10 February, he had received charters of Dundas lands, and provisions and stores found within the tower on its surrender were bestowed on Douglas.[22]

In a statute of 19 January 1450, the Livingstons were accused of responsibility for the treasonable incarceration of the queen, Joan Beaufort, in 1439. On 7 March 1450, the estate of Filde, forfeited by the younger Alexander Livingston, was bestowed upon Alexander Napier, the new comptroller, for his services to the queen and in recompense for the wounds he sustained at the time of her imprisonment in Stirling castle.[23] The clauses in the 'Appoyntement' of 1439 by which the Livingstons sought absolution for the queen's imprisonment were conveniently forgottem or held to have no effect, and there is a certain vagueness about the claim made by James II to the Pope in a letter dated 1 June 1450, that Alexander Livingston had been guilty of 'rebellion and other excesses', although this may be a reference to the faction fighting of 1444–5 in which the queen was definitely on the losing side.[24] The letter also stated that Alexander Livingston was 'expelled from the said kingdom', although there is no evidence for his exact fate. In any event, he did not long survive the family's downfall, for he died between 4 July and 6 November 1451.[25]

The combined family influence of the Livingstons was such that they had aroused the jealousy of others who sought advancement. As the events of the minority show, the Crichtons had no cause to love the Livingstons, and the Earl of Douglas seems to have been prepared to see them fall as the king asserted himself, anxious to demonstrate that his minority was at an end.

Douglas and Livingston have been described as allies in the years between 1444 and 1449, although this may give a misleading impression. It is more likely that Douglas chose to tolerate the Livingstons rather than the Crichtons when he embarked upon his career at court in 1444, because he thought that they could be of more use to him. The Douglases and the Crichtons had crossed swords before, but Douglas could not run the government single-handed, and the Livingstons, with their network of office holding, were the obvious choice for maintaining the machinery of government, although this was in no sense a coalition of equals. Furthermore, the relationship between the two families in the later years of the minority may not always have been harmonious.

In 1447, Sir Alexander Livingston, as justiciar, superintended the surrender of the castle of Lochdoon by the Maclellans, who were Douglas vassals.[26] The castle belonged to the king as Earl of Carrick, therefore Livingston was acting legitimately, but Douglas may have felt that this was an encroachment upon his jurisdiction. The reason for this action is obscure, but the Maclellans were allowed certain expenses for their keepership of the castle, so this does not appear to have been an attack which signified the family's disgrace. Another incident which may have caused some friction between Douglas and the Livingstons was the ousting of John Forrester of Corstorphine as chamberlain. James Livingston had replaced Forrester in that office by 29 June 1448, but as Forrester was an adherent of Douglas, this action may have generated some animosity.[27]

Dr Nicholson has suggested that the arrangement whereby James Livingston's daughter Elizabeth was to marry the young Lord of the Isles was widely regarded as an example of a family of mere baronial rank aiming too high, and that there would have been many voices ready to insinuate to the king that his agreement to such a match was unwise.[28] Certainly, the Auchinleck chronicler states that on 23 September 1449, Elizabeth Livingston,

> the forsaid James dochter that was spousit with the lord of the Ylis come till him sodanlie with few personis with hir and thai met in dumbertane sir duncan persone and led hir with him to kintyre.[29]

This entry in the chronicle, coupled as it is with the arrest of James Livingston, suggests a mood of conspiracy and is worth noting as one of the factors which contributed to the Livingston disgrace.

Marion Stewart, in her study of Richard Holland's alliterative poem, the 'Buke of the Howlat', has argued that it was written under the patronage of Archibald Douglas, earl of Moray and younger brother of William earl of Douglas, probably in the late spring of 1450. The poem, Stewart argues, satirises the Livingston rise to power in the figure of an owl in an assembly of birds, who borrows feathers from the other birds and then becomes so vain that the feathers are snatched back. The moral is clear: the Douglases, as established members of the nobility, were the king's 'natural' counsellors, whereas the Livingstons' rank was too low for them to enjoy an equal privilege.[30] The plans for the Ross-Livingston marriage had evidently been made during the king's minority, and whether or not James saw the issue quite in the terms portrayed by Holland's 'Howlat', he did not seem to be in favour of an alliance between a strong and potentially troublesome northern magnate and the family which he intended to remove from the political stage. The fact that the most prominent members of the Livingston family, Alexander Livingston of Callendar and James Livingston, who had exercised most influence during the minority, and who may be seen to have been most directly involved in the queen's imprisonment, did not suffer execution may seem surprising. However, little is known of Alexander Livingston's fate after his imprisonment except that he did not long survive the family's downfall, and James Livingston was obviously sufficiently alarmed to contrive his escape from royal custody in 1450 and flee to his new son-in-law, John earl of Ross. James Livingston was ultimately received back at court and re-granted the office of chamberlain, but not until September 1455, when James II's hardline supporters, William lord Crichton, James Crichton and William Turnbull, bishop of Glasgow, were all dead. Thus it may be regarded as a rehabilitation born of necessity rather than complete exoneration.

The chief beneficiaries of the forfeiture of the Livingston faction were the queen, on whom the estates of Callendar and Kilsyth were bestowed, and the Earl of Douglas, who obtained large shares of the possessions of the comptroller and the forfeited Dundases.[31] In addition to these rewards, the Douglases had ingratiated themselves so far with the king that they received Crown ratification of a family settlement defining the succession to the earldom, and royal sanction for the marriage of William to his cousin, Margaret of Galloway. Also, William's town of Strathaven was erected into a burgh in barony and he received a gift from the king of £27 9s 4d.[32]

The new queen played an active role in the January parliament of 1450 which forfeited the Livingstons. On 22 January, following the execution of Robert and Alexander Livingston, the three estates confirmed her marriage portion, and on 24 January she pleaded the cause of the prelates in parliament on the question of bequeathing personal estate. The bishops of St Andrews, Glasgow, Dunkeld, Moray, Dunblane, Brechin, Ross and Argyll complained in parliament that the personal estates of deceased prelates were being requisitioned by the king's officers, which made it impossible to settle debts, leave legacies or provide for masses for the soul, because no moveable goods were left with which to pay for these provisions. A drafted charter of redress was read and the queen added her entreaties. Ceremoniously, the king acceded to the requests and a charter was drawn up, under the Great Seal, which gave official sanction to the settlement.[33] The support of Church leaders was essential to James at a time when major political changes were taking place, and the first estate in turn must have realised that the opportunity for seeking concessions had to be grasped.

In the wake of the downfall of the Livingston family, sealed in the January parliament, William lord Crichton may have experienced some nervousness in view of his prominence in the affairs of the minority. It was as a response to the Livingstons' disgrace that Crichton's practical demonstration of loyalty to the king was made, evincing a clear understanding of James II's immediate financial problems. The comptroller's account of 1450 shows a loan of £500 made by Crichton to the king, and on 12 June 1450, Crichton received a charter of the lands of Castlelaw in reward for faithful counsel, service and in recompense for £2080 14s 6d advanced for the expenses of the king's household, in addition to a loan of £400 made by Crichton to the king.[34] Such large sums must have guaranteed Crichton's position and made him indispensable to the king, as no other royal supporter appears to have had the means or the inclination to provide the king with such generous and practical support.

James II's determination to increase the wealth of the Crown and to establish his control after a long minority was apparent in his actions following his marriage, and it is possible that the Earl of Douglas did not understand fully the implications of the king's attitude. In October 1450, Douglas set out for Rome to attend the papal jubilee, travelling by shop to the Continent and then by road to Lille, where he was received by the Duke of Burgundy, and thence to Paris, where he had talks with the French king, Charles VII.[35] He reached Rome in January 1451; and John Law's chronicle states that, by reason of his display of magnificence, Douglas was 'commended by the supreme pontiff above all pilgrims'.[36] On 12 January 1451 Douglas received an indult to choose a confessor, and on 15 January he was granted permission to nominate to ten secular benefices. On the same date, a further indult was granted to William and his brothers and sisters to choose confessors and to Countess Beatrice (William's mother) to have a portable altar.[37] Evidence of Douglas's presence in Rome occurs in a supplication dated 6 February 1451 which reads:

> Lately the Pope granted to William earl of Douglas then present in the Roman court, prorogation for two months to present a fit person for the canon and prebendary of Cambuslang, in the patronage of the earl . . . but the said earl, who is on his journey from Rome back to Scotland, doubts that on account of the dangers of the ways and of the sea, he may not be able to present a fit person within the time of prorogation and therefore supplicates that the Pope would extend the term for other three months with strict prohibition to the bishop, vicar, official or whatsoever others to dispose of the same in any way.[38]

This supplication is very significant in view of the fact that, back in Scotland, events had been running against Douglas in his absence. Law's chronicle states that William Turnbull, bishop of Glasgow, in association with William and George Crichton, conspired against Douglas: 'For by their counsel King James II besieged all the castles of the earl and slew many free tenants of the said earl and received the rest to his peace upon oath'.[39]

The background to this apparently astonishing action by the king may have been the death of Margaret, duchess of Touraine (widow of the 4th Earl of Douglas), who is said to have died at Threave at some time during 1450.[40] She had held the earldom of Wigtown and the lordship of Galloway in life-rent and, legally, they reverted to the crown on her death. The king's attempt to seize these lands may have been prompted by financial considerations, chief of which was the fear that the Duke of Burgundy would withhold further dowry payments as the queen had not received sufficient provision as agreed in the 1449 marriage settlement. The death of the Duchess must have appeared an ideal opportunity to bestow the earldom of Wigtown on the queen and thus increase the value of her tocher. However, on 26 January 1450, a royal

charter had been given to William earl of Douglas of all the lands, lordship
and regalities of Galloway above the water of Cree, resigned by Margaret,
countess of Touraine, through procurators.[41] William styled himself 'lord of
Galloway' from January 1450 and may also have aspired to the earldom of
Wigtown by virtue of his wife Margaret's direct descent from the Duchess.

It is not clear to whom William entrusted the management of his lands and
affairs in his absence. James, the eldest brother after William, appears to have
accompanied him to Rome, therefore the administration of his possessions
may have been left to his other brothers. In his vernacular history, written in
the late 1560s, Bishop Lesley states that William earl of Douglas had travelled
to Rome leaving his brother Hugh earl of Ormond in charge of his lands.[42] In
Douglas's absence, James II, 'be the counsell of thame quha wes with him for
the tyme', summoned the Earl of Douglas to compear upon 'three score days'
warning, which was rather unrealistic considering that they must have been
perfectly aware that Douglas was in Rome, and when he did not appear,
James invaded his lands.

George Buchanan, in his *Rerum Scoticarum Historia*, published in 1582,
goes even further. Buchanan's account is full of the depredations and crimes
of the Douglases, and he states that when Douglas had left for Rome, his
opponents took the opportunity to complain to the king and to persuade him
to summon the earl's procurator to answer the charges. The procurator (who
is not named) refused, and was eventually brought to court by force and
ordered to pay the sums awarded in redress against the Earl of Douglas. The
chancellor, William, earl of Orkney, was sent to see that the rents of the
Douglas estates were received to pay the damages, but he encountered
obstruction and opposition. The Douglas faction were ordered to appear
before the king, and on their failure to do so, were denounced as traitors,
after which the king raised an army and marched into Galloway, seizing
Lochmaben castle and levelling Douglas castle.[43] There is some confusion in
this account, as the chancellor in 1451 was William Crichton, not William
Sinclair earl of Orkney. However, Orkney was involved, as chancellor, in the
proceedings against the Douglases in 1455, and it is probable that Buchanan
was confusing two separate attacks on Douglas lands. Official evidence is
scarce, but there was a justice ayre held at Lochmaben in January 1451,[44] and
the king appeared in Ayr and Lanark on 13 and 16 February respectively.[45]
This is interesting in view of Buchanan's statement that Lochmaben castle
was seized and Douglas castle levelled. As Douglas was warden of the west
march, Lochmaben, although a royal castle, would be within his jurisdiction,
and if it were being held by Douglas men, the king may have decided to
replace the keepers, although there is no official record evidence of this.
Douglas castle was in Lanarkshire, which accords with the king's itinerary,
but Law states that it was the castle of Craig Douglas on the Yarrow which
was attacked, not Douglas castle near Lanark.[46] There does not appear to
have been a concerted 'all out' attack on the Douglases such as the sixteenth-

century chroniclers suggest. It seems that there was a dispute over the administration of the lands of Wigtown and Galloway following the death of the Duchess of Touraine, and an attack may have been made upon Douglas retainers who were obstructing the king, but James had other items of business to attend to in February 1451 which, although not overt attacks on Douglas, hint at a strong royal determination to set limits to the expansion of magnatial power; and this in turn may have rung warning bells in the Douglas camp.

On 13 February, four charters were issued in favour of Gilbert Kennedy of Dunure and one in favour of John Kennedy.[47] Gilbert was given lands in the sheriffdom of Ayr, the keepership of Lochdoon castle and the office of bailie of Carrick. The king also confirmed Gilbert as head of the Kennedy kin, thus giving royal recognition to Gilbert who had been involved in a drawn-out dispute with his half-uncle.[48] The advancement of Kennedy of Dunure, on the borders of Douglas territory, may have been a calculated move designed to secure loyal support in the west which could offset Douglas power. Similarly, on 16 February, Robert Colville of Ochiltree and his wife, Cristiane Crichton, daughter of Robert Crichton of Sanquhar, were given the lands of the baronies of Ochiltree and Oxnam, and lands in the sheriffdom of Roxburgh.[49] There appears to have been hostility already between Douglas and the Colvilles as, according to the Auchinleck chronicler,

> The zere of god lmiii xlix, sir James auchinleck was slane be richert coluile the xx day of aprile and within v or vi days cowartlie gaf our the castell and was hedit and iii sum with him and Incontinent [immediately] efter that he came furth the castell was castin doun be erll william of douglas James son.[50]

James Auchinleck was a Douglas retainer who appears as a witness on royal and Douglas charters in the 1440s. He does not appear on a charter issued by Douglas on 2 May 1449 nor at any time thereafter, and on 26 October 1450 the king confirmed a charter dated 17 October 1449 in favour of John Auchinleck, son and heir of 'quondam' James Auchinleck of that Ilk.[51] Thus the incident referred to and the date given agree with such corroborative evidence as there is, and the extreme action taken by Douglas against Richard Colville in revenge, apparently, for the killing of an old family retainer, was sufficient to indicate that Douglas would not view kindly the king's grant to the Colvilles, who were allied through marriage to the Crichtons.[52] On 31 March 1450, Robert Crichton of Sanquhar had received a royal charter of lands near Moffat in Annandale, and after the death of the 8th Earl of Douglas, Crichton became sheriff of Dumfries on 6 November 1452. Similarly, Andrew Agnew of Lochnaw was created hereditary sheriff of Wigtown on 25 May 1451, and he received a new charter after the death of Douglas. It is also interesting to note that a number of royal charters were granted to Alexander Hume in 1451–2, as he and David Hume of Wedderburn were to be found on Douglas charters and named with him on embassies and safe-conducts.[53] A picture emerges from this evidence of a subtle yet concerted effort on the part of the king to entice Douglas supporters away from him and to build up the position of trusted men in areas within or adjacent to Douglas territory.

John Law's statement that the Crichtons and William Turnbull, bishop of Glasgow, instigated the attack on Douglas's lands in his absence is quite credible given the Crichton's animosity towards Douglas, and Turnbull may have resented the extensive power held by Douglas, the bulk of whose lands lay within his diocese. Turnbull was clearly in favour during the absence of the Earl of Douglas as, on 22 February and 24 March 1451, he received charters of land and ecclesiastical liberties, charters which were witnessed by both William and George Crichton.[54]

Another political figure who had good reason to desire the curbing of Douglas power was George earl of Angus. He was of the Red Douglas line (illegitimate descendants of the 2nd Earl of Douglas), and as such the inheritor of an old animosity towards the Black Douglases, of whom William 8th earl of Douglas was the chief representative. Angus was warden of the east march, and in that capacity he may have clashed with Douglas who was warden of the west and middle marches. Angus was with the king at Melrose on 4 December 1450, and so was probably involved in the proceedings against the absent Douglas which took place that winter.[55]

When news of what had happened reached Douglas, he returned from Rome, but rather than taking ship from Europe to Scotland, he returned through England, availing himself of a safe-conduct issued the previous November. The English herald Garter King was sent to await the earl's arrival in England at the end of February 1451, and if Law is correct in his assertion that Douglas did not return to Scotland until 7 April, then he must have decided to wait south of the border until he could discover the nature of the reception which he was likely to receive in Scotland. John Law states that, on Douglas's return, 'the king forthwith gathered an army against the earl . . . and approached Craig Douglas in warlike fashion, and having taken the castle, razed it to its foundations'.[56]

Law's chronology must be at fault here, as it is unlikely that the king would have attacked the Earl of Douglas personally at this stage, particularly in view of the fact that Douglas was sufficiently back in favour by 17 April 1451 to be named as a commissioner to be sent to England to discuss recent violations of the truce. It is more likely that Douglas remained in England and sent some of his followers ahead to discover what had happened during his absence; indeed Buchanan states that William's brother James was sent for that purpose.[57]

The position of Douglas in the tense months after his return from Rome is important to gauge in view of the subsequent attack on the family by the king. An entry appears in the Auchinleck chronicle which alludes to the Earl of Douglas at this time, although it is unfortunately incomplete, in that the narrative is a continuation of a page now lost. The entry reads:

thai cryit him luftennent and sone efter this thai worthit als strang as ever thai war /
and at this tyme thai gat the erllis sele to consent to the trewis and Incontinent thai
send furth Snawdoun the kings herrod to lundone to bynd up the trewis and als fast
as sir James of Douglas gat wit hereof he past till londone Incontinent / and
quharfor men wist nocht redelye bot he was thar with the kyng of yngland lang tyme
and was meikle maid of.[58]

On the same folio, the chronicler narrates the events of the June parliament
of 1451, therefore it is probable that the preceding fragment belongs to the
same year. An interesting problem arises in interpreting what the chronicler
meant when he wrote 'thai cryit him luftennent'. It has been argued that this
refers to the Earl of Douglas receiving the title and office of Lieutenant-
General, as the 5th earl of Douglas had done in 1437.[59] However, there are a
number of problems with this interpretation. The office of Lieutenant-General
had been held previously only during a minority or when the king was
prevented from ruling effectively due to personal incapacity or enforced
absence from the realm. In 1451, James II could hardly be held to be
incapable of exercising royal power, and he would not have created the Earl
of Douglas Lieutenant-General given the evident atmosphere of mistrust
between them. At no point is Douglas styled Lieutenant-General in extant
official sources. There are numerous charters granted to Douglas of his lands
and offices, resigned into the king's hands and then re-granted in 1451, and his
name appears in charter witness lists in 1451–2 with sufficient regularity to
argue that he could not have held such an important office but fail to be styled
Lieutenant-General on any surviving document.

In this case, the term 'luftennent' was probably used by the chronicler to
indicate that Douglas was to continue acting for the king in the west and
middle marches. In a supplication to Rome, dated 29 January 1450, William
earl of Douglas is found styling himself 'William earl of Douglas and Avandale,
Great Guardian of the kingdom of Scotland and Prince and Lord of
Galloway'.[60] This grandiose string of titles does not include the office of
Lieutenant-General, although the title 'Guardian of the kingdom' is repeated
in later supplications and seems to indicate his duties as warden of the
Marches.

The Auchinleck chronicler's observation that the Douglases were soon as
strong as ever must be a reference to the formal submission of Douglas in the
June parliament of 1451. Douglas had been taken by surprise by the actions of
the king and he must have needed time to assess the situation and decide what
to do. In order to gain a breathing space, he made an overt demonstration of
his loyalty and obedience by surrendering all his lands and titles to the king in
parliament, and having them immediately re-granted.[61] Significantly, the king
continued to hold the earldom of Wigtown until October 1451 when it was
finally re-granted to Douglas, but the only occasion on which Douglas is
styled Earl of Wigtown on a royal charter is 13 January 1452 — the last royal
charter witnessed by him before his murder in February.[62]

Douglas was by now clearly aware of his vulnerability and was determined to seek support and form alliances for his own protection. On 23 April 1451, in the same month as he returned to Scotland, a warrant was issued for a safe-conduct, granted by Henry VI on 12 May, for William earl of Douglas, his brothers James, Archibald and Hugh, and others, to go to England.[63] The safe-conduct was valid for one year, and although there is no evidence of William having used it, his brother James apparently did so. On 11 December 1451, £13 was paid to Garter King of Arms 'lately sent by the king's command to travel with Sir James Douglas on his coming to the king, to bring the said James to the king's presence at Winchester, Salisbury and elsewhere, and then back to Scotland'.[64] This supports the Auchinleck chronicler's cryptic reference to the actions of James, Master of Douglas, during this time, and the involvement of Snowdon Herald is confirmed by the recorded payment of 100s to that officer on 1 July 1451, 'lately with letters'.[65] Also, the Master of Douglas paid a private visit to the English court at Winchester between 14 and 17 July 1451.[66] The reasons for James Douglas travelling to the English court are unknown, although there was evidently some suspicion in Scotland concerning his activities. He may have been initiating the negotiations for the release of Malise Graham earl of Menteith, who had been held captive in England for twenty-four years as a hostage for the ransom of James I.[67]

The connection between Graham and the Douglases was twofold. Euphemia Graham, sister of Malise, married Archibald 5th earl of Douglas, and when he died, she took as her second husband James lord Hamilton, who was a principal adherent of the Douglases. In 1430, Euphemia and her first husband, Archibald, may have been suspected of conspiring to secure her brother's release and Archibald certainly suffered temporary imprisonment.[68] Of all the Scottish nobles, Malise Graham had the best claim to the crown after the king, as Mary of Gueldres had not yet provided James II with an heir. Indeed, if a dynastic claim for Malise Graham was ever considered, it would have been on the basis that he had a better claim to the crown than James II, descended as he was from the first marriage of Robert III. In view of this, if James Douglas were intriguing for Graham's release, his actions may have been construed as potentially treasonable, although there is no reference, in the charges brought against Douglas in 1452 as justification for his murder, to treasonable intrigue with England. Whatever the suspicions in Scotland, it would not have been easy to level such a charge as there was a truce between the two countries at the time, and the king could hardly display open opposition to the return of Malise Graham.

Despite Douglas being named as a commissioner of the truce in April, the Auchinleck chronicler states that 'thai gat the erllis sele to consent to the trewis', which implies that Douglas did not go to England in person, but sent his seal. It is possible that, having been in England the previous month, Douglas did not feel it necessary to return so soon, or he may have felt unwilling to venture far in the light of his recent experience, considering that his interests could best be protected by remaining in Scotland. On 6 July 1451, an English safe-conduct was issued for William Turnbull, bishop of Glasgow, and others, commissioners of the King of Scots. William earl of Douglas does not appear on the list although the earls of Angus, Crawford and Huntly do. On 14 August, a three-year truce was agreed at Newcastle which was ratified by James at Perth on 28 August and by Henry VI at Westminster on 16 September.[69]

The parliament held at Stirling on 25 and 26 October 1451 witnessed the re-granting of the Earldom of Wigtown to William earl of Douglas. To all appearances, the king and Douglas had resolved their differences, and the Auchinleck chronicler wrote that 'all gud scottismen war rycht blyth of that accordance'.[70] However, it was a hollow peace. The king's actions had evidently been too arbitrary to be successful, and he was persuaded to back down. Attacking the possessions of an earl when he was not there to defend them or plead his case would have made other members of the nobility uneasy, fearing that if the king could attack Douglas in that manner, their own positions were similarly vulnerable. James cannot have appreciated losing the contest over Wigtown, which is shown clearly by his reluctance to part with the earldom, and his relationship with Douglas from that point onwards was strained and latently hostile.

Douglas was not slow to appreciate that he must seek allies within Scotland to help him to stand up to the king's animosity, and it was presumably with this in mind that he formed the fateful bond with the Earls of Crawford and Ross. Bonds between members of the nobility were a normal form of activity, and Dr Wormald's study of the practice has shown that the 1440s witnessed the appearance of a number of bonds of manrent.[71] The basic difference between bonds of manrent and earlier feudal agreements was that land was rarely involved in manrent bonds, but rather service and maintenance. It is impossible to form definite conclusions about the Douglas-Crawford-Ross bond as it has not survived and its terms are unknown. However, a bond between three powerful earls was unusual in the context of fifteenth-century bonding practices as bonds were given, normally, to only one lord, generally of a higher social status than the man offering the bond. It was part of the formula that allegiance to the king was stipulated as paramount, and superseded any promise or agreement made to anyone else. There is no other case in the records of this period where three powerful Scottish magnates made a mutual bond, and Charles VII's experience in France where magnates bound themselves to each other in rebellious coalitions would have been known to James, who can hardly have welcomed the development of such a trend in Scotland.[72] Nevertheless, it should not be assumed that James II objected to bonds in principle; indeed he was the only Scottish king known to have made such personal bonds himself.[73] James' objection to the Douglas-Crawford-Ross bond was a specific objection to that particular bond, and it is worth examining the reasons why it was regarded as such a vital issue.

The Auchinleck chronicle contains an entry which describes a revolt involving John earl of Ross, lord of the Isles, which reads:

> the zere of god lmiiiicli in the moneth of merche the erll of Ross and lord of the ylis tuke thir castellis of the king viz Inverness and wrquhart and kest doune the castell of rochwan [Ruthven] in badyenoch And thai said that he gaf the keping of the castell of wrquhart till his gud fader James of levingstoun that was eschapit subtelly fra the king and his counsall out of the abbay of halyrudhouss and was cummand to the lord for supple and succour that resavit him richt thankfully and tuke plane part agane the king for him And said he had the kingis wryt and walx to haf the castell of wrquhart for iii zere And he said that the kingis awne person gart him mary the said James douchter and hacht him gud lordshipe the quhilk he had not gottin bot ewyn the contrar in all thingis.[74]

The problem with interpreting dates in fifteenth-century documents is that the new year was calculated from 25 March rather than 1 January as it is now. In view of this, the extract recorded above with its March date has been taken to refer to 1452, but the Auchinleck chronicle, which will be examined in greater depth later, is not always consistent in this method of dating and in this case strong evidence has been put forward by Dr Grant to show that the chronicler was referring to events in March 1451. The revolt of the Lord of the Isles should be seen in connection with the disgrace of the Livingstons rather than as a response to the murder of Douglas in 1452, and the wording of the entry in Auchinleck supports this view.[75] John earl of Ross and lord of the Isles was married to Elizabeth Livingston, the daughter of James Livingston, chamberlain, and the match had been arranged, apparently, with royal sanction, prior to the fall of the Livingstons. James II must have made certain promises to the Lord of the Isles as part of the marriage agreement — the grant of the keepership of Urquhart castle and the 'gud lordschipe' mentioned. When the Livingstons fell from favour, the king must have rescinded his promises and the Lord of the Isles decided as a consequence to take by force that which he felt to be due to him by the previous arrangement. James Livingston escaped from royal custody in 1450, perhaps fearing the same fate as his brother and cousin, and joined his son-in-law, who launched his attack in the following spring. The Auchinleck chronicler states that Ruthven castle was cast down, an event which must have taken place after 28 April 1451, as on that date the king granted to Alexander earl of Huntly the lordship of Badenoch with the keepership of Ruthven castle.[76]

In March 1451, Douglas was in England on his way back to Scotland from Rome; the king was occupied with the contest over the Earldom of Wigtown and therefore was in no position to take action against the Lord of the Isles. The only gesture which he made was the despatch of John Schethow to Inverness some time before July 1451, 'ad dominum comitem Rossie in negociis regis'.[77] James Livingston was recognised as keeper of Inverness castle in the Inverness account of July 1454 and the bailies accounted for fees paid to him during the whole of the preceding three years. Clearly, therefore,

Livingston, and not the previous keeper, Thomas Ogilvy, was holding Inverness castle in the second half of 1451.[78]

Speculation about the bond made between Douglas, Crawford and Ross has led to many theories, one of which is that it dated from the 1440s, which was a time of Douglas dominance at court.[79] The only writer to put a date to the bond is Sir James Balfour of Kinnaird, writing in the 1640s, who stated that the bond was signed and sealed on 7 March 1445.[80] This statement seems impressively definite until it is considered that there is no evidence given to support it, and Balfour's work is so full of inaccuracies and misdating that very little reliance ought to be placed on this assertion.[81] Also, the Earls of Crawford and Ross were not the same men in 1445 as they were in 1452 (David earl of Crawford died in 1446 and Alexander earl of Ross and lord of the Isles died in 1449), and there is no evidence to suggest that such bonds of alliance were inherited. In the later years of the minority, Douglas was very much in favour and held an influential position at court, therefore it is hard to understand why he would have felt the need to form bonds of alliance in such a climate of security. However, when the king moved against Douglas possessions in the winter of 1450–51, the earl must have realised, with a sense of shock, that his position was not unassailable and that despite the appearance of reconciliation, the king was no longer content to see others form his policies. In this atmosphere of uncertainty it is much more likely that Douglas would have cast about for allies, and the Earl of Ross was an obvious choice, given his recent cause for grievance against the king.

It has been pointed out by Marion Stewart that relations between the Douglases and the Earl of Ross were strained because of the fall of the Livingstons.[82] In Holland's 'Howlat', written under the patronage of Archibald Douglas, earl of Moray, Ross is himself satirised in the image of the 'bard out of Ireland'. Also, there may have been an element of competition between the Douglases and Ross because of their influence in adjacent geographical areas, particularly in the case of Hugh, earl of Ormond. However, when Douglas did come to cast around for support, he and Ross must both have seen the merits of mutual assistance. Expediency mattered, and Ross would have realised that Douglas could provide far more powerful support than his father-in-law, James Livingston. Old enmity probably gave way to pragmatism.

The third member of the bond was Alexander earl of Crawford. There is some evidence that the Lindsays were inveterate troublemakers in this period; the Auchinleck chronicler, when stating that Alexander earl of Crawford died in 1453, called him 'a rigorous man and ane felloun and held ane gret rowme in his tyme for he held all Angus in his bandoun and was richt Inobedient to the king'.[83] After the death of James I in 1437, David earl of Crawford, and Alexander after him, exacted annual and illegal payments from the customs of Aberdeen, Montrose and Banff. There are a number of protests in the accounts that these sums were not due and had been extorted by violence, but these appear to have been to no avail.[84] The battle of Arbroath in 1446 arose out of the aggressive claim of Alexander Lindsay, as Master of Crawford, to the bailiary of the abbey, and he was also involved in the 'herschipe in Fife' which led James Kennedy, bishop of St Andrews, to place his curse on David earl of Crawford.[85]

The Douglas-Crawford connection arose from the marriage of Jean Lindsay, daughter of David earl of Crawford, to the young William 6th earl of Douglas, who was put to death in Edinburgh castle at the 'Black Dinner' of 1440. On 30 October 1445 William 8th earl of Douglas and Jean Lindsay sealed an indenture by which Douglas promised to assist Jean to recover 'her terce of Anandirdale'.[86] Given that the lordship was at that time legally crown property, such a scheme may have had treasonable implications. An instrument proceeding upon the indenture was taken on 14 January 1450 at the church of the Friars of Dundee, and on that same date Douglas witnessed a royal charter at Linlithgow.[87] Douglas and Crawford were, at least to this extent, working together for their mutual benefit, and therefore it must have been natural to invite the Earl of Crawford to join in a bond to advance each other's interests. Alexander earl of Crawford was not at court in January 1451 when the king was involved in the seizure of Wigtown, but he was there on 28 April when Douglas returned from Rome and he was present in the parliament which reinstated him.[88] Rather than there being a cast-iron Douglas-Crawford alliance, it seems that the Black Dinner of 1440 still cast a shadow over the relationship and that the 8th Earl was seeking to strengthen it.

The fact that the bond between Douglas, Crawford and Ross has not survived has induced much speculation about its contents, and it has been tempting to interpret it as a sinister, unusual, and overtly treacherous agreement which boded ill for the king. However, it is more likely that the bond, and the king's objection to it, was far more straightforward. In the context of fifteenth-century bonding practices, a bond of friendship was an acceptable way of settling disputes and matters of contention between interested parties. The crucial point to note in the joining together of Douglas, Crawford and Ross is that these men were not natural allies, and there had been occasions of friction between them in the past. Such friction would have suited James II very well, as he relied, to some extent, on the policy of 'divide and rule' to curb the power of his magnates. Therefore, a bond of friendship, innocuous enough in itself, between three unnatural allies, each of whom had been individually troublesome to the king, must have presented an alarming prospect.

The atmosphere of intrigue at court, with both the king and the Earl of Douglas concentrating on building up their positions and seeking support, indicates that the presence of Douglas there ought not to be interpreted as a sign that he was in favour, but rather that he remained at court in order to protect his interests: he was afraid *not* to be there in view of what had taken place during his absence in Rome. Douglas witnessed a royal charter in

Edinburgh on 13 January 1452, on which he was styled Earl of Wigtown.[89] He was still in Edinburgh on 26 January when he issued a charter of lands to Robert Vaus, and one of the witnesses on this charter was William Lauder of Hatton.[90] Lauder was involved in the lead-up to the final confrontation between Douglas and the king, and it is worth examining the role played by him in greater depth. He was a Douglas retainer who had appeared on safe-conducts with Douglas on 23 October 1450, 12 November 1450 and 12 May 1451.[91] He accompanied Douglas to Rome in the winter of 1450–51 and he was given the task of conveying James II's safe-conduct to Douglas in February 1452. On 18 April 1452, the queen received a charter of lands forfeited by William Lauder of Hatton, who was evidently dead by that date as he is described as 'quondam'.[92] George Burnett, the editor of the Exchequer Rolls, points out that no parliament was held between the death of Douglas in February and the parliament convened on 12 June 1452, and Lauder's forfeiture must therefore have taken place in the preceding parliament held in June 1451.[93] If so, it is not clear what charges were brought against Lauder, but he may have been used as a scapegoat in order to achieve a face-saving 'conciliation' in 1451. It is possible that Lauder was one of the men sent ahead of William earl of Douglas, on his return from Rome, to assess the situation in Scotland before the earl ventured over the border. Lauder may have gone to Craig Douglas, a Douglas stronghold just north of the border, and held it in defiance of the king's officials. James II may consequently have seized the opportunity to make an example of Craig Douglas by attacking it, and the subsequent forfeiture of Lauder is certainly suggestive. In view of this, it is strange that Lauder consented to deliver a safe-conduct to his patron only months later, unless some arrangement had been made with James II, perhaps by which the king had agreed to rescind Lauder's forfeiture. The fact that Lauder was dead by April may suggest that he continued to support the Douglas faction following the murder of the 8th Earl, and perhaps also underlines the sense of outrage which the murder produced in at least one of the supporters of Douglas who may have felt himself to be the victim of cynical manipulation. This is certainly indicated by the fact that the royal forces laid siege to the tower of Hatton in late March or early April 1452.[94] The Auchinleck chronicler describes the safe-conduct for Douglas to come to Stirling as a special 'respit and assouerance'.[95] This indicates that Douglas was facing criminal charges for which he was being granted respite, and the sixteenth-century chroniclers certainly provide a long catalogue of Douglas's supposed misdemeanours. That Douglas, present at court in Edinburgh only one month previously, should have asked for a safe-conduct at all is an indication of the deterioration in the relationship between the king and himself at this time. If James II had only recently received word of the bond between Douglas, Crawford and Ross, this would explain why he chose to confront Douglas and insist on the dissolution of the bond. Douglas, suspecting the reason for the summons, or at least anticipating the king's displeasure, must have demanded a safe-conduct, particularly as Stirling castle was held at that time by his old adversary, George Crichton.

A detailed account of the murder of William earl of Douglas is given in the Auchinleck chronicle. In some of the chronicle's entries, dates and times are vague, but in the account of the murder, the chronicler is very precise, perhaps indicating that the writer was employed at court, possibly as a royal clerk, and therefore was present in Stirling at the time. The chronicler described the safe-conduct as having been given under the privy seal and signed by the king personally. In addition, all the lords who were with the king at that time signed the safe-conduct, following which

> William of Lawder of haltoun passit to the forsaid erll William of Douglas and brocht him to stirling to the king on the monday before fastrennisevyn that was the xxi day of February and this samyn monday he passit to the castell and spak with the king that tuke richt wele with him be apperans and callit him on the morne to the dynere and to the supper / and he come and dynit and sowpit and thai said thair was a band betuix the said erll of Douglas and the erll of Ross and the erll of Crawford and efter supper at sevyne houris the king then beand in the inner chalmer and the said erll he chargit him to breke the forsaid band he said he mycht not nor wald nocht / Than the king said / fals tratour sen thow will nocht I sall / and stert sodanly till him with ane knyf and straik him in at the colere and down in the body and thai sayd that Patrick Gray straik him nixt the king with ane poll ax on the hed and strak out his branes and syne the gentillis that war with the king gaf thaim ilkane a straik or twa with knyffis and thir ar the names that war with the king that strake him for he had xxvi woundis. In the first, Sir Alexander Boyd, the lord Darnley, Sir Andrew Stewart, Sir William of Gremston, Sir Simon of Glendonane and the Lord Gray.[96]

From this account it seems that the earl stayed with the king for two days and it was not until the second day, 22 February, that issue was taken over the bond, or the king realised after long discussion that the matter could not be solved by verbal persuasion. The men named by the Auchinleck chronicler as being with the king and participating in the murder shed some very interesting light on James's position at the time.

Sir Alexander Boyd of Drumcoll was the second son of Sir Thomas Boyd of Kilmarnock. He was knighted between Martinmas 1448 and Martinmas 1449 and in 1456 he was appointed warden of Threave on its surrender to the king, but was removed to Dumbarton shortly afterwards.[97] The Lord Darnley referred to was Sir John Stewart of Darnley, the son of Sir Alan Stewart of Darnley slain by Sir Thomas Boyd. The retributive slaying of Thomas Boyd by Alan's brother, Alexander, may have ended the bloodfeud and would explain why Boyd and Darnley were together at court.

According to the *Scots Peerage*, Sir Andrew Stewart was probably a natural son of Sir Walter Stewart, second son of Murdoch duke of Albany.[98] In 1456 he was granted the barony of Avandale (formerly a Douglas possession) and in the following year he was created Lord Avandale. He held the position of

Warden of the West March and was one of the Scottish conservators of the truce between England and Scotland ratified on 11 June 1457.[99] On 1 March 1460, Avandale was styled King's Guardian on three charters, a title which appears to suggest a personal bodyguard to the king, and on 6 July 1460, on the last royal charter issued before the king's death, Avandale suddenly replaced George Schoriswood, bishop of Brechin, as chancellor.[100] Avandale continued his career in royal service during the reign of James III, seeking and receiving royal letters of legitimation for himself and his brothers, Arthur and Walter, although without specifying their parentage, on 28 August 1472, and again on 17 April 1479.[101] Rewards and political advancement had followed on the heels of Avandale's participation in the murder of Douglas, although old enmities may have been created at the same time which haunted him to the extent that he sought legitimation for his position and protection through loyal crown service for the remainder of his career. On 5 March 1470, Andrew Kerr of Cessford, an old adherent of the Douglases, was indicted for numerous treasonable acts including bringing the exiled James 9th earl of Douglas back into Scotland 'and also for his counsel and consent to the treasonable killing of Andrew lord Avandale, chancellor of Scotland'.[102] Avandale was not killed in 1470, but it was obviously believed that Kerr and others had intended that he should be, most likely as a belated retribution for his part in slaying William earl of Douglas in 1452. The Black Douglas issue was thus far from laid to rest with the formal forfeiture of the family in 1455.[103]

Another participant in the murder of William 8th earl of Douglas is named by the Auchinleck chronicle as 'sir william of gremston', but this ought to be read as Cranston. There is no evidence for anyone of the name Gremston or Grahamston, but there is ample evidence for the presence at court of William Cranston, and the rewards received by the Cranstons in the wake of Douglas's murder are suggestive. William Cranston was the son of Thomas Cranston of that ilk and both men had a demonstrable connection with the Earl of Douglas. On 10 May 1446, William earl of Douglas granted to Thomas Cranston lands on the west side of the town of Sprouston.[104] Following the murder of the earl, Thomas Cranston received a crown grant, on 2 March 1452, of the lands of Greenlaw in the sheriffdom of Berwick.[105] His son William Cranston had received confirmation from William earl of Douglas on 20 August 1443 of a charter, given by Archibald 5th earl of Douglas on 29 November 1434, of the lands of Nether Crailing in the sheriffdom of Roxburgh.[106] William Cranston was a frequent royal charter witness and was employed on embassies to England to negotiate and act as conservator of truces. On 2 March 1452 he received a royal charter giving him the office of coroner in the sheriffdom of Roxburgh, and on 12 April he received a crown grant of lands in the sheriffdom of Peebles which had been forfeited by William Lauder of Hatton.[107] This is further evidence that former Douglas men had withdrawn their support from the earl and placed their allegiance firmly behind the king, whose overt wooing of Douglas followers took place before and after the murder as a conscious effort to curb Douglas power and influence, and prevent its re-establishment.

Sir Simon Glendinning held the lands of Glendinning in Westerkirk parish, north-east Dumfriesshire, on the Megget Water.[108] Glendinning had acted as a conservator of the truce with England on 23 October 1450 and 22 July 1451,[109] and he appeared as a witness on royal charters on six occasions between 1451 and 1459.[110] He also appeared as a witness on a charter by William earl of Douglas to his brother James on 2 May 1449. His motives for taking part in the murder are obscure; possibly he harboured a private grudge against Douglas and as a result the king was able to buy his support against the earl.[111] There survives a royal charter granted by James II to Simon Glendinning and his heirs of £20 of land in the barony of Alde-Roxburgh.[112] Though no date, place of issue or witness list survives and it has been placed in the Register of the Great Seal under the year 1450, it may belong, more rationally, to 1452 as a reward for Glendinning's participation in the murder of Douglas.

Andrew Gray of Foulis had served as one of the hostages for James I in 1424 and had been exchanged for Malcolm Fleming, younger of Cumbernauld, in 1427.[113] He was also one of the train of knights who accompanied the princess Margaret to France for her marriage to the Dauphin in 1436. In 1445, he was created a lord of parliament as Lord Gray, and he was used as an ambassador to England in 1449 and 1451.[114] On 22 January 1452, his name was on a safe-conduct issued to certain Scottish bishops and others to travel on pilgrimage to Canterbury, and William earl of Douglas appears on the same safe-conduct. In 1452, following the murder of Douglas, Andrew lord Gray became Master of the King's Household, and on 26 August he was given permission to build the castle of Huntly (Huntly in the Carse of Gowrie by the Tay, not Huntly, Aberdeenshire).[115] In the Auchinleck chronicler's account of the murder of Douglas, Andrew lord Gray's eldest son, Patrick Master of Gray, also features; and it is the Grays who play a crucial part in the accounts of later chroniclers, particularly Robert Lindesay of Pitscottie's account of the murder.

The *Scots Peerage* states that Andrew lord Gray had a sister who was married to Maclellan of Bombie.[116] No reference for this statement is given and it seems to rest on no better evidence than Pitscottie's account, written in the late 1570s. The gist of Pitscottie's story is that Maclellan, tutor of Bombie, the nephew of Patrick master of Gray, was captured and imprisoned by the Earl of Douglas for failing to join and serve him. Patrick Gray obtained a letter of supplication from the king asking that Maclellan be released and delivered it to the earl personally. Douglas entertained Gray to dinner, but meanwhile, unknown to Gray, Maclellan was being beheaded on Douglas's orders. This example of the brutality of Douglas compelled the king to seek some means of restraining the over-mighty earl, and Douglas was duly summoned to Stirling.[117]

The Maclellans were a family from the Stewartry of Kirkcudbright; there is a reference in the Exchequer accounts to John Maclellan, custumar of the burgh of Kirkcudbright, in 1434. Bombie lies three miles east of Kirkcudbright, and in 1487 one Thomas of Bombie appears as custumar of the town, but the earliest mention of a laird of Bombie of the name Maclellan occurs in 1466 when William Maclellan of Bombie was provost of the burgh of Kirkcudbright.[118] In 1447, the Maclellans surrendered the castle of Lochdoon to Alexander Livingston, but this appears to be the only reference in contemporary sources to the family during James II's reign. Pitscottie's account of the reign of James II is largely a copy of the eighteenth book of Boece, but his story of the tutor of Bombie is original. However, the tale must be viewed with caution as there is no contemporary evidence for the existence of such a man, and because Pitscottie is frequently inaccurate and uses a number of rhetorical devices. It is possible, however, that the story has at least some foundation in fact. Maclellan may have been in the category of small men on or near Douglas estates who suffered for his loyalty to, or for having been bought out by, the king.

The murder of Douglas is unlikely to have been premeditated as, had James really desired Douglas's death, there were more subtle ways of achieving it. To renege on the safe-conduct, which was an assurance to the earl that no harm would come to him, was a violation of the mediaeval code of honour which may have outraged contemporaries more than, for example, the slaying of Douglas in armed combat would have done. It is possible that, when the earl was tackled on the subject of the bond, a heated argument developed between the king and Douglas which ended in the hot-blooded stabbing of the earl by the king 'that had the fyr mark in his face'.[119] James must have been well aware of the enormity of his crime, and the royal itinerary at this time shows that he took the initiative immediately and marched into the south. On 2 March 1452, one week after the murder, the king issued a charter from Lochmaben and another on the same day from Jedburgh. On 4 March, the king was in Dumfries and on 8 March he issued a charter from the Castle of Morton.[120] It is possible that this was a pre-arranged justice ayre, but the itinerary illustrates a flurry of activity which is not mirrored on other occasions; and the most striking feature of the charters issued in the two months following the murder is that they are mostly in favour of men who had some connection with Douglas. Thomas and William Cranston, James Rutherford and James Kerr had all appeared as witnesses on Douglas charters or with him on safe-conducts, and they all received royal charters of lands or offices immediately after the death of Douglas.[121] Similarly, John and Andrew Rutherford and members of the Haliburton, Hume and Hoppringill families, whose names may be linked with the 8th Earl of Douglas on previous occasions, were given grants.[122] Generally, these charters were resignations, re-grants and confirmations, and may be explained as Douglas men making sure of their lands by evincing support for the king.

The exercise of patronage to offset the natural revulsion which would have been felt for the murder showed James' grasp of political realities, and by moving fast he caught the Douglas faction at a disadvantage which he exploited fully. By the time the Douglases recovered from their confusion and challenged the king, the Auchinleck chronicler states that 'thai excedit nocht of gud men vic'.[123] Six hundred is likely to have been an under-estimate, but the general sense is clear: William's brother James, the new Earl of Douglas, did not command widespread support even given the heinous nature of the king's crime.

One explanation for this lies in the nature of the Douglas power base. The Black Dinner of 1440 interrupted the straight Black Douglas descent and shifted the line across to a branch of the family who, under normal circumstances, would have stood little chance of inheriting the earldom. This transfer — a result of the execution of the 6th earl and his younger brother, both minors — may have resulted in a lack of enthusiasm and support for the new line from the tenants and adherents of the 6th earl. Certainly James 7th earl of Douglas and his sons spent most of their time in their Lothian and Lanarkshire strongholds of Abercorn and Douglas, together with Newark in Ettrick forest, rather than the Galloway heartland of the previous Black Douglas line. The more far-sighted of the south-western lairds may have realised that the removal of the Douglas lordship would facilitate their rise to greater power and influence in their own areas, and were prepared to offer more than passive resistance to their erstwhile patrons, as witnessed at the battle of Arkinholm in 1455.[124] The king's success in the south-west in ensuring support for himself, rather than the Douglases, is perhaps explained by the fact that the lordship of the 7th Earl and his sons did not have deep roots in that area. Certainly, they could not command the kind of allegiance which would stir men to take the very drastic step of arming against their king.

NOTES

1. *H.M.C.*, Johnstone, no. 2.

2. NRA (S), Arbuthnott Writs, no. 24.

3. *Foedera*, xi, 235, 242; *Rot. Scot.*, ii, 334, 336.

4. Chron. Auchinleck, f. 122r.

5. Livingston, E. B., *The Livingstons of Callendar* (Edinburgh, 1920). John Livingston appears with Alexander on a charter dated 26 January 1425.

6. This may be Greenyards near Doune, map reference: NN761012, Ordnance Survey 1:50000 1st series, sheet 57.

7. *E.R.*, v, 132.

8. I am very grateful to Norman Shead and Peter Macneill for identifying this as Fildies in Glenfarg. Alexander Livingston received a crown charter of lands in Perthshire, including the lands of Filde which were to be held of the crown as a free

barony. The grant was made at Falkland on 15 February 1449. St Andrews University Library, Calendar of St Andrews Charters, 33.

9. *E.R.*, v, 258, 297, 477. Nairn may have received the keepership of Doune as compensation.

10. Dunlop, *Kennedy*, 102; *A.P.S.*, ii, 61; *E.R.*, v, 479.

11. Fraser, *Keir*, no. 28.

12. Ramsay, Sir J., *Lancaster and York*, ii, 195; *E.R.*, v, 406, 488.

13. *E.R.*, v, lxxx, 471.

14. Smit, H. J., *Bronnen Tot de Geschiedenis van den Handel met Ingeland Schotland en Ierland* (1928), ii, no. 1359.

15. Ibid., ii, 1358.

16. Davidson and Gray, *The Scottish Staple at Veere*, 132.

17. Chron. Auchinleck, f. 122r.

18. *E.R.*, v, 181, 228, 308, 495.

19. Ibid., lxxx; NLS Adv. MSS. B1316/1317. This remission included the Livingstons, and is further evidence of the king's concern to secure support from those who had cause to be disaffected.

20. Chron. Auchinleck, f. 123r.

21. Ibid., f. 122r.

22. *R.M.S.*, ii, 316, 317. After the murder of Douglas in 1452, Sir Archibald Dundas recovered the estates held by Douglas and became sheriff of Linlithgow. His brother Duncan was promoted to the position of deputy to James lord Livingston, chamberlain. *E.R.*, vi, 146, 148, 547.

23. *R.M.S.*, ii, 324.

24. Glasgow University Scottish History Department, Calendar of Scottish Supplications to Rome, 442, 228v.

25. *S.P.*, v, 429.

26. Dunlop, *Kennedy*, 107.

27. *E.R..*, v, 336; *R.M.S.*, ii, 618.

28. Nicholson, R., *The Later Middle Ages*, 350.

29. Chron. Auchinleck, f. 122r. There was a Duncan Pearson associated with Alexander lord of the Isles in a grant from the Exchequer in 1438: *E.R.*, v, 34.

30. Stewart, M., 'Holland's "Howlat" and the Fall of the Livingstons', *Innes Review*, xxvi (1975), 67-79.

31. *R.M.S.*, ii, nos. 508, 316, 317, 357.

32. Ibid., ii, nos. 301, 315; *E.R.*, v, 383.

33. *A.P.S.*, ii, 37-8; *R.M.S.*, ii, 307.

34. *E.R.*, v, 393; *R.M.S.*, ii, no. 363.

35. Dunlop, *Kennedy*, 124.

36. Law, J., De Cronicis Scotorum brevia, 1521. Edin. Univ. Lib. DC7, 63, f. 128v.

37. *C.P.R.*, x, 84, 86.

38. C.S.S.R., 448, 18v.

39. Law, op. cit.

40. Dunlop, *Kennedy*, 131.

41. *R.M.S.*, ii, no. 309.

42. Lesley, *History*, 22.

43. Buchanan, *History*, f. xxxiii.

44. *E.R.*, v, 521.

45. *R.M.S.*, ii, nos. 412–417.

46. Law, op. cit.

47. *R.M.S.*, ii, nos. 412–416.

48. I am indebted to Dr H. MacQueen for this information.

49. *R.M.S.*, ii, no. 417.

50. Chron. Auchinleck, f. 121v.

51. Fraser, *Douglas*, iii, 419; *R.M.S.*, ii, no. 401.

52. *S.P.*, ii, 220.

53. *R.M.S.*, ii, nos. 455, 484, 485, 512, 514, 525.

54. *Glas. Reg.*, ii, 362, 363.

55. *R.M.S.*, ii, no. 404.

56. *C.D.S.*, iv, 1231; Law, op. cit. Craig Douglas was a small Douglas stronghold which stood on the river Yarrow.

57. *Rot. Scot.*, ii, 345. The other commissioners named were: John Ralston, bishop of Dunkeld, John Cranach, bishop of Brechin, George earl of Angus, Alexander earl of Crawford, William lord Somerville, Alexander lord Montgomery, Patrick lord Glamis, Andrew lord Gray, John David of Moray and Alexander Nairn of Sandfurd; Buchanan, *History*, f. xxxiv.

58. Chron. Auchinleck, f. 114r.

59. Grant, A., *Independence and Nationhood* (London, 1984), 192.

60. C.S.S.R., 441, 254v.

61. *A.P.S.*, ii, app. 24–30, 67–71.

62. Ibid., app. 31–32, 71–72; *R.M.S.*, ii, 523.

63. *Rot Scot.*, ii, 346. The others named were: Alexander Hume, James lord Hamilton, William Meldrum, William Lauder of Hatton, Thomas Cranston, Andrew Kerr, James Douglas of Ralston, Alan Cathcart, David Hume, John Ross, George, Alexander and David Hoppringill, William Bailie, George and Mark Haliburton, Alan Lauder, Charles Murray, Thomas Boll, Thomas Graham, James Dunbar, Robert Herries, William Grierson, John Menzies, James Douglas, John Haliburton, Adam Auchinleck, John Clerk, James and Thomas Kerr.

64. *Pell Records*, 30. Henry VI.

65. *C.D.S.*, iv, 1236.

66. Ramsay, Sir J., op. cit.

67. Ramsay, Sir J., *Lancaster and York*, ii, 196; Balfour-Melville, J., *James I*, 294.

Macrae, C., 'The English Council and Scotland in 1430', *E.H.R.*, LIV (1939), 419, 426.

69. *Rot. Scot.*, ii, 347, 354.

70. Chron. Auchinleck, f. 114r.

71. Wormald, J., *Lords and Men in Scotland: Bonds of Manrent 1442–1603* (Edinburgh, 1985), passim.

72. Grant, A., 'The Revolt of the Lord of the Isles and the Death of the Earl of Douglas 1451–52', *S.H.R.*, lx, 169–174.

73. Wormald, J., *Lords and Men*, 152.

74. Chron. Auchinleck, f. 118v–112r.

75. Grant, A., 'The Revolt of the Lord of the Isles', op. cit.

76. *R.M.S.*, ii, no. 442.

77. *E.R.*, v, 465. Accounting period: Michaelmas 1450–July 1451.

78. Grant, op. cit.

79. Grant, *Independence and Nationhood*, 192–3.

80. Balfour, *Annales*, i, 173.

81. For example, the Black Dinner of November 1440 is dated 17 July by Balfour. He states that on 20 January 1449, the king created Alexander Setoun lord Gordon, Earl of Huntly and George Leslie, Earl of Rothes. (Huntly was created in 1445 and Rothes in 1458.) John Cameron, bishop of Glasgow, died in December 1446, but Balfour dates his death, January 1450. He also states that the Earl of Douglas was murdered in Edinburgh castle rather than Stirling. Balfour, *Annales*, i, passim.

82. Stewart, M., 'Holland's Howlat', op. cit.

83. Chron. Auchinleck, f. 112r–112v.

84. *E.R.*, v, 234, 630, 639, 301, 316, 325, 341.

85. Chron. Auchinleck, f. 111v.

86. S.R.O., Calendar of Charters, 321. Also, see Chapter 3.

87. *R.M.S.*, ii, no. 304.

88. *A.P.S.*, ii, 67.

89. *R.M.S.*, ii, no. 523.

90. *Wigt. Chrs.*, 136.

91. *Rot. Scot.*, ii, 340–1, 343, 346.

92. *R.M.S.*, ii, no. 544.

93. *E.R.*, v, xcviii.

94. *Accounts of the Lord High Treasurer of Scotland*, ed. T. Dickson and Sir J. Balfour Paul (Edinburgh, 1877–1916), i, ccxvii.

95. Chron. Auchinleck, f. 114v.

96. Ibid.

97. *E.R.*, vi, 208, 209; *S.P.*, v, 141–142.

98. *S.P.*, i, 150.

99. *Rot. Scot.*, ii, 383.

100. *R.M.S.*, ii, nos. 744, 745, 747; *H.M.C.*, Home, 278.

101. *R.M.S.*, ii, nos.

102. *H.M.C.*, 34, Report xiv.3 — Roxburgh. Misc. Writs, 54. I am indebted to Dr Stephen Boardman for drawing my attention to this reference.

103. It is interesting to note that Kerr was acquitted by a jury among whom were David, earl of Crawford, James lord Hamilton, Sir Alexander Lauder of Hatton and James Auchinleck, all of whose families had traditional Douglas connections.

104. Fraser, *Douglas*, iii, 415; *S.P.*, ii, 587–588.

105. *R.M.S.*, ii, no. 529.

106. *Laing Charters*, 122.

107. *A.P.S.*, ii, 531, 534.

108. Groome, F. H., *Ordnance Gazetteer of Scotland* (Edinburgh, 1882–85).

109. *Rot. Scot.*, ii, 340–41.

110. *R.M.S.*, ii, 490, 491, 492; *Wigt. Chrs.*, 138; S.R.O., GD 25/1/64; Fraser, *Buccleuch*, ii, 61.

111. Fraser, *Douglas*, ii, 419.

112. *R.M.S.*, ii, no. 420.

113. Balfour-Melville, *James I*, 294.

114. *Rot. Scot.*, ii, 345.

115. *S.P.*, iv, 273. Castle Huntly in Longforgan parish, Perthshire.

116. Ibid.

117. Pitscottie, *Historie*, 90–91.

118. *E.R.*, iv, 606, 305; *H.M.C.*, Rep. iv, 539.

119. Chron. Auchinleck, f. 114v.

120. *R.M.S.*, ii, nos. 529, 530; S.R.O., GD 89 no. 10; *Wigt. Chrs.*, 138.

121. Ibid., 136; Fraser, *Douglas*, iii, 406, 417, 419; *Rot. Scot.*, ii, 340, 343; *R.M.S.*, ii, nos. 529, 530, 531, 534.

122. Ibid., 537, 538, 532, 541; S.R.O., GD 157, no. 75.

123. Chron. Auchinleck, f. 115v.

124. See Chapter 5, p. 88.

5

Conflict and Conspiracy, 1452–55

The murder of William earl of Douglas must have stunned his family and followers, and their uncertainty about how to respond was in direct contrast to the decisiveness of the king. William's brother, James, became 9th Earl of Douglas, and one of his first actions following the murder was to come to Stirling on 17 March, where he

> blew out xxiv hornis attanis apon the king and apon all the lordis that war with him that tyme for the foule slauchter of his brother And schew all thair seles at the corss on ane letter with thair handis subscrivit and tuke the letter and band it on ane burd and cuplit it till ane hors tale and gart draw it throu the towne spekand richt sclanderfully of the king . . . and spulzeit all the toune and brint it.[1]

The effect of this defiant display was somewhat lessened by the fact that the king was not in Stirling when it took place, but was, according to the Auchinleck chronicler, on his way to Perth to meet the Earl of Crawford. However, the king had issued a charter from Stirling on 14 March, having returned there following his visit to the south, therefore the Douglas attack was not merely an empty gesture.[2] Some indication of the king's position may be gauged from the list of witnesses on this royal charter, issued on 14 March to David Scott. William Turnbull, bishop of Glasgow, William Crichton, chancellor, Thomas, lord Erskine, William, lord Somerville, Andrew, lord Gray, master of the king's household, Master John Arous, archdeacon of Glasgow and George Schoriswood, rector of Culter were all witnesses, but in view of the magnitude of what had taken place only a month before — the murder by the king of his most powerful subject — the list hardly gives an impressive picture of the king's supporters at the time. There were no earls at court, by the evidence of this charter, and it seems likely that the king was having to work very hard to explain his actions and reassure the political community. When James 9th earl of Douglas came with his followers to Stirling, he clearly expected to find the king there, and had, in fact, missed him by only a couple of days. The force brought by Douglas to Stirling included his brother, Hugh, earl of Ormond and James, lord Hamilton. According to the Auchinleck chronicler, 'thai excedit nocht of gud men vic [600]', which may not be as paltry as the chronicler implies if the relative strength of the king's position was as weak as the Buccleuch charter indicates.

This raises the question of what Douglas hoped to achieve by his act of defiance against the king. How much further would he have been prepared to go if the king had been in Stirling castle? The ultimate action against the king would have been his deposition, but it is not possible to assess whether Douglas ever intended to push that far, although he may have felt that the king had drawn up the battle lines by taking the offensive against the Douglases, therefore he would have very little to lose.

It is not clear where the king was between 14 March, when he issued the charter from Stirling, and 24 March, when he was back in Edinburgh, but if the future James III was born in St Andrews castle in May, this suggests that the king escorted the pregnant queen to St Andrews for safety between his departure from Stirling and his return to Edinburgh, anticipating, correctly, that Stirling would be a storm centre for any Douglas reprisals.[3] There is some disagreement about the precise date of the birth of James III. Thomas Riis points out that as he distributed the Maundy alms in 1474 to twenty-three people (the tradition being that the number of alms reflected the age of the giver), he must have been born in 1451. In addition to this, James III's act of general revocation, an act issued in a monarch's twenty-fifth year, took place in 1476. Against this is the evidence of the 'Golden Charter' granted to James Kennedy, bishop of St Andrews on 14 June 1452 for services rendered and in commemoration of the birth of the young prince in Kennedy's castle at St Andrews. If James III had been born in 1451, there was quite a delay in granting the charter, although Riis explains this by the fact that Kennedy was abroad at the time of the 1451 parliaments.[4] Nevertheless, Stirling was traditionally the residence of the Queen and her children and it is not clear why she should have chosen to journey to St Andrews to have her child in 1451 when there is no obvious reason why Stirling was unacceptable. Also, it seems strange that the queen should choose to occupy the episcopal castle of St Andrews for her confinement at a time when the resident host, Kennedy, was apparently abroad. However, after the murder of William 8th earl of Douglas at Stirling in February 1452, there was every reason to remove the queen, if pregnant at that stage, from the storm centre and into the safe hands of Bishop Kennedy in St Andrews. No previous mention is to be found in the official records of the existence of a male heir to the crown before the 'Golden Charter' of 1452, although evidence for the precise date of his birth remains confusing and inconclusive.[5]

The Auchinleck chronicler's statement that the king had gone to Perth to meet the Earl of Crawford has been seen in connection with the battle of Brechin which was fought on 18 May 1452, although it would hardly have taken the king two months to reach Perth, and he was back in Edinburgh by 24 March,[6] where he appears to have remained until the end of August. A meeting with the Earl of Crawford, if it took place, must have happened sometime before the fight at Brechin, and it is significant that the Auchinleck chronicler does not obviously tie in the battle of Brechin with the aftermath of the murder of Douglas. The description of the battle is the last entry in the original Asloan Manuscript, and is incomplete at the end. It has the appearance of having been tacked on as an afterthought and is given a heading, which is a unique occurrence in the chronicle. The heading reads, 'the battell of ~~arbroth~~ brechyne'.[7] The confusion with the battle of Arbroath is understandable as the earls of Huntly and Crawford were involved in both battles, and there may have been a deep antagonism between the two families, dating from 1446 when David earl of Crawford, the father of Alexander, was killed by a faction which included Alexander earl of Huntly.[8] Following the battle of Brechin, in which the Earl of Huntly proved victorious, the protagonists, according to the Auchinleck chronicler, conducted violent raids in Angus. This is borne out by a transcript of a letter from James II to the sheriff of Forfar, dated 16 January 1455, concerning a complaint by Walter Carnegie that during the fighting between Alexander earl of Huntly and the late Alexander earl of Crawford, Carnegie's mansion was burned and his charters of the lands of Kinnaird were destroyed.[9] Carnegie may have suffered for failing to support the Earl of Crawford in the battle of Brechin, although checking this is extremely difficult as the Auchinleck chronicler names very few of the participants. Apart from the two earls, the chronicler states that the Earl of Crawford's brother, John Lindsay, and the laird of Dundas were slain on Crawford's side, and on Huntly's side, his brother William of Seton.

The issues involved in the battle of Brechin and the reasons why it was fought are rather obscure, but the Auchinleck chronicler provides some clues when he states that

> thair was with the erll of huntlie fer ma than was with the erll of craufurd becaus he displayit the kingis banere and said it was the kingis actioun and he was his luftennend.[10]

The motif of displaying the king's banner was also used by the Auchinleck chronicler in describing the siege of Barnton in 1444 when the Earl of Douglas sanctioned his actions by this device, and it is possible that Huntly was acting as the king's lieutenant in the north at this time. In his account of the battle, John Lesley, bishop of Ross, writing in the late 1560s, stated that Huntly granted lands to numerous followers before the battle of Brechin and he was compensated by the king with the grant of Badenoch and Lochaber.[11] This is certainly a confused interpretation, as the lands of Badenoch and Lochaber and the castle of Ruthven were actually granted to Huntly in April 1451 and therefore could have no connection with the battle of Brechin.[12] In view of the king's policy of rewarding loyal supporters it is curious that the Earl of Huntly does not fare very well in the royal patronage stakes. Had the battle of Brechin been fought, as the later chroniclers suggest, in direct consequence of the slaying of the Earl of Douglas — the Earl of Huntly opposing the Earl of

Crawford on behalf of the king because Crawford had allied himself to Douglas in the notorious bond — then one would expect to see Huntly benefiting materially.

One explanation is that the battle of Brechin has been blown out of proportion, that it was rather less than a battle of national importance and implication, and should be interpreted as a baronial feud. Alexander earl of Huntly may have been a king's man insofar as he was not one of the Douglas faction, but his attitude may best be viewed as self-seeking and opportunist. The destruction of the Douglases would have suited him well, as he must have anticipated rising on their ruins, particularly in the north where there is evidence that the Gordons tried to gain the earldom of Moray following the death and forfeiture of Archibald Douglas in 1455, by attempting to secure the hand in marriage of the widowed Countess of Moray for George, the Earl of Huntly's son.[13] It was not part of the king's plan to see the end of one potentially threatening faction only to witness a new one appearing in the north, and the king's attitude to Huntly is best explained in these terms. If Huntly had been marching south to join the king, then he evidently abandoned the idea because he does not appear at court as a charter witness in 1452, nor was he present in the parliament held in Edinburgh in June, although his son, George Seton, was there.[14]

The sixteenth-century chroniclers portray the king's position in the aftermath of the murder as very precarious, and state that James actually considered fleeing to France, but was dissuaded from this course by the wise counsel of James Kennedy, bishop of St Andrews.[15] Kennedy certainly seems to have been involved in government at this time, as he appears as a witness to a number of charters and on 14 June 1452 he received the 'Golden Charter' of regality rights for the church of St Andrews. This was given

> specially for the birth of the King's eldest son which occurred in the place and principal messuage of the said patron saint [Andrew], and further for kindly services rendered by James Kennedy Bishop of St Andrews.[16]

Far from considering flight from Scotland, James established himself in Edinburgh from 24 March and a parliament was convened there on 12 June, which must have been summoned not later than 4 May if the statutory forty days' notice was given. The three estates proceeded formally to exonerate the king from blame for the murder of the Earl of Douglas, but not surprisingly there was no representation of the Douglases and the parliament appears to have been composed of royalists.[17] The Auchinleck chronicler states that the Earl of Crawford was forfeited in this parliament, but no official record of this survives and it is the chronicler who furnishes the fullest description of the proceedings of the parliament. He writes:

> Item thair was maid in the forsaid parliament three erllis viz Sir James Crichton son and heir to Sir William Crichton that spousit the eldest sister of Moray was beltit erll

of Moray. Item the Lord Hay and constable of Scotland was beltit erll of Erroll. Item Sir George of Crichton was beltit erll of Caithness.[18]

The bestowal of the earldom of Moray on James Crichton was founded on a strong legal claim as he had married Janet, the elder heiress to the Earldom of Moray, although Archibald Douglas, married to the younger co-heiress, Elizabeth, had secured the earldom through the intervention of his father. Thus, with Crichton and Huntly holding earldoms in the north, and William Hay as the newly created Earl of Errol, the Earl of Crawford was surrounded, to all appearances, by men loyal to the king. The same principle of rewarding loyal service and building up a network of interrelated baronial families is evident in the creation of lords of parliament, with Lords Hailes, Cathcart, Fleming of Cumbernauld and Home — men who had been connected with Douglas but had chosen allegiance to the king — being prominent among those receiving the new dignity. Also rewarded were John lord Darnley, Robert lord Boyd, William lord Borthwick and Alexander lord Lyle of Duchal. The Auchinleck chronicler wrote that, in addition to these grants,

> thair was sundry landis gevin to sundry men in this parliament by the king's secret counsall that is to say the Lord Cambell to Sir Colin Cambell to Sir Alexander Home to Sir David Home to Sir James Keyre and till uther sundry war rewardit be the said secret counsall the quhilk men demyt wald nocht stand.[19]

The furious acts of defiance by the Douglas faction described by the Auchinleck chronicler — dragging the safe-conduct through the streets of Stirling behind a horse and fixing a letter on the parliament door by night which set out Douglas's withdrawal of allegiance from the king — furnished James II with the excuse to present a formal show of strength. A general levy was summoned to appear at Pentland Muir, the Auchinleck chronicler assessing the size of the host as 30,000. The army, led by the king in person, raided in the south to Peebles, Selkirk and Dumfries. On 18 July 1452, James was encamped at Corhead with the Scots army, in company with the new Crichton earls of Moray and Caithness.[20] The financing of this campaign had been assisted by William Turnbull, bishop of Glasgow, who diverted 800 marks from the Jubilee offerings at Glasgow Cathedral; and James Kennedy, bishop of St Andrews, made a loan of £50 to the king.[21]

The relative numbers quoted by the Auchinleck chronicler — 600 men in the 9th Earl of Douglas's party for the raid on Stirling and 30,000 in the king's army for his southern raid — are unlikely to be accurate, but the inference is clear: James II had far more support than Douglas notwithstanding the heinous nature of the king's crime. However, having secured the support of parliament and rewarded loyal supporters, King James then committed acts of depredation which may have alienated much of the support which he had so carefully built up. Certainly, the one contemporary note of censure for the king's actions comes as the direct result of the raids in the south in July 1452, in describing which the Auchinleck chronicler wrote that James II 'did na gud bot distroyit the cuntre richt fellonly baith of cornes medowis and wittalis and heriit mony bath gentillmen and utheris that war with him self'.[22] The importance of this alienation of support may be seen in the eventual terms with which the king received the 9th Earl of Douglas back into favour.

Following the murder of his brother, James earl of Douglas evidently decided that his best hope of support lay with the English king with whom he had already had dealings the previous year. On 3 June 1452 English commissioners were appointed to treat with the Earl of Douglas concerning certain articles communicated by Douglas through Garter King and to receive his homage, and on 2 June the Earl's mother, Countess Beatrice, and his sister-in-law Margaret, obtained an English safe-conduct for one year to go to the shrine of St Thomas at Canterbury. It was probably in response to this that James II sent ambassadors to England on 5 June 'in al gudely haste upon . . . secret matiris'.[23]

The Scottish ambassadors petitioned the English chancellor for a safe-conduct for Alexander Nairn of Sandfurd, Nicholas Otterburn and others for a year, and they also asked for a renewal of the safe-conduct for the bishops of Glasgow, Moray and Galloway who were to confer 'upon the secret matiris the qwylks yhour lordeship knawys'.[24] An ambassador sent by Douglas to England received a gift by royal grant of £40, dated 14 July, which was probably connected with the offer of homage.[25] In the meantime, however, Douglas was still in Scotland trying to win support, and while James II campaigned in the south, Douglas was encouraging Donald Balloch, cousin of the late Alexander lord of the Isles, to lead a raid in July 1452 in which he devastated Arran, Inverkip and the Cumbraes. The Exchequer Rolls show that the capture of Brodick castle on Arran took place between 10 July 1451 and 4 June 1453.[26] These lands were crown patrimony, but on 14 April 1452 their revenues had been pledged to William Turnbull, bishop of Glasgow, as surety for the jubilee loan which financed the anti-Douglas campaign, therefore the attack was aimed, almost certainly, at the royalist bishop.[27]

The king was back in Edinburgh by 2 August, where he must have come under considerable pressure from certain sections of the political community to come to some arrangement with Douglas. James II seems to have misjudged the strength of his position, perhaps feeling that the parliamentary exoneration he had received for the murder of Douglas was indicative of general support and approval. In fact, there must have been considerable uneasiness in the minds of many over the circumstances of the murder, and a desire to curb the escalation of hostilities. The less than discriminate raids in the south, which affected royal supporters and Douglas sympathisers alike, had the effect of bringing the king under pressure to end the strife. Awareness of this pressure must have led him to grant concessions and seek support from those ostensibly out of royal favour; and it can hardly have been an accident that the Livingston/Dundas remission was granted at precisely this time. On 27 August, the day before the formal conclusion of terms with Douglas, James II granted a remission to Alexander Livingston and James Dundas, posthumously, and James Livingston and Duncan Dundas, rescinding the forfeiture of January 1450.[28] One of the witnesses on this remission was the chancellor, William lord Crichton, an old adversary of the Livingstons, but the king could not afford enemies and was prepared to offer gestures of goodwill, although James Livingston was not restored to royal service until 1454, the year in which the Crichtons were all but wiped from the political scene.

The king must have realised, albeit belatedly, that he had thrown away what slim advantage he had possessed, as a result of which he was forced to seek an agreement with James, earl of Douglas, which was concluded formally on 28 August, at Douglas castle in Lanarkshire. The document which was drawn up between the two men is known as the 'Appoyntement'; in it, Douglas promised to forgive the king for the murder of his brother, to renounce all treasonable leagues, to carry out his duties as Warden of the Marches faithfully, and to give the king such 'honour and worship' as he could render safely. Above all, Douglas undertook not to seek 'any entrie in the lands of the earldome of Wigtone' without the queen's consent and not to obtain the lordship of Stewarton without the king's leave.[29]

The most interesting points to emerge from the 'Appoyntement' are that the earldom of Wigtown was obviously still a contentious issue, as it had been in 1451; and it also offers some support for the Auchinleck chronicler's claim that William earl of Douglas was murdered because the king objected to his having a league or bond with other earls — 'treasonable leagues'. It is unlikely that James II considered the Douglas-Crawford-Ross bond to be still in effect, but it is clear that he was stating his opposition to Douglas entering into any such bond in the future. A reference to Douglas's links with England may also be intended here, as the 9th Earl had sent a representative to England who had received a royal grant dated 14 July, although it is not clear what business was being transacted.[30] The Earl of Douglas was evidently keeping his options open, as he had a safe-conduct to go to England, dated 22 September.[31]

The earldom of Wigtown by this time appears to have been in the hands of the queen, and the problem with Stewarton was that part of the lands had been bestowed upon Sir Gilbert Kennedy of Dunure on 30 June 1452.[32] Stewarton was part of the patrimony of the Stewards of Scotland; on 21 January 1426, James I had granted the lands to James Douglas of Balvenie (later 7th earl of Douglas) and his wife Beatrice.[33] Some of the lands had been bestowed on Sir Alexander Home by William 8th earl of Douglas on 24 August 1444, and this grant was confirmed by James II on 20 July 1451.[34] Queen Mary and Sir Gilbert Kennedy must have been reluctant to surrender their acquisitions, but the king's position had been eroded badly by the discontent generated by his indiscriminate raids in the south, and he must have been under considerable pressure to back down from his aggressive stance and make concessions. The three estates had been prepared to support the king to the extent of absolving him of guilt for the murder of Douglas, but this does not mean that they were in favour of waging outright war on the Douglas faction.

The dilemma which faced the king at the end of 1452 was that although he mistrusted the Black Douglases and probably wished to crush the power of the family absolutely, he was hampered by a strong reluctance from the political community assembled as the three estates to allow him to proceed unchecked. The fear was that dangerous precedents were being set, and that the king must be made to work with, rather than against, the nobility, and some may have feared a revival of the ruthlessness exhibited by James I. With this erosion of support for the king, Douglas must have realised that he must press home his advantage, exploiting the king's inability or unwillingness to make good the assurances of the 'Appoyntement' in the months following its drafting, during which the king was in Edinburgh and Stirling. To appease those pressing for real concessions and conciliation, James had to agree to terms which he must have resented deeply. It is in the light of his dilemma that the bond of manrent made between the king and Douglas at Lanark on 16 January 1453 should be seen.[35] In this bond, the king promised to restore the earldom of Wigtown to the Earl of Douglas, and he also undertook to promote the marriage of the 9th earl to his brother's widow, Margaret of Galloway. The dispensation for this marriage was dated 27 February 1453 at the petition of James and Margaret and of 'James King of Scots, whose kindred they are'.[36] William earl of Douglas had died without heirs and his brother James would not have inherited those Douglas lands which were part of the patrimony of Margaret of Galloway. In order to keep the Douglas possessions together, therefore, the 9th earl had to marry his brother's widow, although a dispensation was needed as they were within the degrees of consanguinity which forbade marriage under church law. Despite the efforts of the Douglases to keep the Black Douglas lands together through marriage with the sister and heiress of the 6th Earl, no children were born to William and Margaret during their eight-year marriage, and none to James and Margaret. The Douglases were very conscious of the need to establish the family dynasty, and with five adult brothers this should not have been impossible to achieve. However, the two brothers who became earls of Douglas failed to do just that. By 1460, Margaret, 'Fair Maid of Galloway', had returned to Scotland and placed herself at the king's mercy, and if the marriage to James 9th earl of Douglas had actually taken place, a divorce or annulment had evidently been obtained because she was married before 25 March 1460 to John earl of Atholl, the king's half-brother from Joan Beaufort's marriage to James Stewart, the 'Black Knight' of Lorne. This marriage produced children, therefore Margaret does not appear to have been responsible for the failure of William and James Douglas to provide heirs.[37] The very fact that William died without issue must have forced the family to attempt the rather dubious marriage of James to his sister-in-law. It may also indicate that Margaret's loyalty to the family, who were, after all, only enjoying their position as a result of the murder of her brothers, was not taken for granted. If such was the case, it seems incredible that James II should sanction such a marriage willingly as it strengthened the Douglas position at a time when he clearly desired the exact opposite; indeed, Dr Dunlop shrewdly observed the Lanark bond to be 'the gauge of his [James II's] impotence'.[38] One consolation for the king may have been that the 'Appoyntement' and the Lanark bond were not parliamentary agreements, and thus James may have felt that they would be easier to rescind when he was in a position to do so.

It is at this stage, following the Lanark agreement, that Pitscottie recounts the story of the submission of the Earl of Crawford to the king.[39] His account is long and full of details which are picturesque rather than factual, and there is no contemporary evidence — neither the Auchinleck Chronicle nor the official records mention it. Whatever the truth of the matter, the rebel earls of Douglas, Moray and Crawford were restored to favour insofar as their names appeared as conservators of a new truce with England on 23 May 1453.[40] However, before this, on 3 January 1453, an English safe-conduct for nine months was issued to James lord Hamilton, along with James Livingston and Archibald and Duncan Dundas. They appear to have availed themselves of the safe-conduct, as on 19 February payment was made to Garter 'lately sent by the King to the Marches of Scotland, there to ask certain appointments with the Earl of Douglas and also attending on the Lord of Hamelton at London and elsewhere for five weeks and more'.[41]

As the king's commissioner, Douglas sealed the new truce with England at Westminster on 23 May 1453,[42] but another item of personal business was his plan to secure the release of Malise Graham earl of Menteith, who was still serving as a hostage for the ransom of James I. This has been interpreted as an action with sinister overtones, as Malise Graham could be argued to have had the best hereditary claim to the Scottish crown. However, a plot to overthrow the Stewart dynasty was not attributed to Douglas at the time, and Malise Graham would eventually sit in the parliament of 1455 which formally forfeited the Douglases.[43] Graham was the brother of James lord Hamilton's wife, Euphemia, and it was probably largely a family concern to seek his release. However, the prevailing mood of suspicion and unease may have prompted the Douglas faction to obtain safe-conducts on 22 May to visit the 'apostolic thresholds', thus ensuring for themselves an escape route, should they need it.[44]

Alexander earl of Crawford died in September 1453. The Auchinleck chronicler registered the event in the following terms:

Item the zere of god lmiiii liii In the moneth of september deit alexander lyndesay erll of craufurd in fynevyne [Finavon] that was callit a rigorus man and ane felloun and held ane gret rowme [area] in his tyme for he held all angus in his bandoun & was richt Inobedient to the king.[45]

Alexander earl of Crawford was succeeded by his son, David, who was only thirteen years old, his youth effectively dashing any hopes Douglas may have had of reviving Lindsay support for his cause.

Following the apparent rehabilitation of the Douglases as evinced in the Lanark bond of January 1453, there seems to have been some strife and discomfiture within the royalist party, and there is some justification for the Auchinleck chronicler's remark that the hasty settlements of lands and titles granted in the immediate wake of the murder of Douglas were such that 'men demyt wald nocht stand'. The earldoms of Caithness and Moray were such grants. There are no extant charters of erection to show that the earldoms were legally conveyed, and a marginal note was added to John Law's manuscript that 'neither the said James nor George ever had the earldom or possessed the lands of Douglas but they were only called earls'.[46]

James Crichton, whose claim to the earldom of Moray came through his wife as elder heiress of Moray, certainly styled himself Earl of Moray: for example, in the exchequer audit of July 1454 and the parliament of the same month.[47] However, it appears that Archibald Douglas, married to the younger Dunbar co-heiress, had not been ousted from the earldom, as he continued to be styled Earl of Moray, and there is no evidence that James Crichton ever received revenue from the earldom. The king's procrastination must have been resented deeply by Crichton, and the entry in the Auchinleck chronicle which noted the death of James Crichton in August 1454 bears this out. Robert Liddale had been appointed keeper of Dunbar castle between 7 July 1451 and 9 December 1452, but was replaced before 14 July 1453 by James Crichton. In the audit of 5 July 1454, a fee was paid to James earl of Moray and lord Crichton as keeper of Dunbar, and after his death, according to the Auchinleck chronicler, Dunbar castle 'was haldin fra the king a litill quhile and syne gevin till him'.[48]

Admiral George Crichton appears to have been more compliant with the king's wishes over the earldom of Caithness. On 8 July 1452, a charter incorporating George Crichton's southern lands into the earldom of Caithness was granted, but no mention was made of George Crichton's son and heir, James.[49] The Auchinleck chronicler wrote that

within vi days James of Crichton, sone and aire to the said George of Crichton tuke the castell of blakness and his fader in contrar of the king and Incontinent the king in proper persoun put ane sege to the blakness and lay at It ix or x dayis and than it was gevin oure be trety and Sir George was put to Methven and gaf him the landis of Strathurd for the landis that he had conquest in Lothian.[50]

The chronicler assigned these events to May 1454, a view supported by the evidence of a royal charter issued from Blackness castle on 23 May 1454; the Exchequer Rolls show that the siege took place within the audit June 1453 to July 1454 and that a herald of the Emperor, Frederick III, visited James during the hostilities.[51] The reason why James II regarded the castle of Blackness as so important was that it occupied an excellent strategic position on the Forth as a counterpoise to the Douglas strongholds of Inveravon and Abercorn. As George Crichton's heir, the king obtained Strathbrock, but he recognised the need to offer some compensation to James Crichton, and therefore he granted to him the royal lands of Strathord, and James Crichton also succeeded to the ancestral estate of Cairns. This settlement was made in parliament on 18 July 1454.[52] The problems experienced by the king at Dunbar and Blackness illustrate the fact that even members of hitherto staunch royalist families were having doubts about James II in 1453–4, undermining his position quite significantly.

The ranks of royalist supporters who had encouraged the king to attack the Douglases were seriously depleted by the end of 1454. The chancellor, Sir William Crichton, was dead before July 1454, and his son James and cousin George did not long survive him, as they died, according to the Auchinleck chronicler, in August.[53] With the death of Bishop Turnbull of Glasgow in September, the hard core of royal supporters who had helped to initiate and carry through the attack on the Douglases was gone. William Sinclair, earl of Orkney, succeeded William Crichton as chancellor and James Livingston re-appeared in his former post of chamberlain.[54]

James earl of Douglas had, in the meantime, been busy trying to win the support of the remaining member of the 1452 bond, John earl of Ross and lord of the Isles. The Auchinleck chronicler states that Douglas went to Knapdale

> and spak thar with the erll of Ros and lord of Ilis, and maid thaim all richt gret rewardis of wyne clathis silver silk and Ynglis clath and thai gaf thaim mantillis agane and quhat was thar amangis thaim wes counsall to commounis and thai demyt ill all.[55]

The atmosphere of suspicion noted in the Auchinleck chronicle may have been intensified by the actions of the Douglas faction who were fortifying their strongholds of Lochindorb, Darnaway, Inveravon, Threave, Douglas, Strathaven and Abercorn.[56] Archibald Douglas, earl of Moray, fortified the island fortress of Lochindorb, but the king ordered its destruction, which was carried out by the Thane of Cawdor, who appears to have had designs on the large iron gate which Moray had installed. A letter of warrant was issued as early as 5 March 1456 by James II to the Thane of Cawdor to remove the gate and take it back to his own castle, something which must have appeared a small price to pay for Cawdor's co-operation.[57]

In the process of forfeiture against the Douglases in 1455 they were accused of burning Dalkeith, abetting Robert Douglas in his efforts to deprive the king of the succession to Strathbrock and burning the queen's dower lands of Kinclaven and Bonnytoun. In addition to these charges, James earl of Douglas was accused of harrying the grange of the justiciar, Laurence lord Abernethy, who had held a justice court at Lochmaben in 1454 which Douglas apparently regarded as an encroachment upon his authority and interests, although no proceedings from the court have survived to offer specific details.[58]

The murder of the 8th earl of Douglas and the ensuing conflict created considerable turmoil and confusion, and there is no doubt that incidents occurred which, although set against the backdrop of the larger contest, were more in the nature of the settlement of private scores. For example, the royal castle of Lochmaben was in the keepership of the laird of Mouswald; the Auchinleck chronicler recorded that, in August 1454,

> the lard of Johnstonis twa sonnis tuk the castall of Lochmabane apon the lard of Mouswald callit carudderis and his ii sons and other ii or iii men / and all throu treasson of the portar And syne the king gaf tham the keping of the hous to his prophet and how that was men ferleit.[59]

It seems that the action of the Johnstones was the result of some private feud with Carruthers, and the fact that the king condoned the seizure may indicate that he did not regard the Johnstones as opponents or, more specifically, Douglas men; also acceptance of the *fait accompli* would have been less troublesome than diverting attention and resources from the larger issues of the moment — the ultimate defeat of the Douglases. The Johnstones had been minor tenants of Douglas for the lands of Drumgrey in Dumfriesshire, and the laird of Johnstone had ridden with the Douglas force under the command of Hugh earl of Ormond in 1448, when an English invasion was repulsed at Sark. The condoning of the Johnstones' seizure of Lochmaben, which was, after all, a royal castle, may be seen as a deliberate effort to turn the Johnstones from their adherence to the Earl of Douglas, with demonstrable success. When the conflict arose between the king and the Black Douglases, the Johnstones abandoned their patrons and were instrumental in their defeat at Arkinholm. The laird of Johnstone also took part in the siege of Threave castle in 1455, for which the king granted him the lands of Buittle and Sannoch in Galloway.[60]

While the struggle against the Douglases was progressing in Scotland, it was fortunate for James II that the English government was in no position to capitalise on the situation, as the civil strife between the opposing parties of York and Lancaster was keeping the English fully occupied. James II's uncle, the Lancastrian Duke of Somerset, was imprisoned in 1454 and the king sent his stepfather, James Stewart of Lorne, to Somerset with an offer of help in that year, although exactly what he proposed to do is not clear. Thomas Spens, bishop of Galloway, was sent to France to inform Charles VII of the Scottish king's position regarding the Douglases, and he was received at Bourges on 19 and 20 May 1455.[61]

While this diplomatic activity was taking place, the king launched an attack on the lands of Douglas and Hamilton at the beginning of March 1455. The Auchinleck chronicler writes that James

James II and Mary of Gueldres from the Seton Armorial (1591), National Library of
Scotland. This is interesting in showing a likeness of the Queen, although probably not
an accurate one.

James II by an anonymous artist, attributed to the 16th century. Unlike the contemporary portrait on the cover of this book, this representation does not show the fiery red birthmark which covered the left side of the king's face. Scottish National Portrait Gallery.

The father of James II. James I as painted by the same anonymous artist. Scottish National Portrait Gallery.

The arrival in Tours of James II's sister, the Princess Margaret, for her marriage to the son of Charles VII of France, the Dauphin Louis (Chronique de Charles VII).

Isabella, the second sister of James II, who married Francis, duke of Brittany. This portrait of Isabella is from her Book of Hours and shows the arms of Scotland together with those of Brittany, as a heraldic motif.

Charles VII of France is strikingly portrayed in this contemporary illustration from the Diary of Jörg von Ehingen. (Reproduced with the kind permission of the Württembergische Landesbibliothek, Stuttgart).

Henry VI of England from the same source. The Lancastrian Henry VI's preoccupation with the rival Yorkist faction in the Wars of the Roses was exploited by James II.

Philip the Good, duke of Burgundy, by Rogier van der Weyden. Philip assisted James II in his marriage negotiations, provided a dowry for his niece, Mary of Gueldres, and supplied a number of cannon and bombards to the Scottish king, one of which was Mons Meg.

The tomb of James 'the Gross', 7th earl of Douglas, in St. Bride's kirk. James became Earl of Douglas following the execution of his two great-nephews at the 'Black Dinner' of 1440, thus transferring the Black Douglas descent to his family line.

The 'mercat cross' in Stirling where, in March 1452, James 9th Earl of Douglas spoke 'richt sclanderfully' of the king for the murder of his brother William.

Stirling. This view demonstrates the relative positions of town and castle in Stirling, and the extent of the threat had the king still been in the castle when James 9th earl of Douglas arrived in 1452.

Aerial view of Threave castle, near the town of Castle Douglas in Galloway. This was the last Douglas stronghold to surrender to the king in 1455.

Aerial view of Roxburgh, looking east, showing the site of the castle (central mound, skirted by the road) in relation to the rivers Tweed (left) and Teviot (right) and the town of Kelso where the young James III was crowned after the death of his father. The mediaeval town of Roxburgh occupied the open ground beyond the castle, between the rivers and the town of Kelso. (Reproduced by kind permission of Dr. Colin Martin).

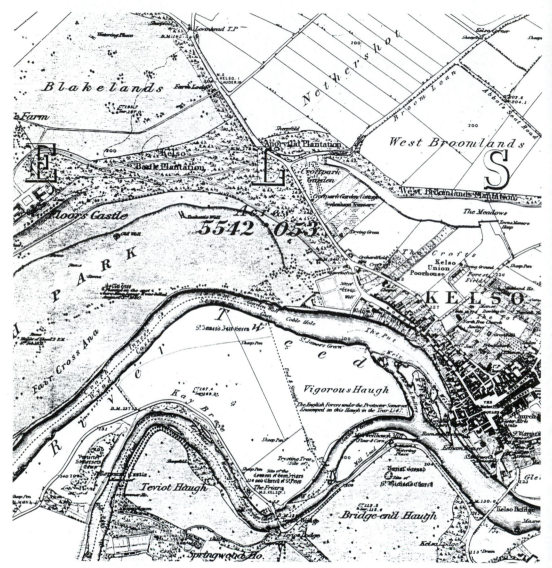

Map of Roxburgh from the first series of Ordnance survey, 1868. The site of the king's death is marked, traditionally, by a holly tree in the modern South Park of Floors castle. The Scottish army would have been deployed in this area with the guns bombarding the castle from across the river. (Reproduced by kind permission of the National Library of Scotland Map Room).

kest doune the castell of Inverawyne and syne Incontinent past till glasgw and gaderit the westland men with part of the ereschery and passit to lanerik and to douglas and syne brynt all douglasdale and all awendale and all the lord hamilton's lands and heriit thaim clerlie and syne passit till Edinburgh and fra thin till the forest with ane ost of lawland men and all that wald nocht cum till him furthwith he tuke thair gudis and brynt thair placis and tuke faith of all the gentillis clerlie.[62]

This decisive action on the part of the king cut the ground from under the feet of the Douglases. James lord Hamilton was in England trying to raise support, although the price asked by Henry VI was that Douglas and Hamilton should swear an oath of allegiance to him. By the time Hamilton returned to Scotland the Douglas castle of Abercorn was under siege. This was a crucial stage in the downfall of the Douglases, as Abercorn was the principal stronghold of the branch of the Black Douglas family which had risen to prominence as a result of the 'Black Dinner' of 1440. The castle occupied a strategic position on the banks of the Forth, close to the royal castle of Blackness, and James II planned the siege carefully, putting to work his beloved artillery. James earl of Douglas seems to have been unable to decide on a course of action against the king in defence or rescue of Abercorn, his vacillation costing him the support of Hamilton, hitherto his most energetic adherent. Hamilton plainly saw no future in the Douglas cause and offered his submission to the king 'throw the menys of his eme James of Livingston . . . and the king Resavit him till grace and send him on Incontinent with the erll of Orkney that tyme chancellor of Scotland till remane in warde In the castell of Roslyne at the kingis will'.

Hamilton's defection was crucial. Abercorn was besieged with artillery and eventually captured and destroyed. Douglas did not appear to defend it, the Auchinleck chronicler remarking caustically that 'men wist nocht grathlie quhar the Douglas was all this tyme'.[63] The problem was that taking arms against the king, however provocative his actions, was ultimately treasonable and the logical outcome of rebellion was the deposition of the king, something which the Douglases had neither the support nor, arguably, the inclination to undertake. The 9th Earl of Douglas was not a man lacking in ability in the martial arts, and had been declared the heir to his brother William in preference to his twin, Archibald earl of Moray, who had hitherto been assumed the elder twin; but by this stage James evidently considered himself to be in an impossible position.

On 24 April the Douglases and their adherents were summoned to appear before the king to answer charges of treason. Parliament convened at Edinburgh on 9 June to proceed with the formal forfeiture of the Douglases.[64] Not surprisingly, they did not appear to answer the charges. James earl of Douglas had fled to England whence his mother, Countess Beatrice, and Countess Margaret, who may at this stage have been his wife, had already escaped. The three remaining Douglas brothers, Archibald, Hugh and John, contented themselves with plundering raids on the borders; on 1 May 1455 they were routed at Arkinholm by a party of southern lairds who included Johnstones, Maxwells and Scotts. Archibald earl of Moray was slain, Hugh earl of Ormond was captured and subsequently executed, and John lord Balvenie managed to escape to England.[65]

The June parliament was prorogued until August to enable the king to take part in the siege of Threave, the last Douglas castle to hold out against the king. Threave was the Douglases' major stronghold in Galloway, having been built between 1369 and 1390 by Archibald 'the Grim', 3rd earl of Douglas. The castle is built on an island and encircled by a curtain wall, beyond which is a ditch, once filled with water from the river Dee. On this occasion the Earl of Douglas did make a last desperate effort to save it by offering it to Henry VI, who made a payment of £100 to Douglas on 15 July 1455 'for succour, victualling, relief and rescue of the castle of Treve'.[66] This was to no avail, as the king attended the siege personally and employed cannon which had arrived from Burgundy for the purpose. The curtain wall round the castle may represent the fortifications made by the Douglases to strengthen the castle, and there is evidence of damage to the wall in the form of two ruined round towers and a wrecked gatehouse.[67] The castle was surrendered eventually, and was given into the keeping of Sir Alexander Boyd for a short while before being handed over to the custody of William Edmonston of Culloden.[68]

The men who benefited most from the downfall of the Douglases were, for the most part, southern lairds who had been tenants on Douglas lands, for example, the Scotts, Johnstones, Maxwells and Kerrs. However, James lord Hamilton, who had remained on the Douglas side almost up to the end, was also rewarded by the king. On 1 July 1455, Hamilton and his wife Euphemia were given a royal charter of the lands of the barony of Drumsergert (Cambuslang) and Carmunnock in the sheriffdom of Lanark, thus benefiting from their timely change of allegiance. George Douglas, earl of Angus, was also a principal beneficiary of the downfall of the Black Douglases. Prior to their forfeiture, he already possessed the lordship of Liddesdale and Hermitage castle, and in 1457, he was rewarded with the lordship of Douglasdale for his services in repelling the Douglas incursion on the east March. In May 1457 he was styled George earl of Angus, lord Douglas, and warden of the east and middle marches, both highly remunerative offices.[69] Angus could expect to receive approximately £200 per annum from the east and middle March wardenships.

Rewards were given in the wake of the Douglas downfall, once the 9th Earl had fled to England and the family had been forfeited formally in the June parliament of 1455, but not to the extent that a concentration of power in one area was the result. It is no accident that the practice of making bonds of manrent starts in James II's reign, as men who were distinguished from their neighbours often simply by a title rather than a notable increase in wealth and resources made written bonds to emphasise their position and status. Bonds of this nature were also used to secure assistance in specific crises, both national and local, and it is in this light that the bond which James II made with James Tweedie of Drumelzier should be seen. On 8 March 1455, a bond of maintenance was given by the king, under the privy seal, to James Tweedie of Drumelzier, in which the king promised

> that we sal mainteine, supple and defend him [Tweedie] and his said house as we walde do oure castellis and housis, and supple and defend him in all his actionis, causes and querellis lauchful, leiful ande honest as oure avun speciale familier ande kyn.

In return, Tweedie's house of Drumelzier should be at the disposal of the king or his nominated leiutenant at any time, and Tweedie himself offered 'speciale manrent ande service for al the dayis of his lyve'. Dr Wormald has pointed out that Tweedie, although an important southern laird, must have been only one of many with whom the king made such agreements in order to ensure the strength of his position in the south.[70] The date of this bond coincided exactly with the king's preparations for his final assault on the Black Douglases for which he needed the support of Tweedie — and no doubt many other southern landowners — who may have had traditional connections with the Douglases.

Throughout the conflict with the Douglases, James II was aware of the need to court support, reward allegiance and punish disloyalty. He must have learned that the indiscriminate raids made in the south during the campaign of late summer 1452 had damaged his position and forced him to compromise, but he emerged from the setbacks of 1453–4 determined to tread the fine line necessary to rebuild sufficient support to crush utterly the power of the Black Douglases. The final onslaught against the Douglases was prefaced with shrewd political manoeuvring, as the king actively courted men with influence in the areas where the Douglases held political sway and would look to their tenants to provide support in their struggle with the king. Initially, the king concentrated on undermining the position of the Black Douglases in the south-west where their lordship was weaker and their hold on the allegiance of their tenants more tenuous. The undermining process appears to have started even before the murder of William 8th earl of Douglas, indicating the king's concern with the rising power of the family, and strikingly illustrated by the involvement of nominally Douglas men such as Simon Glendinning and William Cranston in the murder of Douglas. This process continued, although with more urgency, after the murder, and the bond with Tweedie of Drumelzier is indicative of this political courtship, made even more necessary by the disgruntlement caused by the king's raids of July 1452. The southern lairds, for example the Johnstones and Scotts, were, perhaps, the key to the king's ultimate success, as, assured of rewards and increased power and influence in their own areas, they were instrumental in blocking any attempt at a Douglas resurgence.

NOTES

1. Chron. Auchinleck, f. 115r.

2. Fraser, *Buccleuch*, ii, 49.

3. Macdougall, N., *James III*.

4. Dr Dunlop's itinerary for Bishop Kennedy shows that he was back in Scotland by 24 September 1451, therefore the October parliament could have issued the 'Golden Charter' if Riis's argument for the year of the prince's birth is correct. Dunlop, *Kennedy*, 433.

5. Riis, T., *Should Auld Acquaintance Be Forgot . . . Scottish-Danish relations c.1450–1707*, i, 245; Macdougall, N., *James III. A Political Study*, 17, 81.

6. *R.M.S.*, ii, no. 532.

7. Chron. Auchinleck, f. 123v.

8. Ibid., f. 111v.

9. *H.M.C.*, vii, Southesk, 30. Kinnaird lay in Farnell parish, Forfarshire, 3.5 miles south-east of Brechin.

10. Chron. Auchinleck, f. 123v.

11. Lesley, *History*, 23.

12. *R.M.S.*, ii, no. 442.

13. *Spalding Club Miscellany*, iv, 128–30.

14. *A.P.S.*, ii, 73.

15. Lesley, *History*, 25; Buchanan, *History*, f. xl; Pitscottie, *Historie*, 117.

16. Calendar of St Andrews Charters, 35. St Andrews University Library. Also, see above, p. 76.

17. Those present were William Turnbull, bishop of Glasgow, John Winchester, bishop of Moray, Robert Lauder, bishop of Dunblane, George Lauder, bishop of Lismore, William, prior of St Andrews, Archibald, abbot of Holyrood, Richard, abbot of Dunfermline, George earl of Angus, William lord Crichton, John lord of Lorne, William lord Keith, marischal, Patrick lord Graham, Duncan lord Campbell, Alexander lord Montgomery, William lord Somerville, George lord Setoun, George lord Leslie, John lord Lindesay of Byres, Andrew lord Gray, John Arous, George Schoriswood. *A.P.S.*, ii, 73.

18. Chron. Auchinleck, f. 115v.

19. Ibid. Patrick Hepburn of Hailes, Alan Cathcart, Robert Fleming of Cumbernauld and Alexander and David Hume had all appeared as witnesses on Douglas charters or on safe-conducts issued to the Earls of Douglas and their entourages. Fraser, *Douglas*, iii, 306, 81, 415; *Rot. Scot.*, ii, 340, 341, 343, 346.

20. *Laing Chrs.*, 134. The Corhead referred to in the charter is probably to be identified with Corehead at the head of Moffatdale, map reference — NT 072 125, Sheet 78, Ordnance Survey, 1st Series. I am indebted to Norma Philpott for this suggestion.

21. *R.M.S.*, ii, no. 542; *E.R.*, v, 604.

22. Chron. Auchinleck, f. 115v.

23. *Foedera*, xi, 310–11; *Rot. Scot.*, ii, 357.

24. *C.D.S.*, iv, 1243, app. 22.

25. *Rot. Scot.*, ii, 358; *C.D.S.*, iv, 1245.

26. Chron. Auchinleck, f. 117; *E.R.*, v, 571, 577, 578.

27. *R.M.S.*, ii, no. 542; *Book of Arran*, ii, 46.

28. NLS. ADV. MSS. B 1316/1317. The witnesses are: James Kennedy, bishop of St Andrews, William Turnbull, bishop of Glasgow, Thomas Lauder, bishop of Dunkeld, John Winchester, bishop of Moray, Thomas Spens, bishop of Whithorn, William lord Crichton, chancellor, Alexander earl of Huntly, lord Gordon, William lord Somerville, Andrew lord Gray, Robert lord Hailes. The seals of the burgesses of Edinburgh, Haddington and Cupar were also attached. The way had obviously been cleared for the rehabilitation of Dundas, as on 18 August 1452, Archibald Dundas received a royal remission for plundering the ship and goods of Thomas MacIntyre from the port of Leith 'and all other depredations'. S.R.O. GD 75 no. 339.

29. Tytler, P. F., *History*, ii, 386–7.

30. *Rot. Scot.*, ii, 358; *C.D.S.*, iv, 1245.

31. *Rot. Scot.*, ii, 359.

32. *R.M.S.*, ii, no. 583.

33. *R.M.S.*, ii, nos. 583, 77.

34. Ibid., nos. 77, 484, 485; Fraser, *Douglas*, iii, 426.

35. Ibid., 483–4.

36. *C.P.R.*, x, 130–1.

37. *Rot. Scot.*, ii, 383; *H.M.C.*, Report vii, 708.

38. Dunlop, *Kennedy*, 143.

39. Pitscottie, *Historie*, 104–110.

40. *Foedera*, xi, 334; *Rot. Scot.*, ii, 367 — with the date 30 May. Alexander earl of Huntly also appears on this document.

41. *C.D.S.*, iv, 1266.

42. *Rot. Scot.*, ii, 368.

43. *A.P.S.*, ii, 42, 75; Dunlop, *Kennedy*, 146.

44. *Rot. Scot.*, ii, 362; *C.D.S.*, iv, 1254.

45. Chron. Auchinleck, f. 112.

46. Law, 'De Cronicis Scotorum brevia', f. 130.

47. *E.R.*, v, 645; *A.P.S.*, xii, 23.

48. Chron. Auchinleck, f. 112v.

49. *R.M.S.*, ii, no. 587; *A.P.S.*, ii, 75.

50. Chron. Auchinleck, f. 117r.

51. Fraser, *Pollok*, i, 44; *E.R.*, v, 610.

52. *A.P.S.*, ii, 41. Strathbrock is the modern Broxburn in West Lothian, the lands of Strathord are north-west of Scone, and the estate of Cairns is in Midcalder parish, Lothian.

53. *E.R.*, v, 609; Chron. Auchinleck, f. 112v, 113v.

54. *H.B.C.*, 175, 179.

55. Chron. Auchinleck, f. 117r.

56. *A.P.S.*, ii, 76.

57. *Cawdor Book*, 21–2. The 1458 accounts show that Lochindorb was destroyed by the Thane of Cawdor at a cost to him of £24. *E.R.*, vi, 486.

58. *A.P.S.*, ii, 76. Kinclaven is in Tayside parish in the district of Stormont, Perthshire. Bonnytown was an estate in Forfarshire: Groome, *Gazetteer*, passim.

59. Chron. Auchinleck, f. 112v–113r.

60. Fraser, *Douglas*, iii, 353.

61. Dunlop, *Kennedy*, 154.
62. Chron. Auchinleck, f. 116r: 'ereschery' was a lowland term for highlanders.
63. Chron. Auchinleck, f. 116v.
64. *A.P.S.*, ii, 76.
65. *R.M.S.*, ii, no. 772.
66. *C.D.S.*, iv, 1272.
67. Cruden, S., *The Scottish Castle*,
68. *E.R.*, vi, 203, 209.
69. Fraser, Douglas, ii, 90, 437.
70. *H.M.C.*, Various Collections, v, Tweedy 14; Wormald, J., *Lords and Men*, 152.

6

Diplomacy and War, 1455–60

The Douglases had amassed great wealth in lands and possessions over the years of their rise to prominence, and the forfeiture of the family brought much of that wealth into Crown hands in 1455. Having dealt with the Douglases, at least for the time being, the king was now able to concentrate on returning a measure of stability to the government, and the three estates meeting in parliament on 4 August 1455 were keen to assist him in this. An Act of Annexation was passed in this parliament, the intention of which was to provide the monarchy with a stable foundation of wealth in the form of certain lands, lordships and castle with all the rights, privileges and income that went with them. These were to belong to the crown inalienably; that is, they were not to be used to provide patronage in any form, either fee or freehold, without the consent of the three estates. Nicholson has suggested that the Act of Annexation demonstrated that James II was anxious to ensure that his rich and hard-won acquisitions would not be wasted by grants and alienations made by his successors, the tenor of the act reviving the tradition that the king should 'live of his own',[1] although such anxiety may have been felt more by the three estates who wished to prevent the king from wasting these gains, resulting in the future spectre of systematic taxation or encroachments on the wealth of the nobility when the king was in financial need. This is certainly suggested by the preamble to the statute, 'Forsamekill as the poverte of the crowne is oftymis the cause of the poverte of the realme . . .'[2] The annexations outlined in the statute included forfeited Douglas lands: Ettrick forest, the lordship of Galloway, Redcastle in Ross with other lands north of the Spey 'pertenying tharto', and Threave castle.[3] The major castles of Edinburgh, Stirling and Dumbarton were set aside 'for the kingis residence' and the royal domains of Ballincrieff and Gosford were annexed to the crown. Also included in the act were annexations of the preceding reign: Inverness and Urquhart castles, the earldoms of Fife and Strathearn and the lordship of Brechin.

The newly acquired lands of Galloway were administered for the king by William abbot of Dundrennan as chamberlain of Galloway; George Burnett, editor of the Exchequer Rolls, calculated that in 1456 the gross money revenue from the farmed lands of east and west Galloway was £751 3s 4d. Following the forfeiture of the Douglases, Douglas vassals held their lands directly of the crown, and Wigtown and Kirkcudbright — burghs of regality whose revenues had been received by the Earl of Douglas — became royal burghs.

Ettrick forest, which consisted of the three wards of Ettrick, Tweed and Yarrow, was administered by the crown for a gross money rent of £519 13s 4d, and the queen benefited from this acquisition with two holdings in Yarrow, while James lord Hamilton's wife (widow of the 5th Earl of Douglas) collected a terce from Ettrick forest. The forest's principal messuage was Newark castle, and there are references to courts being held there by James lord Hamilton and Ninian Spot, and to a visit by the king to Newark in the accounts submitted on 13 September 1456.[4]

The 'other lands north of the Spey' referred to in the Act of Annexation were those forfeited by Hugh Douglas earl of Ormond and his younger brother John lord Balvenie. The lands of Ardmannoch, which lay between the Moray and Cromarty firths, fell to the crown. The Earl of Ormond derived his title from the castle of Avoch which stood on the ancient moot hill of Ormond overlooking the bay of Munlochy, and the gross rent of these lands, which included Edirdale's fortress, Redcastle, was calculated at £172 15s 8d in 1460. Ormond also forfeited one third of Duffus in the sheriffdom of Elgin and his brother John forfeited Petty and Brachly, south of the Beauly Firth and Strathdearn (or the valley of Findhorn).

These lands were administered by the crown, although other forfeited Douglas lands in the north were used as patronage. For example, Crimond in Buchan, north-east Aberdeenshire, was forfeited by Ormond, and half of this possession was bestowed on John Dunbar of Westfield and half on Sir William Monypenny. Similarly, the castle of Balvenie in Mortlach parish, Banffshire, and Boharm and Botriphnie (south-east of Elgin) were forfeited by John lord Balvenie. The castle was placed initially in the keepership of Patrick lord Glamis, but was later bestowed on John Stewart earl of Atholl on the occasion of his marriage to Margaret Douglas, widow of the 8th Earl of Douglas, in addition to the lands of Boharm and Botriphnie. These lands were not mentioned specifically in the Act of Annexation and, for the most part, lands annexed to the crown were held and administered for the king and queen in keeping with the tenor of the Act, although the notable exception to this was the bestowal of the barony and castle of Urquhart with Glenmoriston on John earl of Ross and lord of the Isles, to be held in life-rent. This was official recognition of the seizure of Urquhart castle by the Earl of Ross in 1451, James II obviously considering that it would be the less troublesome course to accept the *fait accompli*. By doing so, he no doubt hoped to secure the co-operation of a magnate who was in a position to cause considerable trouble if antagonised, because of his power in an area not easily accessible to the crown. In fact, the Earl of Ross appears to have been loyal to the king for the remaining years of the reign, and by granting the castle and lands only in life-rent, James was ensuring that this was not a permanent alienation.

The financial position of the queen remained a consideration. She received the annexed lands of Brechin and Cortachy (near Kirriemuir, Forfarshire) in security of her dower; and the royal lands of Ballincrieff (north of Bathgate, Linlithgowshire) and Gosford (in Aberlady parish near Haddington), which had been held in 1454 by James Kennedy bishop of St Andrews, were annexed firmly to the crown.[5]

Lands were not the only concern of the three estates in this parliament, as they also dealt with the revocation of all grants of heritable offices made since the death of James I; hereditary wardenships were forbidden and the warden courts were stripped of jurisdiction outside their own particular sphere. In addition, parliament enacted that all regalities then in crown hands were to be merged with the sheriffdoms, a matter which had been raised previously in the parliament of January 1450 when the Livingstons were disgraced.[6] No new regalities were to be erected 'without deliverance of the parliament', a part of the act which appears to relate directly to the Douglases, who had held many of their offices heritably and much of their land in regality. Such legislation was bound to be interpreted as contrary to many people's interests, and in recognition of this, compensation was promised to those who had suffered the revocation of their customs or offices, although there is a dearth of evidence in the official records to indicate how effectively this was carried out.

Following the period of strife with the Douglases, the king was well aware of the necessity to reward loyal supporters of the crown, and he used his right of patronage liberally in 1455. James lord Hamilton benefited from the disgrace of his erstwhile patron and ally with the lands of the barony of Drumsergert (Cambuslang) and Carmunnock within the sheriffdom of Lanark, which had been forfeited by Douglas, and he also received the office of sheriff of Lanark and the lands of Finnart in the sheriffdom of Renfrew, forfeited by the 9th Earl of Douglas.[7] Walter and David Scott of Strathurd were also rewarded for their part in the struggle against the Douglases with a royal charter, dated 10 September 1455, of lands lying in the barony of Hawick. The Scotts participated in the rout of the Douglases at Arkinholm on 1 May 1455, their support having been courted by the king as early as March 1452 when they received a royal grant.[8] The Bishop of Moray, John Winchester, was permitted to retain grants of land in the sheriffdom of Inverness and Banff made to him by Hugh earl of Ormond and John Douglas of Balvenie.[9] The Earl of Angus also benefited from his support for the king during the conflict with the Black Douglases as, on 7 December 1456, he received a grant of the lands of Ewesdale in Roxburgh; and on 8 April 1457 he was granted the lands of the lordship of Douglas. Also, on 28 January 1459, Angus received a royal charter conveying to him the lands of Eskdale, including the chief messuage of Dalblane.[10]

The use of patronage was vital to encourage loyalty and co-operation, but James II never lost sight of the need to enrich the crown, and when he attained his perfect majority on 16 October 1455, he issued an Act of

Revocation. A king's 'perfect majority' was held to be his twenty-fifth birthday and although, in practice, James had been ruling in person since at least 1449, this was the point at which he was deemed, officially, to be in a position to dispense with the restraints of his minority. In the Act of Revocation, James revoked alienations made during his minority which were held to be 'to the prejudice of the Crown'. Exactly who was affected, in practice, is not clear, and the act allows for a number of exceptions: that is, grants conferred on the queen and their second son Alexander (including the earldom of March and lordships of Annandale and Man), the grant of the earldom of Caithness made to William Sinclair earl of Orkney, and certain grants made to John Winchester, bishop of Moray.[11]

Apart from looking to the future prosperity of the crown, the August 1455 parliament was concerned to emphasise the strength of the king's position at that time, as although the Douglas threat had been reduced greatly, the 9th Earl was still alive and being harboured in England, a fact underlined by the last act recorded by this parliament, which forbade all the king's subjects, under pain of forfeiture, from yielding any support to the Douglases, 'proscribed traitors and adherents of the English'.[12] The Douglases had been denounced, but they were clearly still regarded as a potential threat. The battle of Arkinholm, on 1 May 1455, had disposed of Archibald Douglas, earl of Moray, and led to the capture and execution of Hugh, earl of Ormond, but the exiled James, 9th earl of Douglas, was still at large, as was his youngest brother, John, lord Balvenie, in addition to various other members of the family and their adherents who had fled with them, although it is impossible to gauge how many people formed the exiled faction.

Relations between Scotland and England, never cordial, were put under greater strain by the maintenance of the Douglases in England, Henry VI having granted James Douglas a pension. In November 1455, during one of Henry's bouts of insanity, Richard duke of York was appointed Protector, and James II decided to exploit the situation by going on the offensive, with the recovery of Berwick as his overriding goal. On 20 November, in an effort to gain support, James sent instructions to his envoys in France to urge Charles VII to exploit the disturbed state in England brought about by the struggle between Henry VI and Richard, duke of York, by co-operating with the Scots against the English, advocating a simultaneous attack by the French on Calais and the Scots on Berwick.[13]

The parliament which met in Stirling on 15 October 1455 was intensely anti-English in outlook, and much legislation was passed which prohibited the movement of people between the two countries. This problem had been dealt with previously by the warden courts, but these courts had been reduced in influence and power by the legislation enacted in the August parliament. One of the October statutes ordained 'that na Scottisman bring in the realme ony Inglisman', and another that 'na Scottisman sit apon speciale assouerance of any Inglisman'.[14] Not only were the Scots concerned about invasion from

England, but there was also concern that Scottish incursions into England should not be placed in jeopardy, and the failure of the surprise attack on Berwick, which James II attempted in June by diverting some of his army from the siege of Threave, was obviously very much on the king's mind when the statute was passed which concerned 'the punicione [punishment] of thame that warnys of the riding of ane host in Inglande'. Robert Lindsay of Pitscottie relates the story of the interception of the Scottish army by Englishmen pretending to be papal nuncios, who persuaded the king to abandon his planned attack. A letter sent by James II to Charles VII on 8 July 1455 shows that there is some substance to this story and indicates that the attack was abandoned as the result of an English trick. Charles VII replied to James' request for a simultaneous invasion of English territory (the Scots in the north and the French in the south) by pleading that he had problems of his own in France and felt unable to contemplate direct action against the English. The raid on Berwick, abortive though it was, may have been bound up with the final onslaught on the Douglases rather than distinct from it. The pension for James, earl of Douglas, and the obvious fact of his welcome in England as a weapon against the Scottish king, must have rankled with James II, and there was a very real fear that a Douglas 'fifth column' in England posed a constant threat. The weakness of the Lancastrians, following their defeat at the battle of St Albans on 22 May, was one which James was eager to exploit, and it may be that his eagerness to attack Berwick was because he believed that Douglas, or his supporters, had taken refuge there while Threave was under siege. It is hard to say how deep the actual commitment to the raid on Berwick was, and the Scots may have been glad of the excuse to abandon it in order to give their attention to settling domestic issues in the wake of the downfall of the house of Black Douglas.

When it became clear that there would be no immediate help forthcoming from Charles VII, and that he could not pursue a policy of sustained aggression against the English without support, James II had little alternative but to accept overtures for a truce, even though he had far from abandoned his intention to recapture Berwick. Early in 1456, William Monypenny was sent by the French king with proposals for peace between the three kingdoms of France, Scotland and England.[15] Monypenny's name occurs on many occasions in the surviving records. His career is a particular success story and an example of how important the roles of expatriates were in mediaeval diplomacy. William Monypenny was a member of James II's household, regularly employed as a diplomat, and he served both the French and the Scottish courts. From 1439, he was attached to the Dauphin Louis, who had married Princess Margaret Stewart, and he served Charles VII as chamberlain. He travelled principally between France, Scotland and England, and was involved in the marriage negotiations between Isabella Stewart and the eldest son of the Duke of Brittany in 1442, and Eleanor Stewart to Sigismund of Austria in 1447. In that year, on 14 July, Monypenny is styled 'natif d'Escoce, escuier d'escuieres' of the king of France.[16] On 16 October 1449, Monypenny was knighted by the Comte de Dunois at the siege of Rouen, he received a reward in 1450 from Charles VII following the recovery of Normandy from the English, and the grant of Concressault in Berry followed between 1451 and 1458. From James II, Monypenny received a grant of the lands of Halls of Airth in Stirlingshire, which were incorporated into the free barony of Monypenny on 1 May 1450, and on 26 June, he received a grant of the lands of Lethbertshiels, Stirling. Monypenny also benefited from the forfeiture of the Douglases to the extent that on 7 October 1458 he received a charter of the lands of Bordland of Rattray in Aberdeenshire, which had been forfeited by Hugh earl of Ormond (though these lands were resigned in November in favour of St Salvator's college, St Andrews). His elevation to lord of parliament as William lord Monypenny probably occurred towards the end of the reign of James II, and he continued to serve the crown into the following reign.[17]

The protectorate of Richard duke of York ended on 25 February 1456, and this provided the excuse for a temporary check on hostilities. James II, outwardly compliant with the wishes of Charles VII, sent an embassy to England under the leadership of James Kennedy, bishop of St Andrews, and George Schoriswood, bishop of Brechin, but on 10 May, before the embassy could accomplish anything, James wrote to Henry VI renouncing the truce of 1453 on the grounds that it had been violated continually by the English. Undoubtedly there had been devastating raids across the east border. In the account of Patrick lord Hailes, sheriff of Berwick, rendered on 4 October 1456, the fermes of Longformacus and Rachburn (in Lammermuir district, north Berwickshire) were remitted 'propter vastitatem earundem tempore guerre'. Sir Archibald Douglas of Cavers, sheriff of Roxburgh, found nothing to distrain on the castle wards of his sheriffdom and the fermes of Fallinche and Stitchell 'propter guerras Anglicorum', and in the accounts of the earldom of March, the fermes of Cockburnspath and Graden (in Berwickshire) were remitted due to the pillaging of these lands by the English.[18]

A period of aggressive exchanges between the Duke of York and James II occurred between 1455 and 1456. Provocatively, York had revived the claim to English overlordship of Scotland, whilst, for his part, James was goaded by the English maintenance of the Douglases and fired with determination to recapture Berwick. To this end, James courted the support of Charles VII of France, although to no practical effect. The French king was preoccupied with his own problems and exhorted James to seek peace, but although he went through the motions of nominating an embassy to that end, it is clear that James was bent on an aggressive stance. On 10 May 1456, he wrote to Henry VI renouncing the truce of 1453 on the grounds of its continual violation by the English.[19] On 28 June, he wrote Charles VII a letter in which he attempted once more to elicit help and practical support from the French king. The Duke of York's reply to James' renunciation of the truce was scathing in the extreme, but by the time it reached Scotland, James had already taken the field. On 12 July 1456, the king was at Peebles, his force having been 'lately at the water of Calne'.[20] He made a series of raids into Northumberland and then returned home, acccording to the Auchinleck chronicler, 'with gret worschip and tynt nocht a man of valour'; and on 24 August, the Duke of York sent Garter King to complain to James for 'makyng dayly foreis' into England.[21] Such border skirmishing clearly suited James better than a major confrontation with the English forces, and he seems to have been well satisfied with the progress of hostilities, as he took the time to go hunting at Loch Freuchie and Halymill (in Strathbraan, Perthshire) from 26 September to 1 October 1456.[22]

James II's aggressive attitude towards England appears, at least initially, to have had the support of the three estates. A General Council which met in Edinburgh on 19 October 1456 showed a great deal of concern for the defence of the borders, and on 20 October the three estates added their voice to the plea for assistance from Charles VII and sent a letter to which the seals of Bishop Kennedy of St Andrews, William Sinclair earl of Orkney, and the common seal of Edinburgh, were appended. The hostilities of 1456 had evidently been seen as a national campaign in which the whole realm was required to play a part, and the Acts of Parliament contain numerous references to measures intended to train men in warlike pursuits and to establish regular 'wappinschaws' (weapon showings). Football and golf were to be 'cryit doune and nocht usyt' in order to encourage the practice of archery. Also, in 1457, probably as the result of a provision of the General Council which met on 19 October 1456, direct taxation was revived, with the burghs being stented and loans being exacted from merchants.[23] The tax from the burghs and a loan from the burgesses was rendered by Andrew Crawford on 25 July 1457, chiefly in Flemish money.[24] Crawford had been sent to Flanders to raise money for the tax on the security of the Scottish burghs, and on the security of individual merchants for the loan. The money raised was put to use immediately to buy materials for war, including 800lbs of saltpetre and 1500 arrows and arrow heads.[25]

James II spent the Christmas of 1456 at St Andrews and continued to make plans for the recapture of Berwick. In February 1457, he prepared to attack the town, but his intentions were not followed through and negotiations for a truce were opened up, indicating that the Scottish campaign had begun to run out of steam and that enthusiasm was waning as the three estates favoured a more cautious (and less costly) approach. On 20 June, a two-year truce was made, which was ratified by James at Stirling on 6 August.[26] There are a number of possible reasons for this change of attitude. In October 1456, the Yorkists fell from power and Richard duke of York was appointed Lieutenant of Ireland — a post which amounted to virtual banishment. D'Escouchy suggests that the Lancastrian queen, Margaret of Anjou, had proposed a marriage alliance between the two sons of the Duke of Somerset and James II's sisters Joanna and Annabella, and this would have put a halt to hostilities, at least for the period of negotiation.[27] However, it was the failure of Charles VII to offer tangible assistance which seems to have robbed the campaign of most of its impetus, as the amount of correspondence between the two courts indicates that a great deal of importance was attached to such hopes for aid. Charles VII excused himself from sending help on the grounds that he did not know the nature of the country and that the internal affairs of France and the necessity of defending the coastline absorbed all his troops and revenue, although he did promise to send artillery.[28]

Another area in which James II came into conflict with the English was in the dispute over the Isle of Man, where by investing his second son Alexander in the political lordship he revived claims to its suzerainty which had lapsed for more than 100 years. In 1266, the King of Norway had ceded the Sudreys, including Man, to Scotland, but the history of the Scots' possession of Man was fraught and turbulent, and there were numerous struggles with the English over possession. In 1313, Robert Bruce attacked Man, then in English hands, and on 20 December, he granted the island to Thomas Randolph earl of Moray, in free regality, retaining the patronage of the bishopric. The Scottish supremacy was short-lived, however, and sporadic conflict with the English in Man continued, although after the fiasco of Neville's cross in 1346, the Scots made little serious effort to reclaim Man.[29] Henry VI granted the island to Sir John Stanley, giving him also the patronage of the bishopric, and Man was still in the hands of the Stanley family when James II embarked on his attempt to re-establish Scots domination. The excuse for intervention came when an English bishop was provided to the see of Man in 1455, and James, claiming that Man was part of the diocese of Sodor and therefore a Scottish bishopric, sent an expedition from Kirkcudbright, following which he invested his second son, Alexander, in the lordship.[30] The Galloway accounts of 1456 record the disbursement of 36s for a ship that was sent to Man to explore when the king's army was there, and in the following financial year, £5 compensation was paid to Patrick Callander for the wreck of his ship while at the island of Man on the king's service; also a courier received five shillings for carrying letters from Dundrennan to the king at Falkland 'with news of the ships'.[31] The Stanleys appear to have reacted to this provocation by building a curtain wall at Peel castle in Man; and indeed the antagonising of the Stanleys appears to have been the only thing accomplished by the expeditionary force. James II did not succeed in establishing Scottish control of the Isle of Man, perhaps because he did not make a really concerted effort to do so, as his attention was necessarily distracted by other areas of diplomatic activity. The exiled 9th Earl of Douglas took the opportunity of James II's intervention in the Isle of Man to strike back at the king by joining forces with the Stanleys in 1457, invading Kirkcudbright by sea, burning the town and plundering the Marches.[32] In an effort to establish royal supremacy in Galloway, Kirkcudbright had been created a royal burgh in 1455, following the fall of the Douglases, and the Franciscan friars at Kirkcudbright had their friary erected by James II

— the last conventual friary of the Scottish Grey Friars to be founded in Scotland.[33] A strike against Kirkcudbright was therefore a direct attack on a new symbol of royal control in Galloway. The effect of such an action was to underline that the Douglases were still a potential threat, even if their actions consisted of causing a sporadic nuisance rather than presenting a serious danger to the king. In fact, such raids must have been counter-productive for Douglas, as his incursions, such as those at Arkinholm, Kirkcudbright and the marches, were into formerly Douglas territory, hardening the resistance and antipathy of erstwhile tenants and allies. It would appear that one of the Douglas incursions into Scotland resulted in the capture of the young David, earl of Crawford. A charter was given by Crawford on 26 February 1464 to Herbert Johnstone of Dalebank in reward for his faithful service at the time when Crawford was held captive by James 9th earl of Douglas, and in recognition of Johnstone's help in liberating Crawford from captivity.[34] The date of the abduction is not specified, but David succeeded his father, Alexander, earl of Crawford, in 1453 when he was still a child. Alexander was one of the members of the fateful bond which precipitated the death of William, 8th earl of Douglas, but Lindsay support for the Douglases after the murder was not strongly in evidence, and it is possible that James Douglas felt that he could forcibly command that support by seizing the young Earl of Crawford. Alternatively, he may have wished to use Crawford as a bargaining counter with the king, or as an example of what could happen to those who withheld support. The Johnstones had certainly played a major role in the defeat of the Douglases at Arkinholm in May 1455, which may have been the occasion on which the rescue of Crawford took place, although the charter states specifically that Crawford had been in the hands of James, earl of Douglas, and Douglas does not appear to have been present at the Arkinholm skirmish. Whether the rescue of Crawford was effected at Arkinholm or on some other occasion, the fact of Crawford's capture meant that the Douglases were still capable of causing considerable trouble, although resistance to them from the major border families appears to have been resolute. It may be assumed, therefore, that the object of Douglas raids after the forfeiture of the family in 1455 was vengeful rather than a serious attempt to revive support.

James II was not so preoccupied with the Douglases that he neglected other business, and he seems to have been content to delegate the repudiation of Douglas raids to the border landowners while he turned his attention to diplomatic activities. 1458 saw James involved in discussions with France, Castile and Denmark. The parliament which met in Perth on 6 November 1458 appointed the following commissioners to travel to France: William Monypenny, John Kennedy, provost of St Andrews, Patrick Folkart, captain of the Scots Guards, and Robert Pattilok.[35] These commissioners were instructed to negotiate in the dispute between James II and King Christian of Denmark, which had been referred to the arbitration of Charles VII. The problem arose from the terms of a treaty made between James I and Eric of

Norway in 1426 by which it was agreed that Orkney, Shetland and the Hebrides should pay a tribute to the Norwegian king as a renewal of a pledge dating from 1266, when the Scots had agreed to pay 100 marks each year for the transfer of the western isles to Scotland. The agreement had been renewed in 1312, but payments lapsed until 1426, when James I promised to pay the 'annual', although his promise was not fulfilled and the tribute fell into arrears once more. King Christian of Denmark had established himself in Norway in 1451, and in 1457 he was recognised as King of Sweden. Charles VII wished to make an alliance with Christian I in May 1456, but Christian was anxious to settle the matter of the 'annual' with the Scots and asked for Charles' help to that end.

A convention was ordered to be held in Paris at Whitsuntide 1457, but in the winter of 1456/7, Bjarn Thorleiffson, governor of Iceland, along with his wife and companions, was attacked and robbed while seeking shelter from a storm in an Orkney port. King Christian wrote to Charles VII in April 1457 complaining about the outrage, and he stated that Thorleiffson had been taken to James' presence and all his goods and furnishings seized, in addition to the royal tribute and ecclesiastical rents from Iceland which the governor was accompanying to Denmark.[36] As the Earl of Orkney was a vassal of the King of Norway, and the diocese of Orkney and the Isles were suffragans of Trondheim, the attack on Thorleiffson was an insult to Christian I, having been perpetrated on Norwegian territory. The name of William Sinclair, earl of Orkney, is nowhere expressly mentioned, but as Dr Crawford points out, it is very unlikely that such an attack could have been carried out within his earldom without his knowledge. The motive for the attack is not entirely clear, but a number of facts pieced together are certainly suggestive. William, earl of Orkney, had held the office of Chancellor of Scotland from 1454, but his last recorded act in that office was on 20 October 1456, and he was subsequently replaced by George Schoriswood, bishop of Brechin. The attack on Thorleiffson took place in the following winter and the immediate effect was to postpone the meeting scheduled for Whitsun 1457, for upon hearing the news of what had taken place, Christian I requested that the meeting be deferred until after the feast of St Martin, on 11 November.[37]

William earl of Orkney may have believed that the outcome of negotiations between James II and Christian I would be detrimental to his interests in Orkney. James' intention to acquire possession of Orkney and Shetland was not stated formally until 1460, but it is probable that his plans were drawn up much earlier and were known to the Earl of Orkney. Dr Crawford has drawn attention to the fact that the earl had embarked on a long-term programme of land acquisition, buying randomly in Orkney what were termed 'conquest lands'. These were mostly outlying odal lands and such a policy was probably a form of insurance, as the earl would have foreseen a drop in his revenue if Orkney were ceded to Scotland, 'if only because he would be unable to resist the Scottish crown's rights to rents and skatts from the earldom, as he was able to resist the Danish king's'.[38] Christian I's complaints to Charles VII that his repeated demands for redress had received no response may indicate that James II was unable to compel the Earl of Orkney to make amends, but Charles wrote to Christian on 18 May 1457, informing him that the Scottish king had agreed to send envoys on 1 October. This meeting did not take place and Christian, understandably furious, wrote a belligerent letter to James in which he threatened to take the matter to the Pope. In July 1459, Danish and Scottish ambassadors were present at Chinon. No firm agreement was made, although this may have been the first occasion on which the prospect of a Scoto-Danish marriage settlement as a solution to the problem was mooted — a new prospect occasioned by the birth of a daughter to Christian I on 23 June 1457.[39] In December 1459, transumpts of the 1426 treaty were made at Copenhagen in readiness for the next meeting between the representatives of Scotland and Denmark, which took place in the summer of 1460 at Bourges.[40]

The Scots' demands were audacious in the extreme. Hardly a mention was made of the 'annual' except to state that in return for a marriage alliance all claims to the arrears of the 'annual' must be remitted. In addition, the Danish king's right to Orkney and Shetland was to be given to the Scottish king, and the bride was to bring 100,000 crowns with her for her dowry. The Danish ambassadors were obviously in no position to reach an agreement on such terms, and the Scots for their part seem to have been unwilling to have the negotiations continue. They asked for a postponement of four months because Bishop Kennedy, who had set out for the meeting in the spring of 1460 in the company of Alexander duke of Albany, the king's second son, was lying ill at Bruges, and he had in his possession the original documents of the 1266 and 1426 treaties, which were deemed necessary for the negotiations.[41] The death of James II on 3 August 1460 did not, apparently, cause the immediate breakdown of negotiations, but it removed the impetus for the time being.[42]

Foreign negotiations absorbed much time and effort in the last years of James II's reign, but not to the exclusion of everything else. The parliament which met in Edinburgh on 6 March 1458 gave its attention to social and economic matters and to the more effective administration of justice. This emphasis on the prosperity and effective husbanding of the resources of the realm indicates that the political community was concerned to see the king working towards the restoration of normality within the kingdom following the turbulent years of the Douglas conflict, and James was exhorted to direct his energies 'to the quiet and commoune profett of the Realme'.[43] James had certainly been turning his attention to domestic matters, but his overriding concern was to build up the royal house of Stewart to a position of unrivalled wealth and power, and this involved him in considerable conflict with certain members of his nobility.

On 5 November 1457, in the Tolbooth of Aberdeen, an Assize of Error rejected finally the claim of Thomas lord Erskine to the earldom of Mar, and found that the lands of Mar were of right vested in the crown.[44] This dispute had been running since the early days of the king's minority, and had been extremely complex in its evolution, involving a number of members of the nobility. The Earl of Orkney had supported the Erskines in 1449 when Sir Thomas Erskine had delivered a protest on behalf of himself and his father, and was accompanied by the earls of Douglas, Crawford and Orkney as witnesses.[45] The earls of Douglas and Crawford were both dead by 1457, and the king may have felt that a record of pro-Erskine sympathy from his chancellor would not suit his plans for the earldom of Mar. It was, therefore, the new chancellor, George Schoriswood, bishop of Brechin, who acted as King's advocate at the assize. The king was himself present, as he had come north on a justice ayre in October/November 1457, and this may attest to the importance attached by James II to the earldom. The equity of the decision is open to question. George lord Leslie, who held some of his lands of the Earl of Mar, supported the king, and following the favourable result of the case, he became automatically a tenant-in-chief. Three months later, he had been elevated to the earldom of Rothes, and had his lands of Ballinbreich erected into a barony and his town of Leslie Green made into a burgh of barony.[46] The earldom of Mar was settled upon the king's son John, who was infeft during the financial year ending June 1459, although the king took advantage of his possession immediately, as on 12 November 1457 he granted lands in the earldom of Mar and sheriffdom of Aberdeen to Edmund Mortimer.[47]

James II showed great interest in the north following the forfeiture of the Douglases, and the accounts in the Exchequer Rolls, in addition to a number of royal charters, show that James came north in 1456 and 1457, staying at Inverness, Elgin, Spynie castle (the seat of the Bishop of Moray), the monastery of Kinloss, and the burgh of Aberdeen. The king caused extensive repairs to be carried out at Inverness castle under the direction of John Winchester, bishop of Moray, and he sanctioned the continuation of building work which had been initiated by Archibald Douglas at the Moray castle of Darnaway. The island fortalice of Lochindorb, which had been fortified by Archibald Douglas against the king in 1455, did not fare so well; a warrant was issued to the Thane of Cawdor in March 1456 ordering its demolition.[48]

This action by the king, and his general attitude towards the earldom of Moray, brought him into conflict with Alexander earl of Huntly and his son George, master of Huntly. The forfeiture of Archibald Douglas, earl of Moray, in 1455 had resulted in the earldom of Moray falling to the crown. James Crichton, who was married to the elder Dunbar heiress of Moray and who had been 'beltit erll' briefly in 1452, died in 1454, and the king appears to have encountered no opposition to his claim to the earldom from Crichton's family. However, the Earl of Huntly's son George entered into a contract to marry Countess Elizabeth Dunbar shortly after the death of her husband, Archibald Douglas, at the battle of Arkinholm, and he clearly hoped by this to acquire the earldom of Moray in Elizabeth's dowry.[49] Alexander earl of Huntly's wife was Elizabeth Crichton, the sister of the late 'beltit erll', and the

Gordons may have felt that the earldom of Moray was a suitable reward for their loyal services to the crown. However, the king was not noticeably lavish in his rewards to the Gordons, indeed he appeared reluctant to encourage the increase of Gordon power and influence in the north. Consequently, the earldom of Moray was settled on David, the king's youngest son, and the estates continued to be administered by the crown even after the death of the young prince, some time before 18 July 1457. James tried to increase the profits of the earldom of Moray by leasing some of the lands of Darnaway and by appointing four commissioners to revise the rentals of Moray.[50] Continuing royal antipathy towards the Gordons is apparent in the destruction of Lochindorb, which was to have been delivered to Huntly when George married Elizabeth Dunbar, and a further slight occurred when Patrick lord Glamis replaced the Earl of Huntly as keeper of Kildrummy castle. The Gordon response was violent, though ineffectual, and on 7 March 1457, the Earl of Huntly, George master of Huntly and their heirs were granted a remission for their devastation of the lands of Mar.[51]

James II's overall policy in the north-east appears to have been one of 'divide and rule'. He took pains to ensure that no one family would be able to take over the northern lands forfeited by the Douglases and rise to a position of prominence which would present him with problems of control in the future. Moray and Mar were rich and powerful earldoms in terms of both territory and the prestige which they conferred, and the king's intention to keep them in crown hands demonstrated a clear decision to influence the exercise of power in the north-east.

In contrast to his attitude in the north-east, James II's policy towards John earl of Ross and lord of the Isles was placatory. The Exchequer Rolls show that Ross was allowed entry to some of his lands at the age of only sixteen, and his seizure of the castles of Inverness, Urquhart and Ruthven in March 1451 was condoned. Further than this, Ross was invested with the life-rent of Urquhart and Glenmoriston (supposedly annexed to the crown in 1455) and he was made keeper of Urquhart castle.[52] His half-brother Celestine (or Gillespic) also found favour with James II; in 1456 he was presented with a silver collar and chain worth £20 and shortly afterwards he was given the keepership of Redcastle.[53] The comparative freedom granted to the Lord of the Isles should not be construed as arising out of James' magnanimity, but rather from a lack of real choice. A punitive expedition against the Lord of the Isles for his past transgressions would have been costly and unpopular with the political community after the protracted years of struggle against the Douglases, and its success could not be guaranteed. Therefore, James pursued a conciliatory policy towards the problems of the north and north-west.

These actions demonstrate James' ability to tread a fine line between firm action and measures which would invoke dangerous reaction. He carefully endeavoured not to leave himself devoid of support, and would act against certain members of the nobility whom he deemed to be threatening his interests while simultaneously rewarding or advancing others. Clearly, James considered that his position was one which could not simply be taken for granted. The aggressive attitude of his father had antagonised and alienated many of his subjects to the point where few were averse to his removal; and the Stewarts ought not to be seen as an iron dynasty who could not conceivably be challenged. The turmoil of the minority meant that James II had to work hard to establish his personal authority by being seen to fulfil the expectations of those who looked to him for good government.

One important criterion of good mediaeval kingship which James II certainly exhibited was that of travelling extensively throughout the realm and being seen in the localities. In February and March 1457, James travelled to the south-west of Scotland on a justice ayre, and charters were issued from Wigtown, Kirkcudbright and Dumfries.[54] On 23 May 1455, James II had confirmed a charter by James earl of Douglas to his secretary Mark Haliburton of the lands of Glengennet and Bennan lying in the earldom of Carrick. On 3 October 1455, while he was visiting Tongland, James II issued a charter to Mark Haliburton of that ilk of the half of the barony of Trabeath called Glengennet, proceeding on the forfeiture of James 9th earl of Douglas.[55] However, on 31 March 1457, the king granted to his half-brother, James Stewart, the lands of Bedshiel within the sheriffdom of Berwick, which were in the king's hands by the forfeiture of the late Mark Haliburton, and on 19 April, Stewart was given a royal grant of the barony of Trabeath, alias Glengennet, formerly belonging to the forfeited Haliburton.[56] The death and forfeiture of Mark Haliburton may have coincided with the king's visit to the southwest, and it is possible that Haliburton had been in contact with his erstwhile patron, James Douglas. The purpose of the king's visit was undoubtedly to show a strong royal presence in an area only recently deprived of its baronial overlord and to crush any lingering support for the exiled earl. It is also significant that on 24 February 1457, Andrew Stewart, who had received the Douglas title, Lord Avandale, witnessed a charter as Warden of the West Marches, and on 20 March and 28 April he was styled 'King's Guardian', a position directly related to the personal protection of the king.[57]

Evidence of the crumbling of old Douglas support continued in 1458 when the lands of Drumblade (north-west Aberdeenshire) and Towie (Aberdeenshire, near Kildrummy) fell into the hands of the crown through the forfeiture of the wife of Sir James Douglas of Ralston. James Douglas (who is also styled of Lochleven or Lugton) was the brother of Sir Henry Douglas of Lochleven, and he had taken part in the tournament at Stirling in February 1449, where he jousted with knights of Burgundy in the company of James, master — and later 9th earl — of Douglas.[58] Douglas of Ralston was a supporter of the Earl of Douglas, being named on an English safe-conduct obtained by William earl of Douglas on 12 May 1451, but he did not share in the 1455 disgrace of the Douglases, as he was despatched by James II on an embassy to the French court in 1456. It seems that, under cover of this embassy, James Douglas of Ralston was able to intrigue with the exiled Earl of Douglas, or was at least suspected of having done so, for he and his wife fled to England and were forfeited by 1458 for complicity in the treason of the Black Douglases.[59]

The king did not pursue an unbridled vendetta against everyone who had been associated with the Douglases, although one man who appears to have only narrowly escaped the worst consequences of his association with the Douglases was James Lindsay of Covington. On 14 July 1434, James Lindsay was served heir to his father, John Lindsay 'quondam Domini de Cowantoun', and his career in the 1440s was inextricably bound up with the earls of Douglas. Lindsay witnessed a number of Douglas charters and, in a supplication to the Pope for a dispensation to hold two parish churches, dated 3 October 1444, he is styled 'first secretary and counsellor of the Earl of Douglas'. On 11 March 1448, a notarial instrument records James Lindsay's admission to the collegiate church of Lincluden, and he appears as a witness on a number of royal charters under the designation provost of Lincluden.[60] On 12 January 1453, Lindsay was given the office of keeper of the privy seal, witnessing charters in that office until 14 April 1454, after which he disappears from official records, with the exception of a charter issued to him by James II on 3 June 1456.[61] James Lindsay was evidently also a kinsman of the earls of Crawford, and on 18 June 1449, he witnessed a charter by Alexander 4th earl of Crawford to John, 'brother-german' of James lord Hamilton, and he received from the 4th earl the keepership of Crawford castle in Lanarkshire, the bailiary of Crawford-Lindsay and a tenancy in the same lordship, the grant being made in the early 1450s which was the key period of Douglas-Crawford co-operation.[62] Such strong connections with two members of the bond which precipitated the murder of William earl of Douglas in 1452 must have placed James Lindsay in a precarious position in the period of strife against the Douglases, although he held the office of keeper of the privy seal throughout 1453 (the year in which Alexander earl of Crawford died) and the temporary compromise with the 9th earl of Douglas. The office of Keeper of the Privy Seal was a very important one, as it involved effective control of royal patronage, an extremely sensitive area in the early 1450s in the build-up to and the aftermath of the murder of William 8th earl of Douglas. The final collapse of the Douglases in 1455 seems to have heralded James Lindsay's disappearance from active court service, and he may have retired to Lincluden to live down his Douglas/Crawford associations. It is not clear who held the office of Privy Seal following Lindsay of Covington's fall from favour, as the next recorded keeper was Thomas Spens, who did not appear in the office until 1458. However, an intriguing entry concerning James Lindsay exists in the Auchinleck chronicle, and reads:

Item the said quene [Mary of Gueldres] efter the deid of king James the secund tuke master James lyndesay for principale counsalour and gart him kepe the preve sele nochtwithstanding that the said master James was excludit fra the counsall of the forsaid king and fra the court and for his werray helynes and had bene slane for his demeritis had nocht bene he was redemit with gold.[63]

Lindsay's exclusion from the king's council and court agrees with the available record evidence, although the exact meaning of 'helynes' in this context is not clear. It has been suggested that the word has its roots in the teutonic 'hael' and conveys a meaning of subtlety or duplicity. A sarcastic reference to Lindsay's holiness, in the sense of false piety, may be intended, and, in order to escape the penalty of his duplicity (which may be little more than his recorded association with Douglas) Lindsay must at least have been reputed to have given money to the king, although there is no record of this in the exchequer accounts. James II was not prepared, evidently, to reinstate Lindsay to a position of trust, and he had to wait until the king was dead before he could return to court in the service of the queen.

It is clear that James II was selective in his use of patronage, but his awareness of the importance of consolidating loyal support extended to making use of his sisters as instruments of appeasement, and when the two princesses, Annabella and Joanna, returned to Scotland from Europe in the spring of 1458, having failed to secure foreign marriages, Annabella was married to George master of Huntly, and Joanna, who was deaf and dumb, married to James Douglas of Dalkeith, recently created Earl of Morton.[64] The king also provided endowments for his family, as witnessed by the revival of the dukedom of Albany in 1458 for his second son, Alexander earl of March, although this was an honorary title rather than one conveying much wealth and power. Sir John Stewart, half-brother to the king, was created Earl of Atholl before 20 June 1457, and when Margaret Douglas, 'Fair Maid' of Galloway, returned to Scotland and placed herself under James' protection, she was given in marriage to the Earl of Atholl with the forfeited Douglas lands of Balvenie as her portion.[65] This marriage had taken place by 25 March 1460, on which date the king granted a charter to John earl of Atholl and Margaret, his spouse, of the lordship of Balvenie and other lands in the sheriffdom of Banff.[66]

The elevation of James Douglas 3rd Lord of Dalkeith to the earldom of Morton was probably intended to give stability to a family which had been involved in a complex internal struggle for more than a decade. James Lord Dalkeith was in possession of the regality of Morton in Nithsdale when the crown proposed to erect it, along with his other lands, into the earldom of Morton. Lord Dalkeith's great-grandfather, Sir James Douglas, had acquired Morton originally from his brother-in-law, George earl of March.[67] The son of the first Lord Dalkeith had become insane during his father's lifetime and his stepmother and younger brothers used the opportunity to acquire rights prejudicial to the third lord Dalkeith, then a minor. Shortly before his death, the first lord Dalkeith obtained a new charter of the barony of Morton as a regality and he took the investiture to himself and his wife, Janet Borthwick, with remainder to her son, William.[68] Janet viewed her step-grandson's new earldom as a usurpation of her rights, and on 14 March 1458, when the king's intention to create the earldom was announced in parliament, Janet's brother, Lord Borthwick, raised the objection that his sister and nephew had the legal right to Morton, not the Lord of Dalkeith. The reply of Chancellor Schoriswood was that the earldom was not for Morton in Nithsdale, but for Morton in Calderclere, Midlothian.[69] Clearly, many people still thought in terms of land in connection with titles, even though dignities which were essentially of an honorific nature were becoming more common.

Such a title was the one conferred on William Lord Keith, who became Earl Marischal in 1458. This earldom did not carry with it any landed wealth, but it raised William Lord Keith, hitherto a lord of parliament, above his peers, probably as a gesture of gratitude for loyal support in the past which the king hoped would continue, without having required to give Keith much in any tangible sense. Sir William Keith had been made a lord of parliament in 1446, and designated Lord Keith by July 1451. He had been one of the guarantors of a truce with the English in 1457, and the title, Earl Marischal, derived from the judicial office, which had been held by the Keith family for centuries, rather than his estates.[70]

Perhaps the most important creation of 1458 was Colin Lord Campbell, who became Earl of Argyll, the only creation of James II's which was based on territory. Sir Duncan Campbell of Lochawe, who became a lord of parliament as Lord Campbell in 1445, was Colin Campbell's grandfather.[71] Duncan's son, Archibald, predeceased him, therefore when Duncan died in 1453, Colin succeeded him as the second Lord Campbell. His marriage to Isabel Stewart, one of the three co-heiresses of John Lord of Lorne, brought him that lordship in the following reign, and his creation as Earl of Argyll in 1458 appears to have been the result of loyal and diligent crown service, his name appearing as a witness on a number of royal charters. James II clearly felt it wise to reward a loyal and increasingly powerful crown supporter established in the west, above all to form a buffer and act as the king's agent against any possible trouble coming from the Lord of the Isles.

Thus, James replenished the diminished ranks of the higher nobility, although at little cost to himself, and he prepared, from this enhanced power base, to involve himself on the wider stage of diplomacy and aggression. The truce with England, which had been made on 10 June 1457, was disrupted continually by border raids and acts of piracy, one of which resulted in a vessel dispatched by the Bishop of Galloway with a cargo of wine and iron being captured by the English and delivered to the Yorkist Earl of Warwick at Calais. As a result of this, James II sent Rothesay Herald to the English court in October 1457 to demand redress.[72] Breaches of the truce were settled, as far as possible, by commissions, and an indenture was signed at Reddenburn on

29 September 1458, at which the Scots commissioners were Ninian Spot, bishop of Galloway and keeper of the privy seal, the abbots of Holyrood and Melrose, lords Hailes and Borthwick, Patrick Young, Nicholas Otterburn, clerk register, Sir Alexander Home of Dunglass and Andrew Kerr of Altonburn. Also present were the Earl of Angus, Sir Simon Glendinning and the chancellor, George Schoriswood, bishop of Brechin. This indenture demanded the extradition of all the Scots king's rebels who had not renounced their fealty and taken their oath as Englishmen (thus excluding Douglas, who had formally renounced his fealty), and the English commissioners promised to give an answer on 15 January 1459. However, on 23 February 1459, Andrew Hunter, abbot of Melrose, and Rothesay Herald were sent to England again to seek redress for truce violations and for the restitution of £1000 stolen during the talks at Reddenburn![73]

The making and repairing of the terms of the truce continued to be carried out sporadically, and a treaty, signed at Newcastle on 12 September 1459 and ratified at Westminster on 20 February 1460, dealt with an extension of five years to a truce already prolonged until 1463. Such negotiations and extensions have every appearance of being cynical stalling devices while both sides prepared themselves for conflict. On 10 May 1459, the Abbot of Melrose and Rothesay Herald were in England on business for James II, the nature of which is not revealed in the records, but their trip coincided with a gathering of supporters of the Lancastrian cause at Leicester.[74] On 13 July 1459, a safe-conduct was issued for an embassy which included the bishops of Glasgow and Galloway, the Earl of Orkney (obviously restored to some measure of favour) and the Abbot of Melrose, to travel to England to treat for the preservation of the truce. On 15 March, George Schoriswood, bishop of Brechin, had received a safe-conduct to go on pilgrimage to Durham where he was able, no doubt, to discuss with Bishop Booth, the Lancastrian keeper of the privy seal, the 'secret matiris' already broached by the Abbot of Melrose.[75] However, James was clearly keeping his options open by negotiating with both political factions in England, as the Duke of York, still serving as the king's lieutenant in Ireland, sent an envoy to the Scottish court and in return, James sent Archibald Whitelaw, his son's tutor, to conclude a treaty with the duke.[76] Richard duke of York's staunch supporter, Philip, Duke of Burgundy, was also approached, James sending his young half-brother, James Stewart, as negotiator, although he can have been little older than seventeen in 1459. On 27 March 1459, Stewart and his associates received safe-conducts to pass through England to Calais. A few months later, Stewart was being entertained by the Count of Veere, ally of the Duke of Burgundy and the father-in-law of Princess Mary Stewart, lady of Buchan.[77]

By this time, the political affiliations of the king of Scots appear to have swung in the direction of York. Just prior to the Yorkist invasion of England from Calais in July 1460, it was rumoured in Bruges that the Scottish king intended to make a simultaneous attack with an army numbering 30,000, and that one of his daughters had been married to a son of York.[78] Preparations for war were certainly under way in Scotland as may be seen by the importation of bombards from Burgundy (one of which was Mons Meg), the employment of a German gunner and a French armourer, and the expenditure of large sums of money on armaments.[79]

The office of chancellor changed hands once more, it seems, to suit the political wind. Andrew Stewart, lord Avandale, was chancellor by July 1460, thus depriving George Schoriswood, bishop of Brechin, who had been in charge of negotiations with the Lancastrians.[80] James also contemplated the advantage of support from Ireland being brought in from the west, and in July 1460, Andrew Agnew, sheriff of Wigtown, was sent as an envoy to the chieftain O'Neill in Ulster.[81]

On 10 July 1460, the Lancastrian dynasty was overthrown at Northampton, and James took immediate advantage of the resulting turmoil to launch his attack. In England it was reported that James II 'with all his power is expected to lay siege to the town and castle of Berwick-on-Tweed'.[82] However, the object of attack was actually the castle of Roxburgh, although James may subsequently have intended to move on to Berwick. Thus, at the end of July 1460, James laid siege to the castle of Roxburgh. The preparations for war which had been going on for some time enabled him to bring an army into the field with great speed; if his attack on Roxburgh was a reaction to the battle of Northampton, then he mustered an army in approximately a fortnight. It is more likely that the king was carrying out plans which had been made in advance of the battle. Roxburgh held a commanding position between the river Teviot to the south and the river Tweed to the north. The castle stood on a long oblong mound which rose above the surrounding countryside to a height of approximately seventy feet, making it an important strategic stronghold.[83] Roxburgh castle was important both to the English and the Scots. To the English, their possession of Roxburgh was a tremendous psychological advantage, held as it was on Scottish soil, with a garrison maintained at the cost of £1000 per annum in time of truce, and double that amount in wartime.[84] To the Scots, it was an intolerable symbol of English occupation, and over it hung the spectre of James I's ignominious failure to recapture it in 1436. James II eagerly put to use the artillery which he had been amassing busily for a number of years. Unfortunately, it was this very passion for guns and the king's determination to watch his artillery in action which led to his untimely death just two months short of his thirtieth birthday. The only contemporary account of the king's death occurs in the Auchinleck chronicle:

> The zere of god 1460 the thrid sonday of august king James the secund with ane gret ost was at the sege of Roxburgh and unhappely was slane with ane gun the quhilk brak in the fyring/for the quhilk was gret dolour throu all scotland and nevertheless all the lordis that war thar remanit still with the oist [host] and on the fryday after richt wysly and manfully wan the forsaid castell.[85]

There is a tradition that the king was taken to the Friary of St Peter in the burgh, the site of which is shown on the map in the bend of the river Teviot between Teviot Haugh and Bridge-end Haugh, after he had been mortally wounded, in order to receive the last rites. This tradition also states that the Scots were occupying a position near the site of the present castle of Floors, just north of the Tweed,[86] and the place where the king was killed was reputedly marked by a holly tree, the position of which is marked on the map to the north of the river Tweed in the area known as South Park.[87] This would certainly have been a defensible position, from which James II could safely deploy his army and bring the might of his artillery to bear on the castle by firing across the river, a distance well within the range of his bombards. Bishop Lesley, writing in the 1560s, adds the details that a wedge breaking from a gun slew the king and grievously wounded the Earl of Angus, while Pitscottie, also a sixteenth-century writer, states that James was so heartened with the arrival of the Earl of Huntly with his company that he ordered the gunners to discharge a volley, whereupon a fragment from a broken gun severed the king's thigh bone, causing him to die, presumably from shock and bleeding, shortly afterwards.[88]

A more contemporary source, the *Extracta*,[89] states that the fatal salvo was fired in honour of the arrival of the queen at the siege, but the Auchinleck chronicler gives the impression that the queen and the young Prince James were in Edinburgh and were sent for by 'the lordis', the names of whom are unfortunately not recorded. The Auchinleck chronicler states that the prince came to Kelso 'with his modere the quene & bischopis & uther nobillis . . . on the fryday efter the deid of the king'. If the king had been killed on Sunday 3 August, then the prince must have arrived in Kelso on 8 August, on the same day that Roxburgh was taken, and his coronation followed on Sunday 10 August, exactly one week after the death of his father.[90]

The 1460 campaign to recapture Roxburgh from the English appears to have been executed with far more enthusiasm than the 1436 campaign, which broke up amid internal squabbling within the host and between James I and his nobles. In 1460, the Scots were able to capitalise on the chaos in England brought about by the conflict between the Yorkists and Lancastrians, and the impetus of the campaign continued even after the death of James II. Thus, following the crowning of James III at Kelso, 'the forsaid lordis passit to the castell of werk [Wark] & sone thai wan that castell and Incontinent kest it doune to the erd and distroyit It for ever'.[91]

The English border castle of Wark stood on the banks of the river Tweed, a few miles north-east of Roxburgh, and its destruction removed an important English stronghold. However, the Scots did not, apparently, press home their advantage by attempting to recapture Berwick, as the most important task to be faced was the establishment of the minority government for the eight-year-old king, James III.

NOTES

1. Nicholson, R., *Later Middle Ages*, 378; Brown, J., *Scottish Society in the Fifteenth Century*, 37.

2. *A.P.S.*, ii, 42.

3. Professor Nicholson has calculated that the former Black Douglas possessions contributed £1450 besides payments in victuals, and the annexed lands plus the customs should have given the crown a permanent endowment that was worth approximately £6050 per annum in cash. Nicholson, op. cit., 379; *E.R.*, vi, 113–32.

4. *E.R.*, vi, cix–cxvii, 226.

5. Ibid., cxl–cxlii; 265, 360, 514, 217, 221, 376, xc.

6. *A.P.S.*, ii, 36.

7. Fraser, *Douglas*, iii, 429, 430; *H.M.C.*, Report xi, Hamilton 17 (1 July 1455), Hamilton 18 (6 August 1457).

8. See Chapter 5, p. 86.

9. Fraser, *Buccleuch*, ii, 57; S.R.O. Calendar of Charters, ii, 342.

10. Fraser, *Douglas*, iii, 88, 90; *R.M.S.*, v, no. 54; *E.R.*, vi, 556.

11. S.R.O., GD 25/1/65.

12. *A.P.S.*, ii, 43–44.

13. Stevenson, *Wars*, i, 319–22.

14. *A.P.S.*, ii, 44.

15. Stevenson, op. cit; Pinkerton, *History*, i, 486.

16. *S.P.*, vi, 276; *Complete Peerage*, ix, 161.

17. *R.M.S.*, ii, nos. 344, 625, 647, 653; *S.P.*, vi, 277.

18. *Official Correspondence of Thomas Beckynton*, ii, 139–141; *E.R.*, vi, 184, 187, 261.

19. *Official Correspondence of Thomas Beckynton*, ii, 139–41.

20. This is a reference to the river Kale, a tributary of the Teviot. S.R.O., Calendar of Charters, ii, 344; *E.R.*, vi, 226–7, 258.

21. Dunlop, A. I., *Kennedy*, 169.

22. Chron. Auchinleck, f. 119r; *E.R.*, vi, 243.

23. Stevenson, *Wars*, i, 330–1; *A.P.S.*, ii, 45, 48; *E.R.*, vi, xlv–xlvi, 305–7, 384.

24. This worked out at approximately three times the value of Scots money.

25. *E.R.*, vi, xlv–xlvi, 305, 308–10. These materials were delivered to John Dunbar who had held Threave against the king in 1455, but had since been received into favour and employed as a supervisor of military materials.

26. Ibid., 205; *Rot. Scot.*, ii, 378–83.

27. D'Escouchy, *Chronique*, ii, 352.

28. *C.P.R.*, vi, 346, 356; Stevenson, *Wars*, i, 332–51.

29. Moore, A. W., 'The Connexion between Scotland and Man', *S.H.R.*, iii, 404, 406.

30. Thomas Burton was provided to the bishopric on 25 September 1455. The previous bishop, John Seyre, had been consecrated on 11 November 1435, but it is not known when he ceased to be bishop. The Scottish bishop of Sodor or the Isles was John Hector Macgilleon who was provided on 2 October 1441. *H.B.C.*, 255.

31. *E.R.*, vi, 204, 347, 349.

32. Dunlop, *Kennedy*, 176; S.R.O., Treaties with England, 20.

33. *C.S.S.R.*, 663.

34. *R.M.S.*, ii, no. 786.

35. *A.P.S.*, ii, 79.

36. Crawford, B., 'The Earls of Orkney-Caithness and their Relations with Norway and Scotland: 1158–1470' (unpublished PhD. thesis, St Andrews, 1971), 299, 300.

37. A similar incident took place in the winter of 1466–7 at a time when the Danish negotiations had been revived. On this occasion, it was the Bishop of Orkney who was attacked, and this led to the postponement of the marriage negotiations until 1468. Crawford, B., 'William Sinclair, Earl of Orkney, and his Family: a Study in the Politics of Survival', in *Essays on the Nobility of Medieval Scotland*, ed. K. J. Stringer (Edinburgh, 1985), 235–37.

38. Crawford, B., 'The Earls of Orkney-Caithness', 292–5.

39. Ibid., 303, 304.

40. Charles VII drew up a document summing up the negotiations on 8 October 1460, therefore the discussions must have taken place a short time before this date.

41. This was clearly a stalling device, because the documents could have been fetched by other members of the embassy: Crawford, op. cit., 305.

42. Torfaeus, Orcades, 185–6.

43. *A.P.S.*, ii, 52.

44. *A.B.Ill.*, iv, 205–13.

45. *A.P.S.*, ii, 61.

46. *H.M.C.*, Report iv, 495–503; *S.P.*, vii, 274.

47. *A.B.Coll.*, 606. The exact identity of this Edmund Mortimer is not known. He may have been related to Edmund Mortimer, earl of March, who died without legitimate issue on 18 January 1425 in Ireland. Richard, duke of York, succeeded his uncle, Mortimer, as Earl of March, and it is possible that Edmund Mortimer was connected with the Yorkist cause which James II was courting at that point. Chrimes, S. B., *Henry VII*, 73.

48. *E.R.*, vi, 380, 468, 475–6, 221, 469, 482, 521, 220, 380, 486.

49. *Spalding Club Miscellany*, iv, 128–30. The indenture was made at Forres on 20 May 1455.

50. These were: the Thane of Cawdor, Master Thomas Carmichael, canon of Moray, Patrick lord Glamis and John Winchester, bishop of Moray. *Cawdor Book*, 19; Dowden, *Bishops*, 159–60.

51. *E.R.*, vi, 269; *A.B.Ill.*, iv, 203.

52. *E.R.*, vi, 221, 376, 514, 650.

53. Ibid., 124, 518.

54. *Wigt. Chrs.*, 143: 24 February 1457; Ibid., 144: 8 March 1457; S.R.O., RH 1/1/2: 9 March 1457; Fraser, *Carlaverock*, ii, 42: 20 March 1457.

55. S.R.O., GD 25/1/62, 64, 65.

56. *H.M.C.*, Home, 64; S.R.O., GD 25/1/72.

57. *Wigt. Chrs.*, 143, 89; Fraser, *Carlaverock*, ii, 42. Avandale was also the keeper of Lochmaben castle in 1456, and his title 'gardianus rex' may have a parallel in the office, held by David Guthrie in the following reign, of Captain of the royal guard.

58. Hume Brown, *Early Travellers*,

59. Stevenson, *Wars*, i, 243; *E.R.*, vi, 435, 514.

60. Lord Lindsay, *Lives of the Lindsays* (London, 1849), i, 152, 452; *C.S.S.R.*, iv, 1071.

61. *R.M.S.*, ii, nos. 594, 595; NLS, Scc. 5976, Box 6, 14.

62. *Lives of the Lindsays*, op. cit; NLS, Acc. 5474, bundle 58.

63. Chron. Auchinleck, f. 120v.

64. *R.M.S.*, ii, nos. 745, 699; *E.R.*, vi, lviii.

65. *Rot. Scot.*, ii, 383; *C.D.S.*, iv, 498.

66. *H.M.C.*, Report vii, 708.

67. Reg. Honor. de Morton, i, 77–79. The charter was confirmed by David II in 1370.

68. *R.M.S.*, ii, no. 135: 28 February 1440. In her widowhood, Janet obtained two confirmations — *R.M.S.*, iv, nos. 6, 192: 7 March 1450, 22 March 1451.

69. *A.P.S.*, ii, 78; *E.R.*, vi, lvii–lviii.

70. *S.P.*, vi, 40; *R.M.S.*, ii, no. 62.

71. *S.P.*, i, 331–2.

72. *C.P.R.*, vi, 400, 405; *C.D.S.*, iv, 1257.

73. *R.M.S.*, ii, no. 677. At the same time, Marchmont Herald was despatched to the Earl of Northumberland 'about the truce and his answer respecting the security of ships and merchants'. *E.R.*, vi, 498.

74. Ramsay, *Lanc. and York*, ii, 213.

75. *C.D.S.*, iv, 1301; *Rot. Scot.*, ii, 390–1.

76. *E.R.*, vii, 33; Gairdner, *Letters of Richard III*, i, 63.

77. *Foedera*, xi, 420; Manuscript Accounts of Veere, 213–17, November 1459; Dunlop, *Kennedy*, 206. The Buchan title was conferred on Mary on her marriage. James Stewart was created Earl of Buchan in 1469 after the death of his half-sister: *S.P.*, ii, 266.

78. *Milan Papers*, i, 27.

79. *E.R.*, vi, 385–6, 456, 495–99. The exchequer accounts show numerous entries concerning expenditure on the transportation and repair of bombards with brass, copper and iron, canvas for the king's tent and money spent on making arrows and lances in Edinburgh castle. Mons Meg was imported in 1458. Caldwell, D. (ed.), *Scottish Weapons and Fortifications, 1100–1800* (Edinburgh, 1981), 90, n. 12.

80. *H.M.C.*, Home, 278 — 6 July 1460. *E.R.*, vi, 488, 617. Schoriswood ceased to be chancellor after 4 April 1460 — *R.M.S.*, ii, no. 754. At about the same time, Alexander Napier replaced John Learmonth as comptroller — *E.R.*, vi, 656, 658.

81. Ibid., vii, 9; Agnew, A., *Hereditary Sheriffs*, 276–7.

82. *C.D.S.*, iv, 1307.

83. See map, plate 14.

84. *Rot. Scot.*, ii, 360–1.

85. Chron. Auchinleck, f. 119v.

86. Moffat, A., *Kelsae*, 22, 38.

87. Map of Roxburgh, plate 14.

88. Lesley, *History*, 31; Pitscottie, *Historie*, 143.

89. See Chapter 7, p. 128.

90. *Extracta*, 243–4; Chron. Auchinleck, op. cit.

91. Ibid. The Auchinleck chronicler is guilty of some exaggeration when he states that Wark castle was destroyed for ever, as John, duke of Albany, laid siege to it in 1523.

7

James II and the Historians

The reign of James II poses considerable problems for the modern historian, because the lack of comprehensive official documentation has led to a heavy reliance on chronicle sources. Such sources are inherently unsatisfactory, as the only contemporary chronicle is short and fragmented, while the chronicles which deal more fully with the reign and provide the greatest detail about events and personalities were written in the following century and are not concerned with an objective analysis of the reign, but rather with the exposition of a particular political or constitutional principle. The major problem posed by the sixteenth-century chroniclers is the uncertainty about their sources of information, so that many stories which have become incorporated into the standard view of the reign are unverifiable. This does not render the chronicles and later histories useless, but rather it means that a measure of detective work is necessary to trace the growth of particular myths or distortions and, as far as possible, to analyse the motivation behind the writing of the histories.

The Auchinleck Chronicle is the only substantial contemporary chronicle source for the reign of James II of Scotland and is a crucial document for any study of the events of the reign as it provides, in many cases, greater detail than may be found in official sources. Indeed, some of the entries offer the only information now available concerning particular events. The title, the 'Auchinleck Chronicle', was given to the document by T. G. Stevenson in 1877 because the manuscript in which it appears (the Asloan MS.) came from the library of Alexander Boswell of Auchinleck.[1] The entries are not in strict chronological order, therefore to call it a chronicle which, by definition, is a continuous register of events in order of time, is inaccurate, but for the sake of convenience and clarity, the familiar title will be used.

The Auchinleck Chronicle forms only one part of a large folio volume entitled the 'Asloan Manuscript'.[2] The manuscript, written on paper, consists of miscellaneous prose and verse collections which were transcribed from various sources shortly before 1514 by John Asloan, an Edinburgh writer or notary. The manuscript appears to have been acquired in 1730 by Alexander Boswell, as his signature, with that date, appears on the flyleaf of the manuscript. Early in the nineteenth century, the Asloan MS. was brought to Edinburgh and bound at Register House under the supervision of Thomas

Thomson. Unfortunately, as a result, the order in which the pages now appear is, in some instances, clearly incorrect. The Auchinleck Chronicle occupies fourteen folios in the Asloan MS., from folio 109 to 123, and it was edited and printed by Thomson in 1818 for private circulation, although his intention to add notes and illustrations remained unfulfilled at his death and, consequently, very few copies were issued. Those that were contain the Auchinleck Chronicle in two forms: first, with the entries in the order of the original MS., and secondly, with the entries re-arranged in what Thomson believed to be chronological order and given the title, 'A Short Chronicle of James the Second, King of Scots'.[3] However, the very nature of the document defies such strict chronological treatment, and the result of Thomson's efforts has simply been further confusion.

The original manuscript appears to have been imperfect even before it was bound, as a number of the Auchinleck Chronicle's entries begin or tail off in the middle of a sentence, the remainder of which is lost, although it is difficult to gauge whether this involves the loss of one or more folios at any given point. There is also some evidence to suggest that John Asloan's original sources were defective, as some of the entries are incomplete and do not make sense as they read, even when these occur in the middle of a folio. There is an example of this on folio 121r. with an entry which reads:

> James of Douglas sone to the said erll Sir walter of bekirtoune, sir william of setoun, Sir richert of berkirtoun, Schir henry bekirtoun governour to the scottis archeris & alexander bekirtoun with mony utheris gud knychtis and sqwyeris.

Either Asloan was merely copying down a fragment or he was distracted and failed to complete the entry, but this is extremely unlikely unless he was subject to many such distractions!

The value of the Auchinleck Chronicle depends largely on its being contemporary and there is considerable evidence to support this. Where the chronicler's dating may be checked, it is usually impressively accurate. For example, the chronicler states that the battle of Arbroath was fought on 23 January 1446, 'on ane sonday laite'. Sir Patrick of Corntoun was slain in Dumbarton on Saturday 7 August 1451, and William earl of Douglas was summoned to Stirling by the king on 21 February, the Monday before Lent.[4] All these dates and weekdays are accurate, which suggests that the events described were being written about at the time or shortly afterwards.[5] However, the Auchinleck Chronicle's dating does present a number of problems, such as the use of the expression 'that samyn zere' or 'that samyn moneth', as a number of entries begin in this fashion and it is sometimes difficult to ascertain which year or month is meant if the preceding entry is missing. On a couple of occasions, the chronicler is even more vague in his dating, using the expression, 'that samyn tyme'. The most striking example of this is the entry describing the battle of Brechin. This is the last item in the chronicle and it ends in the middle of a sentence, leaving half of the page blank. The

preceding entry concerns border skirmishes in May and June 1449, although
the battle of Brechin took place in 1452, therefore 'that samyn tyme' does not
refer to 1449. The chronicler appears to have been rather confused in his
account of the battle, as the entry is given a heading (the only item in the
chronicle to be singled out in this way) which reads 'the battle of ~~arbroth~~
brechyne'. This confusion is perhaps understandable as the earls of Huntly
and Crawford were involved in both conflicts, and the entry, fragmentary
though it is, is full of detail:

> Item about that samyn tyme the xviii day of maii Thar met and faucht in the feld on
> the mure besyd brechyne The erll of craufurd callit alexander The erll of huntlie
> callit alexander and thair was with the erll of huntlie fer ma than was with the erll of
> craufurd becaus he displayit the kingis banere and said it was the kingis actioun and
> he was his luftennend and schortlie the erll of huntlie wan the feld and slewe the erll
> of craufurdis brother callit Jhon lyndesay of brechyne and the lard of dundas and
> uther syndry gentill men wele till iiixx of cotarmouris on that syd and on that uther
> syd willam of setoun the erllis brother and uthir three or four of gentill men and v or
> sex of zemen and the erll of huntlie held the feld and raid in angus with three or
> foure thousand with him and the erll of craufurd.[6]

The entry has every appearance of being tacked on as an afterthought, but
although there is some vagueness about the year, it is interesting to note that
in the sixteenth century, Lesley dated the battle 18 May 1452 and Pitscottie
dated it Ascension day 1453 — the year is incorrect, but Ascension day 1452
was 18 May.[7] There is also some corroborative evidence for the raid in Angus
which is said by the chronicler to have followed the battle. There exists a
letter from James II, dated 16 January 1455, to the sheriff of Forfar, concerning
a complaint by Walter of Carnegie that during the fighting between Alexander
earl of Huntly and the late Alexander earl of Crawford, Carnegie's mansion
was burnt and his charters of the lands of Kinnaird were destroyed.[8] The
chronicler's statement that the laird of Dundas was slain is interesting, as
James Dundas of that Ilk was forfeited at the time of the disgrace of the
Livingstons in 1450 and was imprisoned at that time in Dumbarton castle,
where he was presumed to have died. On 26 August 1452, the king granted a
remission to the late James Dundas, and his brother Archibald succeeded to
the Dundas estates.[9] Piecing together these strands of evidence, a picture is
formed of a battle fought at Brechin on 18 May 1452 in the course of which a
number of men, including James Dundas, were slain. These men were taking
part in a battle which was a baronial feud rather than a battle of national
importance in which the Earl of Crawford fought against royal authority
represented by the Earl of Huntly, and the battle ought to be seen as
subsequent to, rather than consequent upon, the murder of Douglas. In the
long and very detailed account of the murder of Douglas and the ensuing
conflict, the chronicler makes no mention of the battle of Brechin, an
omission which perhaps demonstrates the dangers of exaggerating the

importance of an event simply because of the accident of a surviving chronicle reference.

Notwithstanding the numerous defects inherent in the Auchinleck Chronicle, it is possible, from a detailed study of the entries, to draw some general conclusions about the nature of the document, and even to recognise some clues to original authorship. At the beginning of folio 109, Asloan wrote the title 'Heir followis ane schort memoriale of the Scottis corniklis for addicoun'. This suggests that Asloan used more than one chronicle source, and the text itself gives the impression that Asloan gathered together all the chronicles he could find and transcribed them. The expression 'for addicoun' probably means that Asloan intended to use these chronicle sources as the basis for a continuation of Walter Bower's 'Scotichronicon'.[10] Thomas Thomson's title, 'A Short Chronicle of James the Second, King of Scots', is highly inappropriate as the Auchinleck Chronicle, while it does deal with events of national importance, such as the conflict between the king and the Black Douglases, and the proceedings of certain parliaments, is far more concerned with recording events of local interest. By far the greatest proportion of the chronicle deals with local incidents ranging from short annalistic entries recording the death of a local man, for example, 'Item, that samyn zere and moneth thare was drownit in the watter of crawmond sir Jhon logane of lestalrig, knycht of the age of xxii zeris',[11] to long, detailed accounts of events with no direct bearing on national politics, but for which the writer clearly had access to first-hand information.

The most interesting and informative aspect of these entries is that many of them have, as a common factor, the west of Scotland. For example, out of seventeen separate entries concerned with feuds and local disorder, eleven relate to the west. A blood feud is described between the Stewarts of Darnley and the Boyds which included a fight at Polmaise near Stirling. Other entries record the slaying of John Colquhoun of Luss at Inchmurrin on Loch Lomond, a detailed account of disturbances in the castle of Dumbarton and the seizure of Lochmaben castle by the Johnstones, to cite only a few examples.[12] In addition to accounts of local violence, other entries show a knowledge of events of local interest in the west. The chronicler noted the proclamation of the privileges of Glasgow University and a papal indulgence in 1451, the first mass said by William Turnbull as bishop of Glasgow in 1449, the outbreak of plague at Dumfries in 1439, and the entry which describes a flood on 25 and 26 November 1454 'the quhilk brocht doun haile houses bernis and millis and put all the town of gowane [Govan] in ane flote quhill thai sat on the houses'.[13]

The west-coast bias is so striking that at least one, if not more, of the original chroniclers must have been living in the west of Scotland, and given their literacy and interest in church affairs, the writers were almost certainly clerics. A clue to the identity of one author may be found in the passage in which the chronicler recorded the death of Thomas Tarvas, abbot of Paisley, extolling his virtues and describing how, on his appointment to the abbacy in 1446, he 'fand the place all out of gud rewle and destitut of leving and all the kirkis in lordis handis and the kirk unbiggit'. The chronicler wrote that Tarvas proceeded to renovate the buildings and increase the wealth and reputation of the abbey, bringing it, by the time of his death in 1459, 'fra nocht till ane mychti place and left It out of all kynd of det and at all fredome'. Some confirmation for this may be found in the Calendar of Scottish Supplications to Rome where, in 1441, Thomas Morow, then Abbot of Paisley, was criticised severely for having 'sold, dilapidated and distrained many of the movable and immovable goods of the monastery. In addition, by his negligence, he allowed regular observance and divine worship to be despised and diminished, the fabric to fall into ruin and the monastery to be utterly devastated'.[14] The complaint against Thomas Morow was raised again in August 1444 and he resigned, being succeeded by Richard Bothwell. The complaint then was that the monastery was 'so destroyed and collapsed in its buildings and structures that it is truly feared that it cannot be restored in the life of man'.[15] Richard Bothwell, no doubt considering the state of Paisley abbey too daunting to contemplate, was translated to Dunfermline in the following year and Thomas Tarvas became Abbot of Paisley, remaining in that office until his death in 1459. The chronicler gives a detailed inventory of the renovations to the monastery instigated by Tarvas, for example, a new slate roof, repairs to the steeple and a new 'staitlie' gatehouse. He also lists Tarvas's acquisitions for the monastery as jewels, fine books, silver chandeliers, a brass lectern and the best mitre and tabernacle in all Scotland. Such detail certainly suggests first-hand knowledge and, coupled with the chronicler's information concerning events in and around Glasgow and Dumbarton, it seems very likely that one of the original chroniclers was a monk of Paisley.

The space devoted by the Auchinleck chronicler to certain entries and the detail with which he furnished his account have led some historians to attach too much importance to events which were simply localised disturbances. The longest single entry in the chronicle is the account of an attack made upon George Lauder, bishop of Argyll, and his party on 29 August 1452 — an account which occupies almost two complete folios.[16] In brief, the chronicler relates that the bishop was journeying from his castle of Achadun, at the south end of the Isle of Lismore, to the cathedral kirk, accompanied by Hercules Scrimegeour, his brother Alexander, and certain others. The purpose of their journey was to deliver a summons to Gilbert McLochlan, chancellor of the cathedral, and Maurice McFadzen, treasurer. Having received word of the bishop's approach and thinking that his purpose was to remove them from their benefice and put in Hercules Scrimegeour, they gathered support and challenged the bishop's party as it approached the church. A violent scuffle ensued, the bishop was threatened, and was released only on condition that there would be no reprisals. This curious incident is also referred to in papal records where there is a mandate, issued on 23 January 1451 to the chancellor, treasurer and official of Argyll to hold an inquiry arising from a complaint by Godfrey McForsan, vicar of St Ferchinus's in Argyll, against Hercules Scrimegeour. If Godfrey's charges were found to be true, the officials of Argyll were empowered to deprive Hercules and to collate his canonry prebend of St Columba in Glassary to Godfrey.[17] According to the Auchinleck chronicler, Hercules Scrimegeour 'had no thing bot a summondis apon Sir Gilbert and apon Sir Morris McFadzane for a sentence diffinitive that thai gaf aganis him of his benefice that he had loysit peceably xv zere with Sir Gotheray McForsan'.[18] Clearly, this incident was part of a continuing dispute which persisted for years. On 3 April 1454, the pope was petitioned, this time by Alexander Scrimegeour, to cause Godfrey McForsan to be summoned and censured for unjustly opposing and hindering Scrimegeour from holding his possessions peacefully.[19]

On 29 April 1462, bishop George Lauder of Argyll supplicated the Pope for permission to live outside his diocese, alleging that he could not conveniently visit his diocese in person 'because of certain ill-wishers and enemies of his'.[20] The Auchinleck chronicler's account of the 1452 incident has an obvious bias in favour of the bishop's party. He regarded the actions of the chancellor and treasurer as outrageous and wrote that they spoke to the bishop 'right dispituouslie with felloun wordis and scorne and for dispyte halsit him in errische sayand bannachadee'.[21] There certainly was a problem of communication with a non-Gaelic-speaking bishop being appointed to a Gaelic-speaking diocese, and this would have been a factor leading to the acrimony described by the chronicler. Originally, 'bannachadee' meant 'blessing of God', but it had come to acquire an offensive meaning approximating to wily, foxlike or crafty.[22] Evidently, this was not the manner in which to address a bishop. The account is long and very detailed, and the chronicler's source of information must have been a member of the bishop's party. However, there is no evidence to suggest the involvement of Donald Balloch or to credit the event with national importance simply because it took place in 1452 when the conflict between the king and the Black Douglases and their allies was being fought out on the national stage.[23]

The emphasis on local history in the Auchinleck Chronicle does not mean that national events are ignored or skimped. There are a number of very detailed accounts concerning Parliaments and General Councils, which may indicate that one or more of the authors worked at court, possibly recording the business of parliament, and where details given may be checked, these are usually quite accurate. The section of the chronicle which runs from folio 114 to 116 deals with the king and the Black Douglases and offers the most detailed contemporary account of the murder of William 8th earl of Douglas by the king and the ensuing conflict. The motive advanced by the chronicler for the murder of the earl was the king's objection to a bond which had been made between the earls of Douglas, Crawford and Ross. Douglas was summoned to Stirling and, on the evening of his second day there (the chronicler even gives the time as seven o'clock), the king instructed Douglas to break the bond and when he refused, the king said 'fals tratour sen thow will nocht I sall / and stert sodanly till him with ane knyf and straik him in at the colere and down in the body'.[24] This is the only instance of reported speech in the chronicle and the whole account is quite remarkably detailed. The chronicler names the lords who rushed in to complete the murder, and states that the earl's body eventually bore twenty-six wounds. All the men named by the chronicler — Sir Alexander Boyd, John Stewart Lord Darnley, Sir Andrew Stewart, Sir Simon Glendinning, Andrew Lord Gray, Patrick Gray and William Gremston (*recte* Cranston) — may be shown to have benefited in the wake of the murder of Douglas with rewards of lands and offices. The chronicler also gives a far more detailed account of the June parliament of 1452 than appears in the printed *Acts of the Parliaments of Scotland*, and he names those who were rewarded with titles, including the new creations of lords of parliament. The impression that these were hastily given grants to win support is conveyed by the chronicler who expressed the opinion that the rewards were such that 'men demyt wald nocht stand'.

It is interesting to note the chronicler's bias at any given point as a reflection of his personal opinion of a particular event or person. The chronicler certainly does not hesitate to criticise the king, describing the murder of Douglas as 'foule slauchter', and when the king led an army down to the south of Scotland in July 1452 to quell the Douglas rebellion, the chronicler stated that he 'did na gud bot distroyit the cuntre right fellonly baith of cornes medowis and wittalis and heriit mony bath gentillmen and utheris that war with him self'.[25]

However, this does not mean that the chronicler was demonstrably pro-Douglas; indeed, he was scathing in his attitude towards James 9th earl of Douglas. In the summer of 1452, the chronicler credited the king with raising an army of 30,000 men, but stated that the Douglas party 'excedit nocht of gud men vic'. Neither figure is likely to be accurate, but the inference is clear. The king, notwithstanding the heinous nature of his crime, was able to command far more support than the Douglases. The 9th earl's lack of decisiveness seems to have annoyed the chronicler and in 1455, when the king was besieging Abercorn, he wrote, cryptically, 'men wist nocht grathlie quhar the douglas was all this tyme'.[26]

Some stress has been laid on the general accuracy of the Auchinleck Chronicle where dates may be checked, although it ought to be pointed out that some of the entries are quite clearly wrong. However, such mistakes provide valuable clues for an overall assessment of the chronicle. An example of this is the entry describing the downfall of the Livingston family at the end of the king's minority. The chronicler gives a very detailed account, naming those Livingstons who were arrested and also their adherents, most notably the Dundases, but when he came to describe the actions taken against the family in the parliament held in January 1450, he wrote 'James of levingstoun sone and air to the said alexander was put to deid and Robyne of levingstoun of lithqu that tyme comptroller was put to deid baith togidder on the castell hill thair heidis strikin of'.[27] Robert Livingston of Linlithgow, comptroller and cousin of Sir Alexander Livingston of Callendar, was indeed executed, but James Livingston was not — it was his younger brother, Alexander, who shared the same fate. However, if news had reached the chronicler that the son of Alexander Livingston of Callendar had been executed, then he must have assumed that it was the eldest son, James. This account appears on folio 122, yet on folio 116, the chronicler, in an entry concerning events of 1455, mentions James Livingston, chamberlain of Scotland, by that time restored to favour, therefore it is unlikely that both entries were written by the same man.

Similarly, the chronicler gets his dates wrong when he records the death of James Stewart of Lorne, the second husband of Queen Joan. The entry reads 'that samyn zere in the moneth of may Sir James Stewart, the qwenes knycht was tane apon the se be the flemyngis befor the son and thair was put to deid and of thaim that come with him viiixx of ynglismen'.[28] The previous entry was dated April 1449, therefore 'that samyn zere' would appear to refer to 1449. However, James Stewart did not die in that year, as a number of safe-conducts were issued to him and his sons (who were to become the earls of Atholl and Buchan) after this date and there is evidence that he was serving his stepson, James II, as an ambassador as late as 1454.[29] In view of this, it is clear that the entry does not belong to 1449 but it may be an accurate account of the fate of James Stewart at a later date.

In addition to the Auchinleck Chronicle's factual inaccuracies, some problems have arisen from a mistaken reading of particular entries, and some of this confusion is due to a lack of consistency in the chronicle's dating. In the fifteenth century, the New Year began on 25 March, therefore when the chronicler wrote 'the zere of god 1445 the xxiii day of January . . .' the year was actually 1446 by modern computation. However, this is not a general rule applicable to all entries in the chronicle, as on folio 109, the chronicler writes 'the zere of god 1443 the x day of March erll James Douglas deit at the castell of abercorn'. As the date given is 10 March, one would expect the year to be 1444 by modern dating, but James 7th earl of Douglas did die in 1443. Dr Grant argues that this very inconsistency has led to a widespread misinterpretation of the date at which John earl of Ross and lord of the Isles led a revolt in the north, seized the castles of Inverness and Urquhart, and cast down the castle of Ruthven. The revolt, according to the chronicler, took place at the beginning of March 1451, which has generally been interpreted as 1452 — the month after the murder of Douglas and connected with a quite different dispute, the fall of the Livingstons.[30]

Interpretations of this nature can have quite radical implications in forming particular theories about the events of the reign, demonstrating that the Auchinleck Chronicle must be used very carefully. Another example of this is the entry which has been seen as a reference to Mary of Gueldres at the beginning of the minority of her son, James III. This occurs at the beginning of folio 121, and the preceding entry on folio 120 concerns events of 1461. It reads, 'of the law and the kingis profettis and of all the Realme and that the king suld cum be him selfe and his and the qwene be hir selfe and hirris / bot the king suld ay remane with the qwene Bot scho suld nocht Intromet with his profettis bot allanerlie with his person'. The two folios are not continuous and Dr Macdougall has shown that the entry may not refer to Mary of Gueldres, but rather to Joan Beaufort who was forced to submit to an agreement known as the 'Appoyntement' in 1439, in which she abdicated political responsibility; and it is to this year and agreement that this entry probably refers.[31] The entry also marks the end of a particular source, as the next item is the laconic recording of the death of Archibald 4th earl of Douglas, Duke of Touraine in 1420 (*recte* 1424), and all the following entries on this page are short and almost exclusively obituaries.

The same event is never described twice in the Auchinleck Chronicle. To this extent Asloan may have been selective when transcribing his chronicle sources, but it is unlikely that he altered his sources when writing them down as, had he done so, the Auchinleck Chronicle would undoubtedly make far more sense and appear more structured than it does. Asloan collected together a miscellaneous selection of prose and verse, much of which, like the 'schort memoriale', is imperfect. These imperfections are not due entirely to missing folios, but also indicate defective source documents. Its deficiencies notwithstanding, the Auchinleck Chronicle is a vital document for the study of the reign of James II, but it cannot stand alone. Many other sources must be analysed to form a clearer picture of the period.

By the fifteenth century, Scotland had developed a chronicle tradition which was the foundation for many later histories which dealt with the reign of James II. In the late fourteenth century, John of Fordun, a chantry priest in the cathedral church of Aberdeen, established an historiographical tradition with an intense patriotic bias, based on a long and largely mythical pedigree of Scottish kings, which emphasised the antiquity and independence of the Scots and attacked the British historiographical tradition, based on the legend of Brutus, espoused in Geoffrey of Monmouth's *History of the Kings of Britain*.[32] Fordun's work inspired Walter Bower, abbot of Inchcolm, to write a continuation, which became known as the 'Scotichronicon'[33] and which Bower began sometime before 1441. The Scotichronicon is much more than a chronicle in the strict sense of a continuous register of events in order of time, as it deals with religion and philosophy in addition to history, with frequent homiletic digressions. The Scotichronicon set the trend, various copies and abridgements were made, and many subsequent histories were largely derivative.

An anonymous poem known as 'The Harp' is included at the end of certain manuscripts of the *Liber Pluscardensis*, a work founded mainly on Bower's *Scotichronicon*. The Book of Pluscarden stops, effectively, in 1437 with the death of James I, although it does contain occasional brief references to events up to 1453 and mentions the death of James II in 1460. 'The Harp' was not composed as an intrinsic part of the chronicle, but was added, presumably, for the purpose of instruction. Dr Lyall, who has studied the various extant manuscripts, argues that the poem was introduced in the context of the minority of James II, although it was written later than 1449, when James assumed full royal authority, according to the evidence of the final stanza:

My soverane Lord, sen thow hes gevin me leif
to fynd faltis that forfaltis to thy crown,
Quhilkis to thi majestie may gane stand or greve,
Thow mak thairfoir gude reformatioun;
Heir I protest be my salvatioun,
It that I say tuichand thy majestie
Is for the proffitt of thy realme and thee.

It is unlikely that 'The Harp' was written any later than 1461 (the last date referred to in the Book of Pluscarden) and F. J. H. Skene, who edited the text in the late 1870s, considered that the poem could be dated to the 1450s.[34]

The poem is concerned with the conventional problems and criticisms of mediaeval kingship — the effective administration of justice, the importance of employing wise counsellors of suitable stature and punishing those officials who transgress their authority — but the author of the poem is at times more specific in his condemnations, for he roundly criticises the king on the subject of remissions. In cases where a crime had been committed for which the law demanded rigorous punishment but the king granted a remission, he had offended against both God and his royal office or, as the poet expresses it:

Bot of a thing all gud men mervallis mare:
Quhen gret consale, with thin awyn consent
Has ordand strayt Justice, na man to spare
Within schort tym thou changis thin entent
Sendand a contre letter in continent,
Chargeand that of that mater mare be nocht:
Than all the warld murmuris that thou art bocht.

This certainly provides proof that the liberal use of remissions was a source of discontent at least as early as the reign of James II, a grievance supported by evidence from official records. In the March parliament of 1458 an act was passed 'Anentis the contentascione of parteis plenyeande of personis quhilkis has remissionis of the king', and the Exchequer Rolls, in the account registered on 19 June 1458, provide some evidence of the scale of remissions. Adam Abell, in his 'Roit or Quheill of Tyme', referred to James II's reputation for good justice, but this is evidently not an entirely accurate view; however, Dr Macdougall has pointed out that the evils of which the author of 'The Harp' complains were endemic in society, that all kings were guilty to some extent of abusing the system, and James II clearly was no exception.[35]

The *Extracta E Variis Cronicis Scocie* is largely based on Bower's own abridgement of the Scotichronicon, although the information for the reign of James II is clearly derived from another source.[36] It is probable that the author of the Extracta was Alexander Myln, who also wrote *The Lives of the Bishops of Dunkeld.*[37] Myln was educated at St Andrews University, later becoming a prebendary of the cathedral of Dunkeld and official of the diocese, and when the diocese was divided into the four deaneries of Atholl, Angus, Fife and Strathearn, he was appointed Dean of Angus. On 28 October 1516, John duke of Albany, regent of Scotland, petitioned Pope Leo X to present Alexander Myln to the abbacy of Cambuskenneth, an appointment which took place officially in 1517. Myln was deeply interested in the study of literature and the furtherance of learning, and was well aware of the importance and value of collections of early muniments, and he had found many of the records and charters of Cambuskenneth (some of them dating from the middle of the twelfth century) in a state of decay. For this reason, he procured a warrant from the king for the transcription of the Cambuskenneth records, and the Register of the Abbey of Cambuskenneth was made in 1535.[38] There appears to have been at least one previous register of the abbey's charters, as certain extracts and transumpts found elsewhere make reference to having been taken 'De libris Registri Cambuskynneth', although they do not appear in the 1535 register. The disappearance of certain records may be attributed to neglect after their incorporation into the register in transcription, and some material must undoubtedly have been destroyed in 1559 when a great part of the abbey was pulled down.

Myln's Latin history of the lives of the bishops of Dunkeld from 1127 to 1515 was dedicated to Gavin Douglas, who had been provided to the bishopric of Dunkeld in 1515 and of whose life there is a short narrative with which the work ends. Gavin Douglas died in September 1522, but Myln wrote of him in the present tense, therefore the *Lives* must have been written before Myln's move to Cambuskenneth in 1517. The *Extracta* must have been written at Cambuskenneth as it seems, apart from the Scotichronicon derivation, to have been a collection of material found in Cambuskenneth which dealt with events of church and state in the reign of James II. The identification of Myln as the author of the *Extracta* is further indicated by the attention given in the work to the bishops of Dunkeld and also to events and personalities in Angus. The section of the *Extracta* relating to Bishop Kennedy, who was translated from Dunkeld to St Andrews, follows the text of the *Lives* exactly,[39] and the bulk of the section covering the years of James II's reign deals with church affairs with largely annalistic entries for the political events. The *Extracta* provides some original material in the account of the battle of Arbroath, the details of which must have come from a local tradition in Angus, and it is in the *Extracta* that the motive for the battle of Arbroath is first explained in terms of the dispute over the bailiary of Arbroath abbey between Alexander Lindsay, master of Crawford, and Walter Ogilvy. The date given does not agree with the Auchinleck Chronicle, which dates the battle very specifically as having taken place on Sunday 26 January 1446, whereas the *Extracta* gives the date 20 January 1447. David Lindsay earl of Crawford was fatally wounded in the conflict, and the *Extracta* is the first source to relate the story of the Countess of Crawford smothering the wounded Walter Ogilvy after the battle as revenge for the death of her husband, notwithstanding the fact that Ogilvy was her brother.

There are a number of original components in the *Extracta*'s account of the fall of the Black Douglases. When William earl of Douglas went to Stirling during Lent, on the king's summons, he was charged by James II with having assisted Alexander earl of Crawford in his rebellion, and urged to break the bond which he had made with Crawford. No mention is made of the Earl of Ross in the *Extracta*'s account of the Douglas bond, and it is not clear to what rebellion of Crawford's the author is referring. The only murderers named in the *Extracta* are Patrick, master of Gray, and William Cranston, and these are certainly two of the men named by the Auchinleck chronicler, but where the *Extracta* departs radically from all other accounts of the murder of Douglas is with the story that the earl, having been laid out in a coffin, could not give up his spirit until a certain serving girl, following Douglas's instructions, took a cross from his neck, whereupon his spirit immediately departed. Douglas was then buried quietly in the place of the Dominicans of Stirling. The author was clearly using a source of oral tradition which was not widely known or was ignored by other writers, as this is the only place where the account appears. The *Extracta* also has the story that the king found himself in such a weak position following the murder of Douglas that he considered fleeing to France, but was dissuaded from this course by the wise counsel of Bishop Kennedy of St Andrews.[40] This became a popular theme, and is repeated in most of the later chronicles, with Lesley, Pitscottie and Chalmers of Ormond all ascribing a major counselling role to Kennedy immediately after the murder of Douglas. Only Buchanan omits the suggestion that James II considered fleeing to France.[41] Douglas was murdered in February 1452 and Queen Mary gave birth to the future James III in May of the same year, in St Andrews castle, which explains Kennedy's involvement at the time.

There are a number of errors to be found in the *Extracta*. For example, the entry recording the death of the Earl of Douglas's brothers states that the youngest brother, John of Balvenie, was put to death, although he actually managed to escape and fled to England; only the Earl of Ormond was executed, Archibald earl of Moray having been killed in battle.[42] There is also some confusion between two of the king's English campaigns, as the writer states that the king was at the river Cale with a great host making for the north of England when he was intercepted by a false English legate who persuaded him to turn back. However, when the king discovered the trick, he invaded Northumberland and carried out depredations 'with fire and sword'. The campaign which saw the Scottish host at the river Cale in Teviotdale took place in July 1456, but the campaign which was thwarted by a false English legate took place in 1455. The *Extracta* entry is dated 1456, therefore the two campaigns have been run into one.

The death of the king at the siege of Roxburgh is described in an entry which states that a salvo was fired at the castle to celebrate the queen's arrival at the siege, and a piece of metal broke from one of the guns as it was being fired, piercing the king's leg and fatally wounding him. The Earl of Angus, who was standing next to the king, was also wounded. Following the death of the king, the castle of Roxburgh was won and then destroyed, and although the *Extracta* contains more details than the Auchinleck Chronicle, the accounts of the king's death and the winning of Roxburgh are substantially the same.[43]

The last entry in the *Extracta* which relates to the reign of James II is a curious one. It reads, 'the misfortune of the king's death, if it may be told, was long before, as is said, foreshown to the king by the late John Templeman who was the father of lord William Templeman, superior of the monastery of Cambuskenneth. Who, whilst (tending?) his flock in the Ochil hills . . .'[44] This is obviously a local Cambuskenneth tradition, only one generation old, and was probably transmitted by word of mouth. The entry is incomplete and the reason for this is not entirely clear. If it was a copy of a chronicle fragment, one might expect Myln, or a monk compiling the *Extracta* under his direction, to have completed it from their own knowledge of the local tradition. It is possible that the manuscript was damaged and the rest of the entry lost, and this seems the most likely explanation. The *Extracta* was not circulated or used to any traceable extent in the sixteenth century, as the original elements are not repeated by later writers, and the manuscript has, even up to this century, been seen simply as an abridgement of the Scotichronicon.[45]

Another chronicle which was derived largely from the Scotichronicon is 'De Cronicis Scotorum brevia', written by John Law before 1521.[46] Law was a canon of St Andrews, and he was later incorporated into the university, which accounts for the attention given in his chronicle to the history of the churchmen of St Andrews.[47] Law made use of a number of short chronicle sources for the section of his chronicle which deals with the reign of James II, and although he wrote in Latin, it is clear that some of his entries are derived from the fragmentary sources later brought together as the Auchinleck Chronicle. For example, under the year 1439, Law describes the dearth and pestilence which afflicted Scotland in that year in exactly the same terms as the Auchinleck chronicler. The figures given for the prices of wheat and meal are exactly the same in both chronicles, and Law also echoes Auchinleck's statement that the plague which affected Scotland in that year was so virulent that those who contracted it died within twenty-four hours. Even stronger evidence for Law's familiarity with at least part of the Auchinleck Chronicle is the fact that he repeats some of the mistakes and inaccuracies found there. For example, one entry reads that in 1454, Gilbert Hay, Earl of Errol died, although the Earl of Errol was called William and he did not die in 1454. Law must have had access to one or more of the sources which were incorporated into the Auchinleck Chronicle by John Asloan, but judging by the selective nature of the similar entries, Law did not use Asloan's collection, as he makes a number of errors which he would not have done had he used the Asloan manuscript. For example, the Auchinleck Chronicle is quite precise about the date of the fall of the Livingstons, but Law confuses this event with the fall of the Boyds in 1469.[48]

Law also makes use of other sources, and these involve digressions, for the most part into papal and European history; however, his chronicle contains some interesting details which do not appear in the earlier sources still extant. For example, he states that William 8th earl of Douglas returned to Scotland on 7 April 1451 from his journey to Rome for the papal jubilee; this is the only source in which such a precise date for his return is given. Law also writes that, when in Rome, Douglas was commended by the pontiff above all other pilgrims; and he makes the very interesting statement that in Douglas's absence, William Turnbull bishop of Glasgow, William Crichton, and George Crichton conspired together and sought to bring about the death of Douglas. It was by their counsel, according to Law, that the Douglas lands and castles were attacked by James II. This seems quite believable as the Crichtons had no cause to love the Douglases, having come into conflict with them on a number of occasions. Similarly, Bishop Turnbull had clashed with this most powerful Scottish magnate, some of whose territory lay within the bounds of his diocese.[49]

Law's account of the murder of Douglas is not as full as that found in the Auchinleck Chronicle, but the details are substantially the same. Both chronicles relate that the murder took place on 21 February 1452 and that Douglas's body had twenty-six wounds. The account of the response of the Douglas faction after the murder also shows agreement of detail between Law and the Auchinleck chronicler, both of whom relate the arrival of James Douglas in Stirling on St Patrick's Day, proclaiming the king's counsellors to be traitors and sounding twenty-four horns. Law's account of the June parliament of 1452 is approximately the same as the Auchinleck chronicler's account, but he breaks off his narration of events in Scotland with his following entry which records the sack of Constantinople in 1453.[50]

Returning to Scottish politics, Law records the death of Alexander 4th earl of Crawford in 1453, and he is the first writer to attach the epithet 'Tiger Earl' to Crawford. He also echoes the Auchinleck chronicler's statement that Crawford held the whole of Angus in subjection and was inobedient to the king. However, Law does not simply supply additional details to the Auchinleck chronicler's account, but also deals with events for which there is no reference whatsoever in Auchinleck. The most notable example of this is Law's account of the events of 1455. There is an entry concerning the battle of Arkinholm, where Archibald earl of Moray was killed and Hugh earl of

Ormond was captured and subsequently executed, and Law notes that the border family of Johnston took part in the battle. This battle is not mentioned by the Auchinleck chronicler, nor is the Act of Annexation passed in the October parliament of 1455, which is mentioned by Law in a brief entry. Thereafter, there is some confusion of detail. Law describes the battle of Lochmaben under the year 1458, but he apparently realised his mistake and corrected the date to 1448 with the note 'bellum de Lochmaben' under the correction. Entries on papal, European and English history follow, and he returns to Scottish history with a short, annalistic entry describing the king's death. He writes, '1460. This year king James the second of Scotland died at Roxburgh on 2 August'. Law is one day out, as the date given by the Auchinleck chronicler, and subsequent chroniclers and historians who mention a date, is 3 August.

The purpose of writing both the *Extracta* and Law's chronicle appears to have been to abridge and then continue the Scotichronicon, using chronicle sources and local traditions. There is no recognisable bias towards James II to indicate a political motive behind the writing of the chronicles, and both writers seem to have been concerned simply with a largely annalistic outline of the reign.

Other brief chronicle sources which deal with the reign of James II, but do not add much which is new or illuminating, are the short chronicle appended to Andrew of Wyntoun's 'Orygynale Cronykyl of Scotland', and 'The Roit and Quheill of Tyme', by Adam Abell.[51] The short chronicle contains only six entries which deal with the reign of James II. The red mark on the king's face is mentioned and the dearth of 1439 is described, although the figures quoted differ from those given in the Auchinleck Chronicle. The next entry concerns the 'Black Dinner' of 1440 when William 6th earl of Douglas, his brother David and their adherent Malcolm Fleming of Cumbernauld were put to death. The author of the short chronicle states that this was done 'James the secund beand Justice', but the king was only ten years old in 1440 and could not possibly have instigated the execution of the Douglas brothers. The following two entries concern Glasgow, mentioning the founding of the University of Glasgow by Bishop Turnbull in 1451, and also the papal indulgence given to Glasgow in the same year. Under 1454, the chronicler recorded the death of William Turnbull and named his successor to the bishopric as Andrew Durisdeer.

The final entry, under 1460, describes the death of James II at the siege of Roxburgh, which the chronicler calls 'the secund sege'. This is a reference to the disastrous first siege undertaken by James I in 1436. The crowning of James III took place, according to the short chronicle, on 'the sanct Laurence day'. This was 10 August, exactly one week after the death of James II on 3 August, and it agrees with the information given by Auchinleck. The short chronicle is anonymous and as the writer stops abruptly in 1482, it seems likely that the chronicle was written at that time.[52]

Adam Abell, a friar of the Observant Franciscan order at Jedburgh, had completed most of 'The Roit and Quheill of Tyme' in 1533, subsequently adding a continuation down to 1537. His work is a short history of Scotland from its legendary beginnings to Abell's own day. Abell's account of the reign of James II, the 103rd king on his list, does not add much of interest to the established picture of the reign, except the statement that James was noted for his attention to justice. There is a lot of confusion in Abell's account; clearly he had no reliable source for the reign. For example, the 8th and 9th earls of Douglas are confused by Abell when he writes, 'the erll of Dowglace brint Stirling and made ane band with the erll of Crawford. Quharfore eftirwart he was slane . . .'[53] The earl responsible for burning Stirling was James 9th earl of Douglas, not William 8th earl, who made a bond with the Earl of Crawford and was slain at Stirling. In common with the *Extracta*, Abell mentions only Crawford when describing the Douglas bond. Further confusion arises with Abell's reference to Mary of Gueldres. He writes of her that 'she marreit eftir ane knight of the kingis surname and to him had James erll of buchan and other barnis'.[54] This is another example of confusion between Mary of Gueldres and Joan Beaufort, and reinforces the impression that Abell was not working from any reliable written source for the reign of James II.

The first chronicler who effectively broke from the dominance of Bower's *Scotichronicon* and wrote an independent Latin history was John Major, whose *Historia Majoris Brittaniae tam Angliae quam Scotia* was published in Paris in 1521.[55] Major, who was born around 1467, studied and taught abroad at the University of Paris before returning to Scotland in 1518 to teach, initially at Glasgow University, and subsequently at St Andrews. He was a theologian rather than a historian and his history was written, primarily, to combat the belligerent ideologies of the rival English and Scottish historiographical traditions. Major was a strong advocate of union between the two countries, which he hoped would be achieved peacefully through marriage between the royal houses. The *History* is not, however, a unified history of Britain, but has the character of two chronicles written in harness. The legendary origins of both the Scottish and the English nations as espoused in their rival histories were dismissed by Major, and his history was intended to serve a didactic purpose.[56] He was not concerned simply with compiling a chronicle of past events, but wished to show 'not only the thing that was done, but also how it ought to have been done'.[57]

Major was concerned about the balance of power between crown and nobility, and his History demonstrates a horror of the over-mighty subject, who instigated feuds which were exacerbated through the involvement of the principal protagonists' vassals and retainers. The monarchy, he believed, ought to rule strongly and effectively, but Major saw the king ultimately as a constitutional monarch who was accountable to his subjects. This was not, however, an advocacy of popular sovereignty in the broadest sense of the concurrence of the whole population with the king's actions, but rather that the prominent members of the community in both church and state ought to advise the king and, if necessary, resist him if he abused his power. There is nothing radically new in this view of government by the king and the three estates, but Major felt that Scottish kings were not dependent enough on parliament, largely through their avoidance of regular taxation which would force a greater reliance on parliament and help to consolidate its role as a consultative assembly.[58]

It is important to recognise these general principles which underly Major's History before assessing the section of his work which deals with the reign of James II. The first political event of the reign mentioned by Major is the 'Black Dinner' of 1440, when William 6th earl of Douglas, his brother David and Malcolm Fleming of Cumbernauld were entertained in Edinburgh castle by James II who, according to Major, 'laid hands' on them and 'caused them to be beheaded'. However, Major adds that he has read 'in the chronicles' that the instigation for the deed came from William Crichton. It is not clear to which chronicles Major is referring, as Auchinleck, the *Extracta* and Law all deal with the Black Dinner in a very short, annalistic manner and offer no opinion concerning motivation or personalities involved. The fact that the dinner took place in Edinburgh castle, the keeper of which was William Crichton, may have been sufficient to found the very credible tradition of Crichton's involvement. The following entry concerns the siege of William Crichton in Edinburgh castle in 1445, but no context, reason or outcome is advanced. Major then jumps to the year 1450 and states that William earl of Douglas travelled to Rome with a large number of noble lords. In his account of the murder of Douglas, Major writes that James II, in a private audience with the earl, asked him to abandon the league he had made with the Earl of Crawford, and he also states that 'A rumour went abroad among many that Douglas was aiming to usurp the royal crown'. This is the first time that such an accusation against Douglas is made, and Major advances a number of reasons to support this fear. The Earl of Douglas had two brothers, Archibald and Hugh, who also held earldoms, thus strengthening the power of the Douglas family. In addition to the 8th earl's immediate family, the earls of Angus and Morton were also Douglases. However, Major fails to note that both of these men were Red Douglases and therefore unlikely to have considered supporting the rival Black Douglases; indeed, they appear to have been loyal to James II throughout the reign. Major names only the Earl of Crawford as having made a league with Douglas, but he does add the vague statement that Douglas had made 'a wide-spreading league with other lords'. The wealth and ambition of the Douglases, according to Major, gave the king cause to fear both for himself and his kingdom, and Major perpetuates the myth that the king considered deserting his kingdom and was dissuaded only by the wise counsel of Bishop Kennedy. Major goes so far as to state that 'Kennedy so carried things that the Earl of Angus, A Douglas by name . . . and most of the other brothers of Earl Douglas, were brought over to the side of the king'.[59] There is no evidence to suggest that the Earl of Angus had ever been anywhere else, and the statement concerning the Earl of Douglas's brothers appears to be a somewhat confused reference to the hollow peace which was made between the king and the Douglases in 1453.

The point which Major is trying to make is that the Douglas faction had grown far too strong, and was able to pose a serious threat to the king. He writes: 'For Scotland, as I see, the Earl of Douglas was too powerful: he had thirty or forty thousand fighting men ever ready to answer to his call'. This contrasts sharply with the Auchinleck chronicler's remark that the Douglas faction, at the time of the Stirling raid, 'excedit nocht of gud men vic',[60] and although this may be an under-estimate, it is likely to be nearer the truth than the figures quoted by Major. However, Major is now launched well and truly into his theme, and there follows a long discourse on the dangers of exalting great magnate houses, especially if 'their territory happens to lie in the extremities of the kingdom'. Powerful lords had no trouble inducing men to follow them because 'the Britons are so kindly affected to their lords', and the men of the borders were used to fighting and accepted it as a way of life. The answer, according to Major, was to reduce the power of the Marcher lords, which would make men less inclined to follow them.[61]

In Major's account, it was the irresolution of James 9th earl of Douglas and his reluctance to fight against the king which resolved the matter without a battle, and not any inferiority of the forces mustered by the Douglases. Had the Douglases chosen to pursue the conflict they would, according to Major, 'have been fighting for kingship'. It was not until the Douglas threat had been removed that James II 'began in truth to reign, and could impose laws upon his people as he would'.[62] Major's account of the events of the reign continues with a description of the 1456 campaign against the English which is a version of the story mentioned in the *Extracta* concerning the tricking of the Scottish army by false English legates who convinced James that he should abandon his invasion.[63] Major states that the English king sent an embassy to James II 'which made many promises; but when James was returned home and saw no fulfilment of these promises, he again gathered a great army and laid England waste with fire and sword'.[64] The death of the king at the siege of Roxburgh is described by Major in a paragraph in which he states that the king was killed by the charge from a cannon, although all the other accounts of the accident say that the gun itself broke and killed the king. Major mentions the wounding of the Earl of Angus at the same time and goes on to relate the taking of the castle by the besiegers. No mention is made of the queen's arrival at the siege.

Major is the first chronicler to offer, at any length, an assessment of the character of the king. He describes James II as strong and valiant with a great interest in warlike enterprises, and he emphasises the king's 'common touch' with his soldiers, stating that 'in time of war he used in the field so great humanity, without distinction of person, that he was not so much feared as revered as a king and loved as a father'. However, Major believed that the king was guilty of carrying this attitude too far, and when he writes that James rode among his soldiers, accepting their offers of food and drink without taking the precaution of having it tasted, confident that none of his men would try to poison him, Major adds that 'in this matter I will not say that I deem him prudent'. Major states a preference for James I, as he regarded James II as rather too fond of warlike activities, although he admits, grudgingly, 'For vigorous kingship, most writers give the first place to this monarch, seeing that he gave himself with all zeal to the things of war and to naught else'.[65]

The disparate elements of chronicle sources and histories dealing with the reign of James II which have been looked at so far form a patchwork of information, but the sixteenth century saw the flowering of a more comprehensive approach to the reign, and it is as a result of the arguments put forward by the sixteenth-century writers that the traditional view of James II was established.

Fordun and Bower's Scottish historiographical tradition was developed by Hector Boece who, in the early 1520s, composed a general history of Scotland entitled *Scotorum Historiae, a prima gentis origine, cum aliarum et rerum et gentium, illustratione non vulgari.*[66] This work was published in Paris in 1527, and it dealt with Scotland's past from its legendary origins down to the death of James I in 1437. Hector Boece, born in Dundee around 1465, was educated at Aberdeen and then Paris where, in 1497, he became a Professor of Philosophy in the college of Montacute. In 1500, Boece was invited by Bishop William Elphinstone of Aberdeen to become the Principal of King's College, and after the death of the bishop in 1514, Boece wrote his *Episcoporum Murthlacensium et Aberdonensium Vitae*, which was published in Paris in 1522. Subsequently, Boece devoted his time to writing his *Historiae*. This work was in keeping with established tradition in that it portrayed Scotland as an ancient kingdom, never subdued by invasion and ruled over by its own independent kings since the mid-fourth century B.C. Boece further embellished the tradition of the mythical kings by naming the first forty of them and describing in detail their deeds and reigns. Factual accuracy was not Boece's aim, his approach being very much in keeping with the essentially rhetorical aims of humanist historiography and the nationalistic spirit of the Scottish mediaeval chronicle tradition. The most striking element of Boece's embellishment of the history of the mythical kings is that many of them suffered punishment, deposition and even death at the hands of their subjects.[67] The numerous precedents offered by Boece for the dangerous principles of resistance and tyrannicide could be interpreted as the advocacy of a general constitutional principle stemming from the Scottish academic tradition of radical political thought, but although Boece was familiar with the work of John Major, there is no evidence that he was influenced by it, or that his *Historiae* embraced in any way Major's sophisticated constitutional theory.[68]

Boece was outlining a moral rather than a constitutional principle and was not advocating seriously an active policy of resistance and tyrannicide to his contemporaries. Had this been Boece's intention, James V is unlikely to have taken the interest he did in Boece's work. The *Historiae* embodied a 'polity of manners',[69] which emphasised the importance of the king's own example for the freedom of the country and the satisfactory administration of justice, a more conventional and conservative theory which would have posed no threat to the monarch or the higher nobility. Shortly after the *Historiae* was published, James V bestowed an annual pension of fifty pounds Scots upon Boece, and in 1530 and 1531, he employed John Bellenden in translating Boece's Latin *Historiae* into the vernacular.

Boece's *Historiae* and Bellenden's translation of it end in 1437 with the death of James I. However, in 1574, a second Latin edition, with a continuation to 1488, was printed in Paris and edited by Giovanni Ferreri.[70] Ferreri was a Piedmontese monk who had come to Scotland in 1528 and had spent some time at the court of the young James V. Between 1531 and 1537, he taught at the monastery of Kinloss, and it is in this period that he may have become familiar with the work of Hector Boece. The seventeen books of Boece's *Historiae* contained in the 1527 edition are extended in Ferreri's edition by two books. The eighteenth book deals with the reign of James II and was translated, for the most part very closely, by Robert Lindesay of Pitscottie in his Chronicles of Scotland, written in the late 1570s.[71] The eighteenth book is a continuation of Boece in the same style as the previous seventeen books and contains a number of passages of set speech and homiletic digressions. By contrast, Ferreri's nineteenth book, which deals with the reign of James III, does not have the same character, as it is shorter and more annalistic in form.

The authorship of the eighteenth book is uncertain. It is possible that Boece wrote it himself, or a continuator with a strikingly similar style. Boece did not die until 1536, and he may have written the eighteenth book after the appearance of Bellenden's translation in 1533. The difference between the eighteenth and the nineteenth books in terms of length, detail and style would indicate that the latter was an addition, probably by Ferreri himself. Bellenden is unlikely to have been the author of the eighteenth book as it was written in Latin and, having translated Boece's *Historiae*, he would almost certainly have written any continuation in the vernacular. For the nineteenth book, Ferreri follows Bishop Lesley's *History* fairly closely, but the eighteenth book, while there are similarities with Lesley, differs in a number of details and is a fuller and more detailed account of the reign. The eighteenth book espouses the instructive purpose of Boece's *Historiae*, and many of the stories which were adopted and used by later writers were invented or embellished to fit these rhetorical aims. The theme of the over-mighty magnate occurs in the eighteenth book, with the Douglases portrayed in a very bad light for failing to keep in check large numbers of thieves and murderers who lived within the bounds of Douglas territory. The problems of James II's minority are explained solely in terms of the conflict between Sir Alexander Livingston (styled 'governor' throughout the text) and Chancellor Crichton. Arising from this conflict appear a number of stories, for example that of the queen smuggling her young son out of Edinburgh castle (the keeper of which was William Crichton) in a bundle of clothes and escaping with him to Stirling castle which was held by Livingston. The abduction of the young king while hunting in Torwood near Stirling, by Crichton and his men, and the removal of the king back to Edinburgh, is another example of the Crichton/Livingston hostility, and these stories endure, becoming incorporated firmly in the view of the reign put forward by later writers.

Although Pitscottie follows the text of the 1574 edition of the eighteenth book of Boece very closely, there are a number of slight divergences and one passage which is definitely from another source. The Scottish Text Society edition of Pitscottie's *Historie*, edited by Aeneas Mackay in 1899, made use of a number of different manuscripts of the work, none of which is Pitscottie's original.[72] The oldest of these is designated MS.A by Mackay and provides the bulk of the text for the S.T.S. edition. However, MS.A contained a number of gaps and was supplemented by the much fuller, but later MS.1. The passage of interest in the eighteenth book, which is not to be found in the Ferreri edition of Boece, concerns the execution of Maclellan, tutor of Bombie, by William 8th earl of Douglas. Briefly, the story is that Maclellan, who was the nephew of Patrick, master of Gray, refused to give his assistance to the Earl of Douglas in ravaging the countryside or in any way opposing the king's authority. Douglas, furious at Maclellan's refusal to ride with him, took him from his house and held him in the castle of Douglas as a prisoner. On hearing this, Patrick Gray obtained a written supplication from the king that Maclellan be released, and Gray delivered the supplication to Douglas personally. Douglas received Gray and gave him dinner before attending to the king's letter; but during the meal Maclellan was beheaded in another part of the castle. When Patrick Gray enquired after his nephew, he was met with the callous retort, 'Schir patrick ze ar come a litill to leit bot zondar is zour sistir sone lyand bot he wantis the heid, tak his body and do with it quhat ze will'.[73] Patrick Gray, fearful for his own position, waited until he had mounted his horse and was outside the castle wall before he rebuked Douglas, and he was pursued by Douglas men almost to Edinburgh, although his horse proved swifter and he reached the king in safety.[74]

This story provides the principal motive in Pitscottie's text for the summons of Douglas to Stirling, although there are a number of problems inherent in the account, not least of which is whether or not Pitscottie was the author of the story. The oldest manuscript of Pitscottie's *Historie* used by Mackay (MS.A) does not contain the story of the tutor of Bombie, which is taken from MS.1, a later manuscript with a number of additions which were probably made by a writer other than Pitscottie. The absence of the story from the earlier manuscripts of the *Historie* may indicate that he was not the author, and it is worth noting that the story is the only digression of any appreciable length from the text of Ferreri's edition of Boece. Had Pitscottie wished to make additions and insert extra stories into the eighteenth book, he would surely have done so on more than one occasion.

Contemporary evidence for Maclellans of Bombie has already been discussed in Chapter 4; but it may be worth noting that on 25 June 1526, a respite for nineteen years was issued under the privy seal to Douglas of Drumlanrig, Gordon of Lochinvar and others, for assistance given by them to Alexander Forrester and his accomplices, and for the slaughter of Maclellan of Bombie in Edinburgh.[75] It is possible that this slaying of a Maclellan of Bombie by a Douglas was a fresher tradition known to Pitscottie, or a transcriber of his work, which he applied to an earlier Douglas and Maclellan. The contemporary Auchinleck chronicler does not mention the incident, nor do any of the earlier chronicles.

Ferreri's edition of Boece does not seem to have been widely available, as Bishop John Lesley, when writing his *History*, commences with the reign of James II, thus continuing Boece from the point where the 1527 edition ended.[76] John Lesley, Bishop of Ross, was a staunch supporter of Mary Queen of Scots. He wrote his vernacular history in the late 1560s while living abroad as a Marian exile, as his support for the ill-fated queen had cost him his position in Scotland, and it is understandable, in view of this, that his royalist sentiments are very apparent in his writings. Lesley was one of the editors of the first edition of the parliamentary records of Scotland, published in 1566, and he used these as the framework for his narrative. It appears that he also had access to a copy of John Major's *History*, for there are a number of similarities between the two accounts; for example, he follows Major's line in his approach to the Crown/Douglas conflict, stressing the evils of too much power vested in great magnates who could raise armies of friends and retainers of a size to challenge any force which the king might muster. Lesley had good reason to portray James II favourably, but the Douglases, although they are described as powerful, are not shown as the lawless opponents of the king's authority who appear in the eighteenth book of Boece, but rather as co-operating with the king until they were attacked in 1450–51. However, once the Douglases, following the murder of the 8th Earl, rose in opposition to the king, Lesley's line is clear and the conflict is greatly exaggerated. Lesley follows Major in reporting that the king considered fleeing to France, but was dissuaded by James Kennedy, bishop of St Andrews. Lesley also credits Douglas with raising an army of 30,000 men and states that the king's army was considerably smaller. However, encouraged by Alexander earl of Huntly's recent victory at Brechin and by the wise counsel of the Bishop of St Andrews, the king ordered Douglas to submit or give battle. There is a considerable amount of confusion in Lesley's account, but the dilemma was resolved by the defection of James lord Hamilton from the Douglas camp and the consequent capitulation of the 9th earl. In common with Major, Lesley

takes this opportunity to deliver a homily on the preservation of the true line
of the kings of Scotland, by God's grace, without bloodshed.[77]

In addition to Major's *History* and the parliamentary records, Lesley
describes a number of events which are drawn from other recognisable
sources. For example, when praising James II for his efficient administration
of justice, Lesley echoes Adam Abell when he writes, 'he causit the rashe
bushe kepit the cow'.[78] A similar remark is made by Walter Bower about
James I, and it is possible that it was a well-known colloquialism which Abell
and Lesley ascribed to James II, although it does not accord with the
sentiments expressed in the poem 'The Harp'.

Lesley's *History* also contains similarities to entries in the Auchinleck
Chronicle. The feud between the Stewarts of Darnley and the Boyds is
described, and also the slaying of John Colquhoun of Luss. Feuds which were
of local rather than national importance were incorporated into the overview
of the reign simply because of the availability of the chronicle sources in
which they were mentioned. A number of mistakes which occur in the
Auchinleck Chronicle are repeated in Lesley's *History*, in particular the
statement that James Livingston was executed in the Livingston downfall.
However, Lesley mis-dates the Livingston forfeitures which happened in 1450
to 1448, and he does not appear to have had access to anything more than a
brief section of the Auchinleck Chronicle as incorporated in the Asloan MS.

The parliamentary framework of Lesley's *History* may be checked with
existing parliamentary records and, where this is possible, the dates, places
and items of business generally correspond, although Lesley does not associate
the January 1450 parliament with the disgrace of the Livingstons because the
Livingstons are not mentioned expressly in the records. However, much of the
legislation enacted in this parliament is particularly pointed in view of the
Livingston disgrace — for example, the statute 'of rebellione ageynis the
kingis persone or his autorite' and 'of punicione of officaris that wilfully
trespassis the ministracion of thar office'.[79]

Lesley also pays some attention to English history, describing at some
length the conflict between the factions of York and Lancaster. He states that
James II received a letter from Henry VI asking him to raise an army and take
the castles of Wark and Roxburgh, which were being held by the supporters
of Edward earl of March. According to Lesley, James responded, 'partlie
moved at King Henries desire partlie also becaus the said twa castells were
lyand with the landis and shires promeisit him be King Henry'.[80] Lesley's
account of the death of the king at the siege of Roxburgh does not add
anything new to the conventional view, and he ends this section of his *History*
with a character assessment of the king which portrays James II very
favourably. He writes:

> of harte he was couragious, politique in councell, in adversite nothing abashed, in
> prosperitie rather joyfull nor proude in peace just and mercyfull, in warre sharpe

and feirce, in the fielde bolde and hardie . . . he had greit trubles in civil and intestine warres in his youthedde; bot in the tyme of his later daies, his realme was in quiet prosperous estaite.[81]

The first writer to supersede Boece's *History*, rather than simply attempt a continuation or abridgement of it, was George Buchanan, whose *Rerum Scoticarum Historia* was published in 1582.[82] Buchanan, born in 1506, spent most of his life, prior to 1561, on the continent. He had studied as a pupil of John Major, but had abandoned 'the theologian's arid scholasticism in favour of the Erasmian brand of evangelical humanism current in Paris in the 1520s'.[83] Sometime around 1560, for reasons which are not clear, Buchanan rejected Catholicism and France, returning to Scotland where he became involved, in a lay capacity, with the Reformation Kirk's General Assembly. By that time, Buchanan was a staunch Calvinist and humanist, he was placed in charge of the formal schooling of the young James VI between 1570 and 1582, and his *History* was a work written primarily as a justification of the deposition of Mary Stuart in 1567 and as an instructive manual of political guidance for the young king. Buchanan was concerned with the moral influence of the king over his subjects, and to illustrate this, he used a history of good and bad kings — virtue versus tyranny. The tenor of his argument was that the king was accountable for his actions to the nobility who had the right to restrain or even depose him if he acted tyrannously. Given this point of view, one might expect to find a different picture of the reign of James II emerging in Buchanan's account from that found in Lesley, who was a staunch royalist and a despiser of the over-mighty magnate. James II had murdered personally his most powerful earl, having first guaranteed his safety by issuing a safe-conduct, surely ideal material for Buchanan's anti-tyrannical views. However, in his assessment of the character of James II, Buchanan writes that the king

> engaged almost from infancy in foreign or domestic war . . . had displayed such self-command in adversity and in prosperity, such bravery against his enemies and such mercy towards his suppliants, that his death was universally lamented by all ranks; and it appeared the more severe because, after having overcome so many misfortunes and raised expectation to the highest pitch by his virtue, he was suddenly cut off.[84]

This almost rhapsodic appraisal of James II is counterbalanced by Buchanan's view of the Douglases, as chief representatives of the nobility, to whom Buchanan devotes considerable attention. The five earls of Douglas who were active during the reign of James II are each dealt with in turn. Archibald 5th earl of Douglas is censured immediately on the grounds that he failed to restrain the men of Annandale, who ravaged and wasted all the neighbouring counties, and his son William, the young 6th earl, is also criticised for being at the root of the disorder and breakdown of justice in the localities. By comparison, James 7th earl of Douglas, escapes quite lightly; Buchanan admits that he did not actually retain the Annandale robbers supported by the preceding earls of Douglas, although he is criticised for failing to suppress them with sufficient energy. The accession of William 8th earl witnessed the Douglas power, in terms of land and possessions acquired, stronger than it had ever been, and Buchanan is quick to point out that 'insolence accompanied this wealth and bands of robbers pillaged everywhere, whose leaders, it was believed, were not unconnected with the projects of Douglas'. The censoriousness of Buchanan's attitude towards the Douglases becomes more pronounced in the lead-up to the murder of the 8th earl, and reaches its height with the statement that oppressions under Douglas and his adherents increased as they

> indulged in every species of licentiousness, respecting nothing either sacred or profane, murdering whoever was obnoxious to them, and sometimes, with wanton and gratuitous cruelty, torturing those who had never offended them, lest their souls, softened by the disuse of crime, should become humanized.[85]

Such exaggerated language is hardly useful for gaining a historical perspective on the reign of James II, but it does offer an insight into Buchanan's view of the reign. The portraits of virtuous kings amd vicious tyrants in Buchanan's *History* are far from original, and although he wished to see the restriction of the judicial and administrative responsibilities of kings, he did believe in the moral influence, good or bad, which a king had over his subjects. The ideal of popular sovereignty advanced by Buchanan was not as radical as it may appear, because a closer examination of his line of argument reveals that checks and limitations on the power and actions of the king were to be exercised, not by the people as a whole, but by the nobility, the king's 'natural counsellors'.[86] Because of this, Buchanan looked for the same standards of virtue in a nobleman as he did in a king. A magnate who rose to a position of power and then abused that power was equally guilty and worthy of condemnation as a tyrannical king, and Buchanan must have seen the pre-eminently powerful Earl of Douglas as a superb illustration of this point.

Buchanan is not the first writer to condemn the Douglases for supporting lawless bands in their territory, as the same accusation is made, although less vehemently, in the eighteenth book of Boece;[87] but Buchanan extends and embellishes the story. There are a number of similarities between Buchanan's *History* and the eighteenth book of Boece; for example, Buchanan writes that John Innes, bishop of Moray, and Henry Lichton, bishop of Aberdeen, acted as mediators between Livingston and Crichton.[88] Boece gives exactly the same names, although John Innes never held the bishopric of Moray and is being confused with John Winchester. A number of incidents described in the Auchinleck Chronicle also appear in Buchanan, such as the Boyd/Darnley blood feud and the fight at St Johnston on midsummer day between Sir William Ruthven and John Gorme Stewart of Atholl. The latter is described only in Buchanan's *History* and the Auchinleck Chronicle, although many of the other stories common to both writers appear also in the eighteenth book of Boece and Lesley's *History*. There are also some original entries in Buchanan's *History* which do not appear in any previous account; for example, on folio 23, Buchanan writes that John Lyon was put to death in the market place of Dundee by Alexander earl of Crawford.[89] This incident is not dated, but it appears immediately after the recording of the death of Queen Joan in Dunbar, and it may be assumed from this that Buchanan was referring to an incident which took place in 1445, although there is no corroborating evidence for it. Buchanan also makes some consistent mistakes with proper names; for example, he calls Hugh earl of Ormond, George, and refers to Margaret of Galloway as Beatrix, which is probably a confusion with the mother of the 8th earl of Douglas, who was called Beatrice. The accuracy of such details would hardly have been considered important by Buchanan, and the major effect of his *History* for the reign of James II was to entrench the view of the lawlessness of the Douglases to such an extent that later writers had little option but to be influenced by it, even when it conflicted with their personal bias in describing the events of the reign.

David Hume of Godscroft experienced this dilemma when he wrote his *History of the Houses of Douglas and Angus*, which was published in Edinburgh in 1644.[90] His account is very obviously pro-Douglas, for he endeavours to provide favourable interpretations for the actions of the earls of Douglas, even when they had been condemned by previous writers. Archibald 5th earl of Douglas, despising Crichton and Livingston as 'new' men, but unwilling to oppose them forcibly for fear of causing civil war, retired to his own lands. Of his actions there, Godscroft explains that he was concerned that his own privileges and liberties, which had been conferred upon him by royal grants, should not be infringed, and under his regality rights, all those living on his lands were answerable only to his courts. The men of Annandale, so roundly condemned by Buchanan, felt free to spurn the authority of the upstarts Crichton and Livingston, having respect only for the Earl of Douglas. Godscroft could not entirely condone the ravages of the men of Annandale, however, and he conceded that Douglas should have taken firmer measures to restrain them. When describing the career of William 6th earl of Douglas, Godscroft considered that the repeated complaints lodged at court concerning the ravages of the adherents of Douglas were biased and exaggerated, and he questioned why the spoliations of the Islemen and the various other episodes of violence and bloodshed should not have caused equal condemnation. Godscroft, not surprisingly, made no connection between the execution of the 6th earl and his brother and the succession of their great-uncle James to the earldom, and James 7th earl of Douglas is dealt with very briefly, Godscroft confining himself to a description of the earl's family. A fuller account is provided of the career of William 8th earl of Douglas, although it is largely derived from Buchanan. Godscroft tries to explain the murder of Douglas at the hands of the king by arguing that it was premeditated and at the instigation of William's enemies, especially Patrick

Gray, seeking revenge for the execution of his nephew by Douglas — evidence of Godscroft's familiarity with the story of Maclellan, even if he does not elaborate. The reasons for the murder are given by Godscroft as the private conference held by Douglas with the King and Queen of England on his return from Rome, Douglas's vehemence in revenge for the murder of his cousins and of his servant, John Auchinleck, his execution of Lord Herries and the tutor of Bombie and his support for thieves and robbers. In his analysis of the motives behind the murder of Douglas, Godscroft does not dwell on the league made with the earls of Crawford and Ross, although he does mention it in his account of Douglas's confrontation with the king prior to the murder, with Douglas expressing surprise that the bond should give offence. The picture of the scheming and brutality of William 8th earl of Douglas had been established so well that even Godscroft, who was concerned to portray the Douglases in as good a light as possible, was obliged to accept it. The Douglases, following the 8th earl's murder, were moved to rebellion and the general reaction to the deed was that it 'incensed the whole common people'. This is the closest Godscroft comes to a condemnation of James II; and he repeats the story of James Kennedy, bishop of St Andrews, dissuading the king from fleeing the realm. By the time Godscroft wrote his *History*, the magnitude of the king's peril following the murder had been exaggerated and incorporated firmly into the accepted view of the reign. David Chalmers of Ormond, who had written a history of Scotland while in France as a Marian exile in the 1570s, went so far as to state that James actually went to France to renew 'the auld Lig and Band', but no later historian repeats this.[91] Of the 9th earl of Douglas, Godscroft states that had he been 'as politicke as hee was powerfull, the King might have beene set beside his Throne'.[92]

A contemporary of Godscroft was William Drummond of Hawthornden, who wrote his *History of the Five Jameses* in the 1640s, although it was not until 1655 that it was published in London, six years after Drummond's death.[93] The work has the character of a collection of biographies, the structure of which is fairly uniform in each case: the king's accession, domestic and foreign policy, miscellaneous events of interest and the king's death, followed by a short character assessment. Drummond had access to the histories by Lesley, Buchanan and Ferreri, but does not appear to have drawn on any independent sources for his assessment of James II, adding little of interest. It seems that his *History* was intended for use as royalist propaganda for the cause of Charles I, as Drummond was summoned to defend it before the Covenanters.[94]

The reign of James II also received some attention in the work of Sir James Balfour of Kinnaird, a contemporary of Drummond of Hawthornden. As the title, *Annales of Scotland in Historical Works*, suggests, the work is in chronological form.[95] Balfour used the printed Acts of the Parliaments of Scotland as the framework for the *Annales*, and he also appears to have read Lesley's and Buchanan's histories. Balfour's dating is extremely unreliable, as he frequently describes events under the wrong year and gives precise dates which do not accord with earlier evidence and have the air of having been selected at random. Professor Donaldson has described Balfour as 'a student of antiquities and heraldry . . . best known as a collector — and forger — of mediaeval charters'.[96] For example, Balfour dates the execution of the 6th earl of Douglas and his brother in Edinburgh castle as 17 July 1439, whereas all the earlier writers who mention this event date it November 1440. The imprisonment of the Livingstons is dated 8 December 1448 by Balfour, although the attack on the family actually occurred in the autumn and winter of 1449–50; and he also mis-dates the king's marriage to Mary of Gueldres under 1448. Many of Balfour's errors are inexplicable if he had access to copies of Lesley's or Buchanan's histories as, although the events related in the *Annales* are clearly derived from the sixteenth-century histories, the mistakes indicate that Balfour did not have copies to hand when writing, but relied on his memory of what he had read. For example, no other writer makes the mistake that the 8th earl of Douglas was slain in Edinburgh rather than Stirling castle. Balfour is also the only writer to put a date on the bond made between the earls of Douglas, Crawford and Ross. He gives the date 7 March 1445; but in that year, the earls of Ross and Crawford were not the same men as in 1452 when the bond suddenly became an issue, both earls having died and been succeeded by their sons, and personal bonds do not appear to have been inherited. In the absence of the actual bond it is impossible to know its contents, but Balfour's description of it as 'an offensive and defensive league and combination against all, none excepted (not the king himself)' is unlikely, as surviving bonds almost invariably carried the conventional rider placing allegiance to the king above any conditions laid down in the bond. The only notable exceptions are bonds involving the Earl of Ross in his capacity of Lord of the Isles, and these follow the Irish practice of making no allusion to the king. In 1445, with the king still a minor and the 8th earl of Douglas dominant at court, it is hard to understand why he would have felt any need to form such an alliance, and given Balfour's palpable inaccuracy, it is not possible to place any reliance on either the date or the content of the bond given in the *Annales*.

One of the most influential writers in terms of establishing a traditional view of Scottish history which endures up to the present day was Sir Walter Scott. In his *Tales of a Grandfather*, Scott condensed Scottish history into a short volume which has been used as a convenient overview of Scotland's political past, although it espouses many of the moralistic, didactic views of previous writers such as Buchanan and Pitscottie.[97] Scott was not a historian, and his book was written from the standpoint of a grandfather instructing his grandson on Scotland's past, passing appropriate judgement on those whose actions shaped that past. Much of the work is derivative, and Scott adds little to his account of the reign of James II which is new. He consolidates the view that the Douglases were over-mighty magnates, stating that, 'in personal wealth and power, the Earl of Douglas not only approached to, but greatly exceeded the King himself'. Scott was impressed by the chivalric image of the middle ages, and the reputation of the Douglases as adept in military pursuits presented Scott with a dilemma as he struggled between the view that the Douglases were 'always gallant defenders of the liberties of Scotland during the time of war', and the problem of their hostility to the king, the rule of law, and their eventual refuge in England. Scott gives long, detailed descriptions of battles, laced with passages of direct speech illustrating acts of valour. In his description of the tournament at Stirling in 1449 in which James Douglas met and fought Burgundian knights, Douglas's military skills are praised enthusiastically, with no reference being made to the fact that Douglas lost the contest! The conflict between the king and the Black Douglases is explained in terms of the growing power and arrogance of the Douglases and their arbitrary behaviour in punishing those whom they considered to have wronged them. Scott reproduces the stories of William 8th earl of Douglas's execution of Colville and Herries, and builds up to the ultimate demonstration of Douglas high-handedness in the story of the tutor of Bombie, which appeared first in Pitscottie's *Historie*.[98] Scott takes the opportunity to moralise on the flagrant flouting of justice and the rule of law by both the king and Douglas, although ultimately he accepts the established line that James II was to some extent justified in that he was forced to respond to intolerable Douglas arrogance and aggression. In his assessment of the character of the king, Scott states that James II

> did not possess the elegant accomplishments of his father; and the manner in which he slew the Earl of Douglas must be admitted as a stain upon his reputation. Yet he was, upon the whole, a good prince, and was greatly lamented by his subjects.[99]

NOTES

1. Stevenson, T. G., *The Auchinleck Chronicle* (1877).
2. National Library of Scotland, Ms. Acc. 4233; see full text, Appendix 2.
3. Thomson, T., *A Short Chronicle of James II King of Scots* (Edinburgh, 1819).
4. Chron. Auchinleck, f. 111v, 112r, 114r.
5. Cheney, C. R., *Handbook of Dates* (1945).
6. Chron. Auchinleck, f. 123v.
7. Lesley, *History*, 23; Pitscottie, *Historie*, 118.
8. *H.M.C.*, vii, Southesk, no. 30.
9. *Royal Letters and other Historical Documents selected from the Family Papers of Dundas of Dundas*, ed. W. Macleod (Edinburgh, 1897).
10. *Johannis de Fordun Scotichronicon cum supplementis et Continuatione Walteri Boweri*, ed. W. Goodall (Edinburgh, 1759).
11. Chron. Auchinleck, f. 112r.
12. Ibid., 109, 110, 112.

13. Ibid., 112, 122, 109, 113.

14. Ibid., 113; *C.S.S.R.*, iv, 748.

15. Ibid., 1049.

16. Chron. Auchinleck, f. 117–118.

17. *Calendar of Entries in the Papal Registers relating to Great Britain and Ireland: Papal Letters*, ed. W. H. Bliss *et al.* (London, 1893), vol. x, 470.

18. Chron. Auchinleck, f. 118.

19. *C.P.L.*, x, 692.

20. *C.S.S.R.*, 550.

21. Chron. Auchinleck, f. 118.

22. I am indebted to Anne Johnston for this information.

23. Nicholson, R., *Later Middle Ages*, 362.

24. Chron. Auchinleck, f. 114.

25. Ibid., 115.

26. Ibid.

27. Ibid., 122.

28. Ibid., 121.

29. *Rot Scot.*, 347; *Proceedings and Ordinances of the Privy Council of England*, ed. H. Nicolas, vi, 63–4.

30. Grant, A., 'The Revolt of the Lord of the Isles and the Death of the Earl of Douglas, 1451–1452', *S.H.R.*, LX, 169–174.

31. Macdougall, N., 'Bishop Kennedy of St Andrews: a reassessment of his political career', in *Church, Politics and Society*, ed. N. Macdougall (Edinburgh, 1983), 18–19.

32. Mason, R., 'Scotching the Brut', *History Today*, 35.

33. *Chron. Bower.*

34. Lyall, R. J., 'Politics and Poetry in Fifteenth and Sixteenth Century Scotland', in *Scottish Literary Journal*, vol. 3 (1976), 5–29; *Liber Pluscardensis*, ed. F. J. H. Skene (Edinburgh, 1877–80).

35. Macdougall, N., *James III* (Edinburgh, 1982), 274–5.

36. *Extracta E Variis Cronicis Scocie*, Abbotsford Club, 1842, 237–244.

37. Myln, A., *Vitae Dunkeldensis Ecclesiae Episcoporum*, Bannatyne Club, 1831.

38. *Cartulary of Cambuskenneth, 1147–1585*, Grampian Club (Edinburgh, 1872).

39. Myln, *Vitae*, 18–24.

40. *Extracta*, 242.

41. Lesley, *History*, 23; Pitscottie, *Historie*, 116; Chalmers of Ormond, G, NLS Adv. MS. 16/2/20; Buchanan, *History*, f. xl.

42. *Extracta*, 243.

43. Chron. Auchinleck, f. 119.

44. *Extracta*, 244.

45. Drexler, M., 'The Extant Abridgements of Walter Bower's Scotichronicon', *S.H.R.*, lxi, 1982, 62–74.

46. Law, J., 'De Cronicis Scotorum brevia', Edin. Univ. Lib. DC 763, f. 128.

47. Durkan, J., 'St Andrews in the John Law Chronicle', *Innes Review*, xxv, 1974.

48. Chron. Auchinleck, f. 109, 112; Law, f. 128, 130, 132, 129.

49. See Chapter 4, p. 58.

50. Law, f. 130.

51. Short Chronicle appended to Wyntoun, B.M.Royal MS. 17 DXX, f. 307; Abell, A., 'The Roit and Quheill of Tyme', N.L.S. MS. 1746, f. 109–110.

52. Macdougall, N., *James III*, 276.

53. Abell, f. 110.

54. Ibid.

55. Major, J., *A History of Greater Britain*, S.H.S., 1892, 381–386.

56. Mason, R., 'Kingship and Commonweal: Political Thought and Ideology in Reformation Scotland' (Unpublished PhD. thesis, University of Edinburgh, 1983), passim.

57. Major, *History*, cxxxiv.

58. Mason, 'Kingship and Commonweal', op. cit.

59. Ibid., 383.

60. Chron. Auchinleck, f. 115.

61. Major, op. cit., 384.

62. Ibid., 385.

63. *Extracta*, 243.

64. Major, op. cit., 385.

65. Ibid., 386.

66. Hector Boethius, *Scotorum Historiae* (Paris, 1527).

67. Innes, T., *Essay*, 140–1.

68. Mason, op. cit., 102.

69. Ibid., 106.

70. Hector Boethius, *Scotorum Historiae*, 2nd edition (Paris, 1574).

71. R. Lindesay of Pitscottie, *The Historie and Cronicles of Scotland* (S.T.S., 1898–9), i, 13–147.

72. Ibid.

73. Ibid.

74. Ibid., 89–92. Patrick, master of Gray, had two sisters, Margaret and Christian, who were married, respectively, to Robert 1st lord Lyle and James Crichton of Strathurd, therefore neither could have been the mother of Maclellan of Bombie.

75. *Criminal Trials in Scotland from 1488 to 1624*, ed. R. Pitcairn (Edinburgh, 1833), i, appendix. I am indebted to Dr Ken Emond for this reference.

76. J. Lesley, *The History of Scotland from the Death of King James I in the Year 1436 to the Year 1561* (Bannatyne Club, 1830), 11–32.

77. Ibid., 24–26.

78. Ibid., 24–26.

79. *A.P.S.*, ii, 35.

80. Lesley, op. cit., 31.

81. Ibid., 32.

82. Buchanan, G., *The History of Scotland*, translated, J. Aikman (Glasgow and Edinburgh, 1827–29), vol. ii, book xi, chapter iii, folios 1–50.

83. Mason, R., op. cit.

84. Buchanan, *History*, f. 1.

85. Ibid., ff. ii, ix, xviii, xxvii.

86. Mason, op. cit.

87. Boece, *Historiae* (1527),

88. Buchanan, op. cit., f. xiii.

89. Ibid., f. xxiii.

90. Hume of Godscroft, *The History of the Houses of Douglas and Angus* (Edinburgh, 1644), 139–209.

91. Chalmers of Ormond, *Ane Cronikill of the Kingis of Scotland* (Maitland Club, 1830).

92. Hume of Godscroft, op. cit.

93. Drummond of Hawthornden, *History of Scotland from 1423 Until 1572* (London, 1681), 35–71.

94. Rae, T. I., 'The Historical Writing of Drummond of Hawthornden', in *S.H.R.*, liv (1975), 22–62.

95. Sir James Balfour of Kinnaird, *Annales of Scotland in Historical Works*, ed. J. Haig (London, 1824–5), i, 166–89.

96. Donaldson, G., *Scotland: James V–James VII* (Edinburgh, 1965), 262.

97. Scott, Sir W., *Tales of a Grandfather* (Cambridge, 1926).

98. See above, p. 136.

99. Scott, op. cit.

8

The Character of the King

In his account of the reign of James II, Bishop John Lesley includes a brief character assessment of the king, writing that

> of harte he was couragious, politique in councell, in adversite nothing abashed, in prosperitie rather joyful nor proude in peace just and mercyfull, in warre sharpe and feirce, in the fielde bolde and hardie . . . he had greit trubles in civil and intestine warres in his youthedde; bot in the tyme of his later daies, his realme was in quiet prosperous estaite.[1]

The overriding impression, according to Lesley, was of a formidable king, no stranger to aggression and war, but with a concern for the execution of justice within his kingdom. However, that is by no means the whole story, and more may be divined about the king's character than the vague impressions offered in Lesley's *History* by tracing the course of James II's emergence onto the political stage and his reactions to the people and events surrounding him.

James II was thrust into the kingship unexpectedly early, in circumstances which could scarcely have been less favourable. The assassination of his father, James I, by a faction including some of his own courtiers, coupled with the civil strife and faction fighting which ensued, gave James II a precarious base on which to build his position and establish his authority when he assumed personal control of his kingdom. Notwithstanding this inauspicious start, by the time that James II met his untimely death at the age of only twenty-nine, he had established himself, and consequently the Stewart dynasty, in a position of strength and authority such as they had not previously enjoyed. Unlike his father, James II was born and raised entirely in Scotland and grew up with an awareness of the traditions, requirements and aspirations of the political community. This awareness stood him in very good stead, as he was clearly able to appreciate the signals of discontent and grievance on occasions when he had miscalculated or ventured too far, and showed remarkable aptitude for redeeming potentially dangerous situations. He did not do this by displays of timidity or capitulation, as here was a Stewart king who believed in his own worth, but, mindful of his father's fate, he endeavoured never to alienate too many of his nobility to the extent that he was completely isolated or devoid of support.

James II is remembered, chiefly, for his struggle with, and eventual defeat of, the Black Douglas family. This conflict absorbed much of the king's attention for the brief years of his personal rule; but the fact of his ultimate success should not obscure the difficulties and dangers which faced him during those years when the outcome appeared, at times, far from a foregone conclusion. The king made a number of mistakes and miscalculations, one of which was the initiation of the dispute with the Douglases by launching an attack on the Earldom of Wigtown, the overlordship of which was particularly complex. It may be that James was seeking to prove a point in an earnest game of power politics with his most powerful subject, the Earl of Douglas, who had become active at court at a crucial time when the young king was a few years short of being able to exercise personal control, but old enough to be aware of what was taking place around him and to have become frustrated by his lack of real power. Through having to back down in the dispute over the earldom of Wigtown, James II probably harboured a deep grievance. Indeed, he demonstrated a grim determination to acquire Wigtown throughout the power struggle with the Douglases in a manner which may have had less to do with the actual value of the earldom than a demonstration of deep personal pride and an unwillingness to admit defeat.[2]

Having decided on a course of action, which may initially have been little more than a desire to bring the Douglases to heel, James II laid his plans carefully, gauging the extent of support available to the Douglases, and exploiting the weaknesses in their power base, many of which resulted from the rift in the family following the Black Dinner. The differences and resentments caused by the Black Dinner within and between the south-west based 6th Earl's affinity and the Lothian and Lanarkshire based 7th Earl's family and followers may have been obscured over the centuries, but ten years was not a long time for the healing of such deep wounds, and James II clearly grew up well aware of how to exploit them and turn men who appear on paper to have had Douglas connections, against their feudal superiors. Such political manoeuvring was shrewd and calculating, although in essence it was simply capitalising on the evident unpopularity of the Douglases with some of their tenants. The sixteenth-century chroniclers relate a number of incidents indicative of Douglas high-handedness and ruthlessness, such as the story of the tutor of Bombie and the execution of Richard Colville,[3] the details of which, although they may not be entirely accurate, nevertheless suggest that the Douglases were guilty of the feudal sin of not giving good lordship in some areas of their vast domains.

The dramatic murder of William 8th earl of Douglas at Stirling while under safe-conduct demonstrated that James II could abandon calculation and judgement for violent emotion, although it may be that Douglas himself failed disastrously to read the king's mood and react accordingly. Douglas knew James well, having been in his company frequently since at least 1444, with ample opportunity to judge his character and mood swings. The murder of Douglas took place on the second day of talks at Stirling, during which the intransigence of both sides must have built up to the angry outburst which led the king to stab Douglas. James cannot have premeditated such an outcome, as the murder of Douglas was far from being a solution to his problems.

Nor were the difficulties faced by the king solved by the parliamentary declaration of Douglas's guilt issued in June 1452. This was a royalist parliament with no Black Douglas representation, although this does not mean that the three estates unreservedly approved the king's action — particular discomfort must have been caused by the fact of Douglas having been under royal safe-conduct — but acknowledged that the deed was done and that the king must be supported. The murder of the 8th Earl was almost certainly spontaneous and hot-blooded, but the king was helped in that the position of the Douglases was regarded by many, if not with outright hostility, then at least with considerable unease or envy. The curtailment of Douglas influence was undoubtedly welcomed by those who expected the consequent enhancement of their own positions, such as the Scotts and the Johnstones in the south-west, and the Red Douglas earl of Angus.[4] However, politically active magnates cannot have been insensitive to the implications of the king's hostility towards the Douglases for their own positions in the future; consequently, some effort was made to temper the king's actions and bring him to settle the conflict. Such pressure forced James II to agree to the Lanark bond with James 9th earl of Douglas in January 1453, although he seems to have taken care, quite deliberately, to ensure that this was not an agreement made in parliament and endorsed by the three estates, thus making it easier to rescind later. Political cynicism was not alien to James II.

Indeed, James had a calculating mind, demonstrating the ability to weigh up people and situations in order to use them to his best advantage. Impatience and frustration sometimes broke through this reserve to devastating effect, but strength and determination seem to have been his dominating characteristics. His ultimate success is partially explained by the fact that he was not launching a general attack on the nobility, never alienating the political community to the extent his father had done. It was not James II's intention to decimate the nobility; he pursued an active policy of creating earldoms and lordships, albeit only after he had become embroiled in the struggle with the Douglases, many of these creations having every appearance of being tactical. For example, the position in the north of the Earl of Huntly caused the king some uneasiness. There is no evidence for Huntly ever having acted against the king, but James seems to have regarded him with suspicion, perhaps feeling that Huntly's overriding concern was the enhancement of his and his family's position in the north-east. The creation of the earldoms of Rothes, Marischal and Errol was no doubt intended to surround the principal Huntly estates and forestall any trouble from that direction.

James II was aware of the potential trouble spots in his kingdom, and conscious of the limits of personal control imposed by climate and geography. In a country where government was necessarily decentralised. James was concerned that the magnates to whom he delegated authority should be reliable, and therefore anxious to prevent any noble family rising to a position of power and influence above the others. Most of the peerage creations of James II were achieved without giving very much away. Argyll was the only earldom which may be described as territorial, the others being essentially honorific. The peerage titles assumed during the minority were accepted and recognised, with the king adding to the ranks of lords of parliament although, again, it cost him little to do so. Social distinction through title was a marked feature of the reign of James II, and, as Dr Wormald has demonstrated, it was no accident that the practice of making bonds of manrent begins in his reign, as men with little to choose between them territorially would seek to emphasise their superior standing in written bonds of service and protection.[5] It was not only the king's subjects who were making bonds with one another, as James himself acknowledged their social and political importance by entering into such agreements himself. In January 1453, James II entered into a bond with James 9th earl of Douglas, ostensibly to settle the conflict between himself and the Douglases on terms favourable to both.[6] On 8 March 1455, the king entered into another bond, this time with James Tweedie of Drumelzier, which may have been one of many made at that time as James sought support in his final onslaught against the Douglases.[7] However, these bonds were not generalised grantings of manrent or maintenance with no immediate aim in view; they were made as a direct response to the specific political crisis facing the king in his struggle with the Black Douglases and should not be seen in the general context of bonds of manrent.[8] Nevertheless, the bonds demonstrate that dialogue rather than imperious dictation was called for and acknowledged by James II in the more sensitive stages of negotiations with his subjects in times of crisis, or when he simply could not take for granted the absolute strength of his position.

James II's relationship with the three estates seems, on the whole, to have been one of reasonable co-operation. Parliament was held every year of the king's adult reign, and while the assembly displayed, on occasions such as June 1452, a noticeable royalist bias, the king did not escape a measure of mild criticism in the statute of 1458 which declared that, as the rebels and breakers of justice had all been removed from the realm, the three estates,

> with all humilite exhortis and requiris his hienes to be inclynit with sik diligence to the execucione of the statutis actis and decretis abone writtyn that God may be emplesit of him and all his lieges spirituale and temporale may pray for him to gode and gif thankyng to him that sende thame sik a prince to their governor and defender.[9]

However, this is no more than a mild rebuke, showing concern at the lack of implementation of statutes, which was not peculiar to this parliament or the reign of James II. Similarly, the 1455 Act of Annexation which exhorted the king to 'live of his own' was demonstrating an attitude to the management of crown resources which was conventional rather than radical. The regular assemblies of the three estates and the attendance there of men who owed their positions as lords of parliament to the king suggests that James II distributed patronage sensibly and secured greater authority for his actions through frequent consultation of the political community. Naturally some voices were more influential than others: for example, the Crichtons, Bishop Turnbull, James Livingston and Bishop Schoriswood.

James II's perception of himself and his position as a European monarch was far from timid and self-effacing. Scotland was not a rich or powerful country, therefore James' requests for assistance from the King of France, suggestions of military tactics and offers to mediate in the dispute between Charles VII and his son, the Dauphin Louis, may seem highly impertinent, but James II grew up in a court where his father, having lived in England and travelled to France, was comfortable in the world of foreign diplomacy. Scottish magnates, such as the Earls of Buchan and Douglas, had fought in France and received French honours, in addition to which four of James' sisters were married to European potentates: Margaret to the Dauphin of France, Isabella to the Duke of Brittany, Eleanor to Duke Sigismund of Austria and Mary to the lord of Veere. James himself married the niece of the Duke of Burgundy and daughter of the Duke of Gueldres, therefore he too felt comfortable on the European stage and displayed no sense of inferiority, clearly regarding himself as a prince of consequence. Indeed, his behaviour towards contemporary rulers could be very arrogant. King Christian of Denmark found James' terms in the early stages of negotiations over Orkney and the payment of the 'annual' excessively demanding, and a letter sent on 10 May 1456 to the King of England renouncing the truce of 1453 was deemed by Richard, duke of York, to be an 'overweening and insensate epistle'.[10] In his quest for allies against England, James exhorted 'confederate princes . . . [to] concur with us against the English, who are the principal disturbers of the peace of all Christendom'. Among those from whom James seemed to expect assistance were Charles VII of France and Ludovico Sforza, Duke of Milan, and he undoubtedly wrote similar letters to other European princes at the same time.[11]

The warlike aspect of James II's character is noted by most of the writers who have dealt with his reign, most notably Buchanan and Lesley, with some justification, as there were a considerable number of sieges and battles, of varying scale and intensity, many of which saw the king in personal attendance. The written evidence for sieges consists of chronicle references supplemented by occasional details in the exchequer accounts of expenses incurred for materials. Precisely how the various sieges came about, the way in which they were conducted and when and how they were resolved are rarely described in detail. However, Mr Stell observes that James II exhibited the earliest successful 'blitzkrieg-type siege operations involving the use of artillery'.[12] Siege warfare began early in the reign of James II. In 1444, while still in his minority, the young king was taken to witness the proceedings and lend credibility to the faction which held him, at the siege of Methven castle. Little is known of this siege beyond the noting of the king's presence there, but the castle was probably being held by a supporter of William lord Crichton, who was out of favour with the ruling faction,[13] and who was himself besieged in Edinburgh castle for a number of weeks in 1445. The Crichtons had also been the target of the Douglas attack on the tower of Barnton in 1443, at which, following a five-day siege, William earl of Douglas appeared and 'schew the kingis banere'. This device was intended to confer legitimacy on the earl's claims on Barnton, and the tower was duly surrendered.[14] After the assumption of James II's majority, there followed a number of sieges, the first of which was a response to the attack launched on the Livingston family and their adherents in 1449–50, when Archibald Dundas 'stuffit' the tower of Dundas and held it in defiance of the king for several weeks. On this occasion, it was William earl of Douglas who once more took charge of the siege until the tower was surrendered at the end of April 1450; however, most of the sieges which took place during the reign of James II were connected with the Douglas dispute and aimed at that family.

The first of these was the siege of Craig Douglas. According to John Law, James II responded to his failure to take the earldom of Wigtown during the 8th earl of Douglas's absence in Rome by laying siege to the castle of Craig Douglas. This action was intended as retribution and warning to the homeward-bound Earl William, as the castle was held by his supporters. This does not seem to have been a particularly protracted siege, and beyond Law's reference, there is no evidence for the king's actual presence there, although it does show that James II was swift to use siege warfare as a weapon to punish defiance and resistance to his will. Similarly, the siege of Hatton, to which there is only a brief reference in the *Treasurer's Accounts*,[15] indicates that James was wreaking revenge on William Lauder of Hatton, who had delivered the safe-conduct to his patron, William earl of Douglas, to come to Stirling in February 1452. Hatton seems to have defied the king following the murder by maintaining his allegiance to the Douglases, and James II no doubt sought to make an example of him at a time when he was striving to cut the Douglases' support from under them.

James II's problems were not confined to the actions of his adversaries. During the period when the king was compelled to back down and concede some ground to the Douglases, it was his own supporters, most notably the Crichtons, who experienced a sense of betrayal as their grants and concessions of 1452 seemed to be ignored. In particular, James Crichton's investiture in the earldom of Moray was apparently rescinded, with Archibald Douglas continuing to hold possession of the earldom and the title. Crichton's animosity towards the king as a result of this is demonstrated by the fact that when he died in Dunbar in August 1454, the castle 'was haldin fra the king a litill quhile and syne gevin till him'.[16] James Crichton replaced Robert Liddale as keeper of Dunbar before 14 July 1453, and in the exchequer audit of 5 July 1454 he received a fee for his keepership of Dunbar, being styled James earl of Moray and lord Crichton.[17] There is no documentary evidence giving details of the siege of Dunbar beyond the Auchinleck chronicler's reference, but the incident demonstrates the king's plight at this time — facing conflict and rebellion both from the Douglases and from some elements within the ranks of his own supporters — problems which were far from over with the surrender of Dunbar.

If all was not well with the king and his supporters, then neither was the mood within the Crichton family harmonious. The problem, as with Dunbar, was with the younger Crichtons. Admiral George Crichton, who had been 'beltit' Earl of Caithness in the July 1452 parliament, appears to have been at odds with his son James, as he received a charter on 8 July 1452 in which all his lands in the southern part of the kingdom were incorporated into his new earldom, but no mention was made of his only son's inheritance of these.[18] In May 1454, during James II's temporary reconciliation with the Douglases, George Crichton went so far as to resign all his acquired lands into the king's hands, making him his heir.[19] For his son James this was the last straw. Within six days of his father's action, James Crichton fortified the castle of Blackness against the king, apparently holding his father captive in the process, and the Auchinleck chronicler records that

> the king in proper persoun put ane sege to the blakness and lay at It ix or x dayis and than It was gevin oure be trety and Sir George was put to Methven and gaf him the landis of Strathurd for the landis that he had conquest in Lothian.[20]

The fact that the king himself was concerned to attend and raise this siege testifies to its importance. Not only was this a far from timely rebellion on the part of a supposedly loyal supporter which threatened the position of George Crichton, a demonstrably consistent king's man, but Blackness castle itself was seen as a crucial strategic stronghold with its commanding position on the banks of the Forth and its closeness to the two Douglas strongholds of Abercorn and Inveravon. It was in order to control Blackness, thereby facilitating any attack on the neighbouring Douglas castles, that James II placated and granted concessions to the Crichtons.

The Douglas castles of Inveravon and Abercorn were attacked and besieged in 1455 during the final assault on the Douglases which was to drive them out of Scotland. Very little written evidence exists for the siege of Inveravon beyond a laconic entry in the Auchinleck chronicle: 'The zere of god 1455. In the begynnyng of merche, James the secund kest doune the castell of Inverawyne'.[21] The exchequer accounts record the purchase of equipment for the siege and demolition of Inveravon,[22] although the exact duration of the siege is not recorded. The king almost certainly attended personally, as he was present at the siege of Abercorn, the conquest of these Douglas strongholds being of crucial importance to him. Inveravon does not appear to have been a protracted siege, as James followed its capture with a series of raids and skirmishes, returning to besiege Abercorn by the beginning of April. In a letter to Charles VII, James reported that he had laid siege to Abercorn in Easter week (Easter Sunday fell on 6 April in 1455), and he also described to the French king the collapse of Abercorn's towers as a result of continual artillery assault.[23] The Auchinleck chronicler adds the information that the siege was conducted with the assistance of a 'gret gun the quhilk a franche man schot richt wele'. The chronicler also records the death of Allan Pantour whom he describes as the most ingenious man in Scotland. Unfortunately, his ingenuity did not prevent him from being slain by one of the guns 'throu misgovernyng of himself' in an ominous foreshadowing of the fate suffered by the king in 1460. The siege lasted for a month, the castle eventually being taken by storm, and it was an important turning point in the fortunes of the Douglases as, within seven days of siege being laid to Abercorn, James lord Hamilton, hitherto the Douglases' staunchest and most powerful supporter, abandoned their cause. It is possible that he despaired of James 9th earl of Douglas's ability to hold out against the king, indeed his non-appearance in defence of his beleaguered stronghold disheartened his supporters, and the Auchinleck chronicler remarks disapprovingly that 'men wist nocht grathlie quhar the Douglas was all this tyme'.[24] The attitude of James II to the defenders of Abercorn was mixed. The chief officers were hanged for their defiance, but the less significant of those within the castle were spared. The castle itself was destroyed.

The king's success in seizing Abercorn must have elated him no less than the news that, while he was conducting the siege, a Douglas border raid was defeated at Arkinholm on 1 May by a group of southern lairds, resulting in the slaying of Archibald earl of Moray and the wounding of Hugh earl of Ormond who was later executed. The only major Douglas stronghold which remained unconquered was the island fortress of Threave. James II's clear enjoyment of active participation in sieges led to his personal involvement in the siege of Threave, following the parliament of June 1455 which formally forfeited the Douglases. An effort was made by Douglas to save Threave when he offered it to Henry VI in return for a grant of £100, issued on 15 July 'for succour, victualling, relief, and rescue of the castle of Treve',[25] but to no avail as, having been under attack for some weeks from the king's artillery, which included a 'gret bombard', the garrison surrendered.[26]

Although the use of artillery was an important factor in the conduct of sieges in the reign of James II, negotiated political settlements ended many sieges rather than sheer military force. James appears to have had an impressive collection of artillery, most of which were bombards (used specifically for battering down walls) manufactured in the Low Countries.[27] Certainly, the king's guns merited the appointment of William Bonar as master of the artillery by 1458.[28] Dr Caldwell points out that James II's interest in artillery was not confined to large guns, as he exhibited an awareness of the value of smaller guns in the field by attempting in the October parliament of

1455 to have members of the higher nobility provide such 'cartis of weir' themselves.[29] The response to this was probably unenthusiastic. 'Turning up to the royal host armed to the back teeth was one thing, dragging a cart of guns along was another that the barons were not going to have imposed on them lightly'.[30]

The use of sieges to secure his ambitions was not confined to domestic disputes, as James II also employed them in his dealings with the English. In pursuit of his ambition to be overlord of the Isle of Man, for example, James ordered an attack on Peel castle, held for the English king by the Stanley family who fortified the curtain wall at Peel in response to James II's aggression.[31] However, it was at Roxburgh that James concentrated his most determined siege against English occupation of a castle on Scottish soil. The Yorkist victory at Northampton on 10 July 1460 over the Lancastrian dynasty presented James II with a golden opportunity to move against the English-occupied strongholds in Scotland, an opportunity which he wasted no time in seizing. By the end of July, the Scottish king had laid siege to Roxburgh, the English having anticipated an attack on Berwick and concentrated their defences there. Artillery was once more extensively employed, putting to use the Duke of Burgundy's gifts of cannon, one of which was almost certainly the famous Mons Meg, now on display at Edinburgh castle. The history of Mons Meg is comparatively well documented. The gun was made in 1449 by Jehan Cambier at Mons for Philip duke of Burgundy, who gave it to James II, sending it to Scotland in May 1457 with an escort of fifty men-at-arms.[32] James II would almost certainly have employed all the artillery at his disposal in such a concerted effort to take Roxburgh, personally supervising their deployment when, unfortunately, a faulty gun broke apart when it was fired and an iron fragment struck the king, causing him to fall victim to one of the hazards of mediaeval warfare — weakened or badly cast ordnance.[33]

James II was only twenty-nine years old when he was killed at Roxburgh, having enjoyed a mere eleven years of personal rule. Because of the scarcity of documentation, personal letters and detailed descriptions, it is initially difficult to form a clear picture of the king's character, and we see him, necessarily, as a rather shadowy figure. It is only by reading between the lines of official documents and chronicles that the man emerges, his actions and motives governed by shrewd calculation, fierce personal pride and the strong passionate temper which, in conjunction with the striking red birthmark, earned him the Auchinleck chronicler's description of 'James of the fiery face'.

NOTES

1. Lesley, *History*, 32.
2. For a fuller account of the Wigtown dispute, see p. 55–56.

3. See above, p. 68.

4. See above, p. 88.

5. Wormald, J., *Lords and Men*, passim.

6. See above, p. 82.

7. *H.M.C.*, Various Collections, v, Tweedy, no. 14. Also, see above, p. 89.

8. I am grateful to Dr Stephen Boardman for his interpretation of these political bonds.

9. *A.P.S.*, ii, 52.

10. *Off. Corr. of Thomas Beckynton*, ii, 139–41.

11. *Milan, State Papers*, i, no. 36.

12. Stell, G., 'Late Medieval Defences in Scotland', in *Scottish Weapons & Fortifications 1100–1800*, ed. Caldwell, D. H., 39.

13. See above, p. 32.

14. See above, p. 29.

15. *T.A.*, i, ccxvii. See above, p. 65.

16. Chron. Auchinleck, f. 112v.

17. *E.R.*, v, 506, 645.

18. See above, Chapter 5, p. 84.

19. Chron. Auchinleck, f. 117r.

20. Ibid., f. 117r.

21. Ibid., f. 116r.

22. £15 14s 10d was expended for diverse instruments, carriages, iron, ropes and pipes for the destruction of the castle of Abercorn and the tower of Inveravon. *E.R.*, vi, 12.

23. This letter was dated 8 July 1455 and is printed in Pinkerton, *History*, I, 486–8.

24. Chron. Auchinleck, op. cit.

25. *C.D.S.*, iv, 1272.

26. See above, p. 88.

27. Caldwell, D. H., 'Royal Patronage of Arms and Armour Making in Fifteenth and Sixteenth Century Scotland', in Caldwell, *Scottish Weapons*, op. cit., 74.

28. *E.R.*, vi, 383.

29. *A.P.S.*, ii, 45.

30. Caldwell, op. cit., 74.

31. See above, p. 100.

32. Gaier, C., 'The Origin of Mons Meg', in *Journ. Arms & Armour Soc.*, v (1967), 425–31; Stevenson, R. B. K., 'The Return of Mons Meg from London, 1828–1829', in Caldwell, *Scottish Weapons*, 419.

33. See above, p. 111–112.

The Itinerary of James II

Key: Places where James II issued charters, (e.g., <u>Perth</u> (53)).
Non-underlined place-names are for reference when mentioned in the text.

Appendix 1:
The Itinerary of James II

Numbers of Royal Documents Issued From Each Place on the King's Itinerary.
(in order of volume)

Edinburgh	346	Kirkcudbright	2
Stirling	127	Irvine	2
Perth	53	Crichton	1
Falkland	23	Melrose	1
Linlithgow	14	Ayr	1
Aberdeen	13	Lochmaben	1
Inverness	10	Jedburgh	1
Methven	5	Castle of Morton	1
Glasgow	3	Arbroath	1
Dundee	2	Kildrummy	1
Dalkeith	2	Blackness	1
Lanark	2	Tongland	1
Peebles	2	Spynie	1
Dumfries	2	Brechin	1
Dunfermline	2	Lauder	1
Wigtown	2		

Appendix 2:
The 'Auchinleck Chronicle'

This series of fragments (analysed in Chapter 7) forms part of the Asloan MS. (NLS MS. Acc. 4233). As it is a vital source for the reign of James II, its text is given in full below.

Heir followis ane schort memoriale of the scottis corniklis for addicioun.

f. 109r

Item It is to wit that the scottis Regnit befor the pictis iic lxv years and three monethis The pictis Regnit lm lxi year fra thai began or thai war distroyit. Scotland was a kinrik before tha Incarnacioun ccccxliiii years.

The zere of god 1428 [this should read 1438] the 20th day of september Allan Stewart lord Darnley was slane at polmais thorne be sir Thomas Boyd under ane assouerance taken betuix tham

The zere of god 1439 the 7th day of July. sir Thomas Boyd was slane be Alexander Stewart buktuth and his sonis and mathow Stewart with his brother and uther sundry

That samyn zere the thrid day of august the lord Kalendar Sir Alexander Levingstoun that tyme beand in the castell of Sterling with the qwene / Tuke the qwene and put hir in ane chalmere and kepit hir stratlye thairin / till scho was lowsit be the thre estatis at the counsall haldin at striuling that samyn zere the last day of august and that samyn tyme he tuke sir James Stewart the lord of lornis brother and William Stewart and put tham in pittis and bollit thaim / at that samyn counsall sir James was borowit be the lord Gordon sir Alexander Setoun lord of the Isles, Sir William of Crichton that tyme chancellor under the pane of thre thousand

f. 109v

The samyn zere the 24th day of september John of Colquhoun the lord of Luss was slane in Inchemuryne [Inchmurrin, on Loch Lomond] underneth ane assouerance be Lauchlane McClanis and Murthow Gibson.

The samyn tyme thar was in Scotland a gret derth for the boll of quheit was at xls and the boll of ete mele xxxs and werraly the derth was sa gret that thair deit a passinge peple for hunger and als the land Ill the wame Ill was so violent that thair deit ma that zere than ever thair deit under iii pestilens or yit in ony uther seikness in scotland and that samyn zere the pestilens come in scotland and began at drumfres and It was callit the pestilence but mercy for thar tuk it nain that ever recoverit bot thai deit within xxiiii houris

160

The zere of god 1443 the 10th day of March erll James Douglas deit at the castell of abercorn to the takin thai said he had in him four stane of talch and maire

Thar faucht on mydsomere day in sanct Johnston Sir William Ruthven, John gorme Stewart of Atholl quhar thair was slane William of Ruthven and ane man with him on his syd and na ma and on the tother syd the said John gorme gilcrist makynare and of thaim slane out of hand of gentill men and yemen xviii and ma and mony hurt in perell of thair lyf. That gat away and this bargane was done on the north Inche of sanct Johnston / all for the takin of a man for thift that the said William tuke

f. 110r

The samyn zere forsaid tha 15th day of July, Sir Robert Sempill than beand in the castell of Dumbarton and sherrif deput to the lord Erskine and Patrick Galbraith beand in the ower bailze havand the entre be him self at wallace towre and the k(ep)ing of the ower bailze the said Sir Robert put out the said sir Patrick clerlie fra all governans of the castell subtelly and gart him remuf his geir and on the morn the said Patrick past agane to the castell and gat entre to remuf the laif of his gere and had in with him bot iii or iiii unharnest men Nevertheless he tuke the portar and wan the ower bailze clerlie on force and was commendit for his takin and supleite be the toun of Dumbarton and schortlie he put out the said Sir Robert of the nether bailze and remanit yit with the hale castell efter that.

Item, that samyn zere the 22nd day of august Erle William of Douglas, James son, at the command of James II, come to bernetoun in lothian with ane gret ost and with him the forsaid kingis counsall beand with him and his houshald and schortlie he askit the hous on the kingis behalf and schew the kingis lettres of commandement to ask It and suthlie Andrew Crichton than beand thair in captain answered sayand that the hous was in the kingis hand and Nicol of Borthwick and James of Crichton war under burrowis to the shiref / Sir William of Crichton and thai put in be him on the kingis behalf and said thai wald nocht gif him the hous bot gif it were of the sherrif's bidding and then the erll remanit about the

f. 110v

hous in proper person iiii days and iiii nights and on the fifth day he schew the kingis banere and than thai gaf it our condicionaly that thai suld haf fredome vi days to remuf thair gudis and thaimself and he kest it doune within iiii days efter

Thar was ane counsall generale haldin at Stirling the ferd day of novembre in the hender end of the quhilk counsall thai blewe out on sir William of Crichton and sir George of Crichton and thar advertence and Incontinent efter the out blawing Sir George and Sir William tuke away Sir John Forrester's gudis that is to say schepe and nolt and syne Sir George tuke the erll of Douglas' horses and brynt his grangis of Abercorn and Strabrok and uther five placis and brynt the samyn tyme the black nestis [Blackness].

The zere of god 1445 the last day of May, Sir James Stewart of Auchingowne was slane and ane with him at drumglas besyd Kirkpatrick be the laird of duchall and Alexander the lyle and thair childer and erdit in the kirk of Dumbarton and that samyn tyme Robyn Boyd send Sir Alexander Cunningham / chaplane to Robyn kalendare to the kirk of Cardross to Sir James' wife efter that he had cummyn fra the slauchter of hir husband and bad hir cum to the castall and said thai suld send hir hame in a bait and warrand hir for thai gart hir trow thair was men waitand hir on hors and fut to tak hir / and schortlie throu Sir Alexander's fair language and hechtis scho passit with him and sone within vi days efter for diseis scho toke hir child ill and was

f. 111r

deliverit befor hir tyme ix oulkis of ane knaif child that liffit nocht ane houre and was erdit besyd his fader in the kirk forsaid.

1446 thar decessit in the castall of Glasgow Master John Cameron, bishop of Glasgow apon zule ewyne that was bishop xix zere. The samyn zere, Archibald of Dunbar tuke the castell of halis on sanctandrois day the apostle and syne cowardlie gaf It ower to the master of douglas sodanlie.

Thar was ane parliament haldin at perth the v day of June by king James the secund and Remanit thar bot iii days and was continewit till Edinburgh becaus of the siege that was liand about the castell on the kingis behalf and Sir Wiliam of Crichton was in till it / and held it ix oulkis and than gaf It to the king throu trety and the xv day of July the qwene his moder deit in Dunbar and was erdit in the charterhous of Perth and incontinent the lord Hailes gaf our the castell of Dunbar throu trety. This quene forsaid was callit Jane and scho was the duke of somersydis dochter that king James the first spousit in yngland for till help to lous him furth of It and he gat on hir James that was king and ane nother son callit alexander and scho baire baith thir sonis on a nycht.
Item he gat with hir vi dochteris the eldest was callit Margaret that was baith wys and wertuis and was spousit with the dalphin of France. The secund was

f. 111v

callit Elenor and was spousit with the duke of brettan.

The zere of god 1445 the 23rd day of January the erll of Huntley and the Ogilvies with him on the ta part and the erll of Crawford on the tother part met at the zettis of Arbroath on ane sonday laite and faucht and the erll of Huntley and wat Ogilvy fled and thair was slane on thair party Sir John Oliphant laird of Aberdalghy; Sir William Forbes; Sir Alexander Barclay; Alexander Ogilvy; David of Aberkerdath with uther sundry and on the tother part the erll of Crawford himself was hurt in the feild and deit within viii days / bot he and his son wan the field and held it and efter that a gret tyme held the Ogilvies at gret subjectoun and tuke thair gudis and destroyit thair placis.

Item thair was ane richt gret herschipe maid in fyf be thir personis The erll of Crawford, James of Livingston, that tyme kepar to the king and captain of Stirling The Ogilvies all Robert reach, the laird of Kadzoch and uther sundry and this herschipe was maid on sanct androis land be the maist force and Incontinent efter bishop James Kennedy cursit solempnitlie with myter and staf buke and candill contynually a zere and Interdytit all the placis quhar thir personis ware and the samyn day xii moneth that this hereschip was maide thair happinnit the said batale betuix thaim and the forsaid erll of Craufurd lay four days abone the zerd and thair durst no man erd him quhill the forsaid bischop send the prior of St Andrews and

f. 112r

he had nocht gottin bot ewyn the contrary in all thingis.

The samyn zere the 16th day of August thar was slane John of Sandelandis son and are to the lard of Caldor. In that tyme bot 20 zeris of age and his Eme James and ane man with tham

Item that samyn zere and moneth thare was drownit in the watter of crawmond sir John Logan of Restalrig, knycht, of the age of 22 zeris.

Item that samyn zere Sir Patrick of Corntoun was slane in Dunbarton on setterday the 7th day of August be Allan Hog that tyme portar

That samyn zere the privilege of the universite of Glasgow come to Glasgow throw the Instance of king James the secund and throw Instigacoun of master William Turnbull that tyme bischop of Glasgow and was proclamit at the croce of Glasgow on the trinite sonday the 22nd day of June And on the morne thair was cryit ane gret Indulgence gevin to Glasgow at the request of thaim forsaid be paip nycholas as it war the zere of grace and with all Indulgens that thai mycht haf in rome contenand iiii monethis begynnand the ix day of July and durand to the x day of november.

Item the zere of god 1453 in the month of september deit Alexander Lyndesay erll of Crawford In fynevyne that was callit a rigorous man and ane

f. 112v

felloun and held ane gret rowme in his tyme for he held all Angus in his bandoun and was richt Inobedient to the king.

Item 1454 thar decessit in the moneth of August, Gilbert Hay erll of Erroll.

Item the samyn zere and moneth thair decessit in Edinburgh Sir George of Crichton and in the samyn month and zere Sir James lord of Crichton decessit at Dunbar and It was haldin fra the king a litill quhile and syne gevin till him and in the samyn month and zere decessit John Hamilton that was callit quhissilberry and was a licht man in his tyme. Item in the samyn zere and month decessit in Stirling Andrew Cunningham, son and heir till William of Cunningham of Glengarnock and the samyn Andrew spousit Margaret Campbell, Sir Duncan lord Campbell's dochter and tuke viiic merkis of touchers and arit the land.

And in the samyn month and zere decessit Sir Alexander Ramsay, lord of Dalhousie and in the samyn month and zere decessit John of Park, laird of that Ilk. Item that samyn zere and month decessit Sir William Keith that was callit ane gentill knycht and a wertuous. Item the samyn zere and month the laird of Johnston's twa sonis tuk the castall of Lochmaben apon the laird of mouswald callit carudderis and his ii sons and other ii or iii men / and all throu treasson of the portar

f. 113r

And syne the king gaf tham the keping of the hous to his prophet and how that was men ferleit

Thar was ane richt gret spait in clyde the 25th day and 26th day of november The quhilk brocht doun haile houses bernis and millis and put all the town of Gowane in ane flote quhill thai sat on the houses.

The zeir of god 1448 the 25th day of February the master of Douglas callit James and twasum with him That is to say James of douglas brother to the laird of Lochleven and the laird of Haukat [Hawkhead] faucht in the barres at Stirling aganis twa knychtis and ane sqwyar of Burgunze and thir ware thair names Sir Jakkis de lalane, Sir Symond de lalane and the laird of longawell [Longueville] that was the sqwyre and this was befor king James the secund.

That samyn zere the 23rd day of October was the battel of lochmaben stane within the parrische of St. Patrick Quhar Hugh of Douglas erll of Ormond was chieftan on the scottis syd and with him Sir John Wallace of Craigie the lord of Johnston the lord of Somerville's son and heir David Stewart of castell myll [Castlemilk] the sherrif of Ayr with uther sundry gentillis of the westland and thair men was callit iiiim And on the Inglis syde the younger Percy Sir John of Pennytoune Sir John Herntoun war chiftanis and with thaim sex thousand of Inglis men quhare thar chiftanis war tane and xvc men with thaim / slane

f. 113v

drownit vc And on the scottis syd xxvi slane and tane / bot na man of reputacoun war tane nor slane bot Sir John Wallace deit efter that he come hame throu misgovernance.

Item 1456 Cunningham and Dalrympill faucht in the barras of Stirling befor king James the secund

That samyn zere the thrid day of December thair decessit in Glasgow master William Turnbull bishop of Glasgow that brocht haim the pardon of it.
Item that samyn zere the last day of august deit in Glasgow Master Walter Stewart that was lord prowand.
Item that samyn zere and month decessit in brechyne Master John Crennock [Cranach] bishop of Brechin that was callit a gud actif and wertuis man and all his tyme wele governand.

The zere of god 1459, the penult day of June decessit at Paisley Thomas Carvas, abbot of Paisley the quhilk was a ne richt gud man and helplyk to the place of ony that ever was for he did mony notable thingis and held ane noble hous and was ay wele purvait he fand the place all out of gud rewle and destitut of leving and all the kirkis in lordis handis And the kirk unbiggit / The body of the kirk fra the bricht stair up and put on the ruf he biggit and thekit It with sclait and riggit it with stane and

f. 114r

thai cryit him luftennent and sone efter this thai worthit als strange as ever thai war / and at this tyme thai gat the erllis sele to consent to the trewis and Incontinent thai send furth Snawdoun the king's herrod to lundoun to bynd up the trewis and als fast as Sir James of Douglas gat wit hereof he past till londone Incontinent / and quharfor men wist nocht redelye bot he was thar with the king of yngland lang tyme and was meikle maid of

The zere of god 1451 the 25th day of June thar was haldin a parliament in Edinburgh be king James the secund To the quhilk parliament the forsaid erle William of Douglas come and put him body landis and gudis in the kingis grace and the king resavit him till his grace at the Request of the qwene and the three estatis and grantit him all his lordshippis agane outtane the erldome of wigtoun That is to say galloway fra the watter of Cre west and stewartoun outtane the landis of pedynnane Of the quhilk the erllis moder had conjunct feftment and charterit him now of all the laif of his lordschippis and gaf him and all his a fre Remission of all things bygane to the day forsaid. And all gud scottismen war rycht blyth of that accordance.

That samyn zer Erll William of Douglas wes slane in the castell of striuling be king James the

f. 114v

secund that had the fyre mark in his face. The forsaid king James send owt of Stirling with William Lawder of haltoun [Hatton] a speciale assouerans and respit under his preve sele and subscrivit with his awne hand and all the lodis that war with the king that tyme gaf bodely aithis to kepe that respit and assouerance and subscrivit Ilk man with thair awne hand and all the lordis that war with the king that tyme war oblist suppos the king wald brek the band forsaid / that thai suld let it at thair power. This beand done the forsaid William of Lawder of haltoun passit to the forsaid erll William of Douglas and brocht him to Stirling to the king on the monday before fastrennisevyn that was the 21st day of February and this samyn monday he passit to the castell and spak with the king that tuke richt wele with him be apperans and callit him on the morne to the dynere and to the supper / and he come and dynit and sowpit and thai said thair was a band betuix the said erll of douglas and the erll of Ross and the erll of Crawford and efter supper at sevyne houris the king then beand in the Inner chalmer and the said erll he chargit him to breke the forsaid band he said he mycht nocht nor wald nocht / Than the king said / fals tratour sen yow will nocht I sall / and stert sodanly till him with ane knyf and straik him in at the colere and down in the body and thai sayd that Patrick Gray straik him nixt the king

f. 115r

With ane poll ax on the hed and strak out his branes and syne the gentillis that war with the king gaf thaim Ilkane a straik or twa with knyffis and thir ar the names that war with the king that strake him for he had xxvi woundis. In the first, Sir Alexander Boyd the lord Darnley Sir Andrew Stewart Sir William of gremston [Cranston] Sir Simon of Glendonane [Glendinning] and the lord Gray

The zere of god 1452. The 27th day of March Sir James of Douglas erll James secund son for the foule slauchter of his brother erll William of Douglas come on sanct Patrikis day in lentryn to Stirling and blew out xxiiii hornis attanis apon the king and apon all the lordis that war with him that tyme for the foule slauchter of his brother And schew all thair seles at the corss on ane letter with thair handis subscrivit and tuke the latter and band It on an burd and cuplit It till ane hors tale and gart draw It throu the towne spekand richt sclanderfully of the king and all that war with him that tyme and spulzeit all the toune and brint It. And thair was with him his brother the erll of

Ormond and the lord Hamilton and na ma lordis and thai excedit nocht of gud men vic all this tyme the king was in Perth passand to the erll of Craufurd.

That samyn zere Thar was ane parliament haldin in Edinburgh the 12th day of June by King James

f. 115v

the secund and thair was forfaltit Alexander Lindsay The erll of Crawford and lord Lindsay bath land lyf and gudis and in that samyn parliament thar was put on the nicht on the parliament hous dure Ane letter under Sir James of Douglas sele and the sele of the erll of Ormond and Sir James Hamilton's declynand fra the king Sayand that thai held nocht of him nor wald nocht hald with him with mony uther sclanderous wordis calland tham traitors that war his secret counsall and than this parliament was continewit for xv dayis and chargit all maner of man till be at Edinburgh baith on fut and hors Ilk man for him self baith in burgh and land under the pane of ded and tinsall of thair landis.

The quhilk day thai apperit all and semblit at pentland Mure and war noumerit xxxm and the king him self passit on southwart with the ost to peblis, selkrig, drumfres and uther sundry partis and did na gud bot distroyit the cuntre richt fellonly baith of cornes medowis and wittalis and heriit mony bath gentillmen and utheris that war with him self.

Item thair was maid in the forsaid parliament three erllis viz Sir James Crichton son and heir to Sir William Crichton that spousit the eldest sister of Moray was beltit erll of Moray

Item the lord Hay and constable of Scotland was beltit erll of Erroll.

Item Sir George of Crichton was beltit erll

f. 116r

of Caithness. Item thair was maid vi or vii lordis of the parliament and banrentis In the first the lord dernlie, The lord halis, the lord boyd of Kilmarnok, the lord Fleming of Cummyrnald, the lord Borthwick of that Ilk, The lord Lyle of dowchale, the lord of Cathcart of that Ilk.

Item the lord of Lorne John Stewart talzeit all his landis to the male and surname in the said parliament.

Item the lord of Cathcart deit in the samyn tyme.

Item Sir George of Crichton annext all his landis to the erldome of Caithness that samyn tyme.

Item thair was sundry landis gevin to sundry men in this parliament by the kingis secret counsall that is to say the lord cambell to Sir Colin Cambell to Sir Alexander Home to Sir David Home to Sir James Keyre and till uther sundry war rewardit be the said secret counsall the quhilk men demyt wald nocht stand.

The zere of god 1455 In the begynnyng of merche, James the secund kest doune the castell of Inverawyne and syne Incontinent past till glasgw and gaderit the westland men with part of the ereschery and passit to lanerik and to douglas and syne brynt all douglasdale and all awendale and all the lord hamiltouns landis and heriit thaim clerlye and syne passit till Edinburgh and fra thin till the forest with ane ost of lawland men and all that wald nocht cum till him furthwith he tuke thair gudis and brynt thair placis and tuke faith of all the gentillis clerlie and all this tyme

f. 116v

the lord hammiltoun was in England till have gottyn suple and couth get nane bot gif the douglas and he wald have bene Inglis men and maid the aith and Incontinent efter the king passit in proper persoun and put ane sege till abercorn and within vii days lord hammiltoun come till him till abercorne and put him lyf landis and gudis in the kingis will purelie and sempillye throw the menys of his Eme James of Livingston that tyme chalmerlane of Scotland and the king Resavit him till grace and send him on Incontinent with the erll of Orkney that tyme chancellor of Scotland till remane in warde In the castell of Roslyne at the kingis will and thus he left the erll of Douglas all begylit as men said and men wist nocht grathlie quhar the Douglas was all this tyme the king remanit still at the sege and thair was mony hurt and nane slane till sanct Georgis daye outtane Allan Pantour that was that tyme the mast Ingenious man that was in Scotland and mast subtell in mony divers thingis and was slane with ane ganze throu misgovernyng of himself and was richt mekle menyt be the king and mony uther lordis. Thus the king remanit still at the sege and gart strek mony of the towris doun wit the gret gun the quhilk a franche man schot richt wele and falzeit na schot within a faldome quhar it was chargit him to hit and

f. 117r

The king gadderit ane gret ost and past In England and did gret scaith and wan mony towris and houses

Item the 12th day of May, James the brother of erll William of Douglas that was slane in the castell of Stirling come to Knapdale and spak thar with the erll of Ross and lord of Ilis and maid thaim all richt gret rewardis of wyne, clathis, silver, silk and English cloth and thai gaf thaim mantillis agane and quhat was thar amangis thaim wes counsall to commounis and thai demyt Ill all

Item that samyn moneth and zere Sir George of Crichton resignit all his conquest landis in the kingis handis and maid him his aire and within vi days James of Crichton, sone and aire to the said George of Crichton tuke the castell of blakness and his fader in contrar of the king and Incontinent the king in proper persoun put ane sege to the blakness and lay at It ix or x dayis and than It was gevin oure be trety and Sir George was put to Methven and gaf him the landis of Strathurd for the landis that he had conquest in Lothian.

The hereschipe of Inverkip be Donald of the Isles viz. Balloch with the powere of the Isles with him and thai said John of Douglas ane bastard son till archebald erll of Douglas was with thaim thai war vxx of galays wele told and ma and of men v or vi thousand. This hereschipe was done the said zeire

f. 117v

The x day of July and thair was slane of gud men xv and of wyfis twa or thre and of barnis thre or foure and of hors v or vic and of oxin and ky xm and ma and of schepe and gait a thousand and ma and thai brynt that tyme certane townis In Inverkip viz. about the kirk. Item this said Donald with his ost of the Isles heriit all Arran and wan the castell of Brodick and kest it down to the erd and heriit baith the Ilis of Cerayes the samyn tyme. Item thair tuke crauchmet of Bute the samyn tyme viz. 1c bollis of male 1c bollis of malt 1c martis 1c merkis of silver

Ane thousand iiiic lii the 29th day of August thair was cummand to the cathedral kirk master George of Lauder that tyme bishop of Ergyle fra his castall of Auchindoun efter that he had bene in the Isle of Lesmore that tyme 30 dayis and maire and thair was in his company that samyn tyme Master Hercules Scrimegeour persoun of Glassar Sir John McArthur and Sir Adam his parish priest and Alexander Scrimegeour the personis brother and the lordis awne servandis of houshald and nane utheris for the lord come for gud trety and trastit nain evil. This person forsaid brocht ane summondis apon Sir Gilbert McLathane that tyme chancellor of the forsaid cathedrall kirk and apon Sir Morris McFadzane that tyme treasurer of the said kirk. The quhilk Sir Gilbert and Sir Morris gadderit all hale the clan lathane and all utheris that thai mycht

f. 118r

purches and send to thir men word that the forsaid bishop come with the forsaid clerk and put thaim out of thar benefice and to put In the forsaid master Hercules and thus thai Informit the people wranguisly and begylit thaim for the person had no thing bot a summondis apon Sir Gilbert and apon Sir Morris McFadzane for a sentence diffinitive That thai gaf aganis him of his benefice that he had loysit peceably xv zere with Sir Gotheray McForsan becaus that this summondis was apon his chennonis the lord passit in proper person till haf maid gud tretye. And als fast as this lord with thir persons forsaid come nere the kirk within the quarter of ane myle The forsaid Sir Gilbert and Sir Morris come with all the power that thai mycht be in fere of were apon the forsaid lord the bishop and his company and spak till him self richt dispituoslie with felloun wordis and scorne and for dispyte halsit him in errische sayand bannachadee and dispytfully reft fra him the forsaid master hercules and pullit him fra his hors and brak the lordis belt and tuke the clerke and his brother and harllit and led thaim away rycht dispytfully and band the gentill man and thocht to strik of his hed and quhen this foull surpris was done till god and haly kirk than the lord wald have past on his fute till his kirk thai stert befor him sayand that and he schupe to gang thair away that thai suld sla him and alll that war with him and thai war all about him and wald nocht let him pass ony gait till he was oblist till assolze thaim of all

f. 118v

thing that was done thare and for dreid of his lyf and his mennis he grantit throw consall of rure alanson and utheris that war with him and than thai come with a flyrdome and said that thai come for na Ill of him ne his childer and thai held the clerk and his brother and on the morne gart thaim swere that thai suld never follow him nother of summondis nor of uther thing that was done to thaim be thaim self na na utheris bot held thair bullis and thair silver and a silkyn twys and all uther graith that thai had that was oucht worth viz. gownis, clokis, hudis, bannettis and uthir small geire.

The zere of god 1451 In the month of March the erll of Ross and lord of the Isles tuke thir castellis of the king viz. Inverness, our'cuart and rothwane in Badenoch and stuffit the castell of Inverness and Urquhart and kest downe the castell of Ruthven in Badenoch and thai said that he gaf the keping of the castell of Urquhart till his gud fader James of Livingston that was eschapit subtelly fra the king and his counsall out of the abbay of halyrudhous and was cummand to the lord for supple and succour that resavit him richt thankfully and tuke plane part agane the king for him and said he had the kingis writ and walx to have the castell of Urquhart for iii yeres and he said that the kingis awne person gart him marry the said James' douchter and hecht him gud lordschipe the quhilk

f. 119r

biggit ane gret porcioun of the steple and ane staitlie zethous and brocht hame mony gud Iowellis and clathis of gold silver and silk and mony gud bukis and maid staitlie stallis and glasynnit mekle of all the kirk and brocht hame the staitliest tabernacle that was in all Scotland and the maist costlie. And schortlie he brocht all the place to fredome and fra nocht till ane mychti place and left It out of all kynd of det and at all fredome till dispone as thaim lykit and left ane of the best myteris that was in Scotland and chandillaris of silver and ane lettren of brass with mony uther gud Iowellis

Item the 16th day of August king James the second maid his first wayage in England with vic thousand men and brynt and heriit xx mylis within the land and wan and distroyit xvii towris and fortaliceis and remanit on the ground of England vi days and vi nychtis and thair persewit thaim never Englishman with Ill nother be day nor nycht and come hame with gret worschip and tynt nocht a man of valour.

Item Incontinent the Englishmen war gadderit wele till iiii or vc thousand and come to the marche and thair discordit and passit hame with ane gret vellany viz. the Duke of York, the erll of Salisbury with mony uther sundry gret lordis of the land

The zere of god 1460 the thrid sonday of August king James the secund with ane gret ost was

f. 119v

At the sege of Roxburgh and unhappely was slane with ane gun the quhilk brak in the fyring for the quhilk was gret dolour throu all Scotland and nevertheless all the lordis that war thar remanit still with the ost and on the fryday efter richt wysly and manfully wan the forsaid castell and tynt nocht a man may in the wynning of it.
And than the lordis Incontinent send till Edinburgh for the Prince and the said Prince with his modere the quene and bischopis and uther nobillis come to Kelso on the fryday efter the deid of the king and remanit thar quhill he was crownit and quhill the forsaid lordis passit to the castell of werk and sone thai wan that castell and Incontinent kest it doune to the erd and distroyit it for ever. Item in the tyme of the coronacoun of the king thair was maid ma than a hundreth knychtis.
Item in the monetn of January in the zere forsaid the prince of England and the Queen of England come in Scotland to get help and supple aganis the Duke of York and thai come to Drumfres and the Queen of Scotland, the Duke of gillerlandis dochter met

the forsaid prince and his modere at kyncloudane and thai remanit thair togidder x or xii days and thai said that thai war accordit on baith the sydis and in the meyne tyme

f. 120r

The duke of York and the erll of Salisbury and the Duke's son war slane with uther divers lordis of thair company

The zere of god 1460 the erll of ergyle Colin Campbell passit in Lorne for the redempcoun of his cousin John Keir of Lorne The quhilk was tane be his brother Allane of Lorne of the wod, sister son to downe balloch. And schortlie this erll forsaid with his ost come to the Isle of Kerewra quhar this Allan had his brother in fessynans and his entent was to distroye him that he mycht have succedit to the heretage. And schortlie thai come sa suddanlie apon the forsaid Allan in the said Isle that he mycht nocht pass away with his schippis in the quhilkis war a hundreth men and this said John Keir was bound and his men was slane to the noumer of iiii or vxx and brynt thair schippis and Redemit his cosing and restorit him to his lordship and the tother chapit richt narowly with his lyf and iiii or v personis and this was the first slauchter efter the deid of king James the secund.

The samyn zere the 23rd day of Februar king James III held his first parliament at Edinburgh to the quhilk parliament come thir lordis under-writtin That is to say the lord of the Isles and erll of Ross and all the lardis of the Ilis lord dernlie and the lord Kalendare The lord Hamilton and thai did litill gud in the forsaid parliament Bot that thai ordanit sessionis to sit first at Aberdeen syne in

f. 120v

perth syne in Edinburgh and thai left the King in keping with his modere the queen and governing of all the kinrik. And thairfor the lordis said that thai war littill gud worth bath spirituale and temporall That gaf the keping of the kinrik till a woman and Incontinent the Queen eftir this parliament put in new keparis in the castellis of Edinburgh, Stirling and Dunbar viz. in Edinburgh Androw keyre In Dunbar lord Hailes In Blackness and Stirling Robert Liddale.

Item the said Queen eftir the deid of king James the secund tuke master James Lindesay for principal counsellor and gart him kepe the preve sele notwithstanding that the said master James was excludit fra the counsall of the forsaid king and fra the court and for his werray helynes and had been slane for his demeritis had nocht bene he was redemit with gold.

Item eftir the deid of the forsaid king the lord of the Isles past till Inverness and tuke the kingis fermes and all wittalis of the kingis and proclamit all the gudis and the landis of the kingis in till his handis and gaf remissions and respittis and for thir caus he was summond to the parliament under the pane of forfalt And comperit nocht and than thai supersedit his caus quhill the feist of sanct John the Baptist and continewit the forsaid parliament till that day to be haldin in Aberdeen
Item the lord of curthous come till Edinburgh till

f. 121r

of the law and the kingis proffettis and of all the Realme and that the king suld come be him selfe and his and the Queen be hir self and hirris bot the king suld ay remane with the Queen Bot scho suld nocht Intromet with his proffettis bot allanerlie with his person.

The zere of god 1420 [1424] Archibald erll of Douglas and the duke of turane decessit in France and In the samyn tyme and place decessit John Stewart, erll of Buchan and constable of France James of Douglas son to the said erll sir walter of bekirtoune Sir William of Setoun sir richert of bekirtoun Schir henry bekirtoun governour to the scottis archeris and alexander bekirtoun with mony utheris gud knychtis and sqwyeris Item that samyn zere Robert stewart decessit in the castell of Striuling and lyis in dunfermling Item duke murthok decessit at strivling walter stewart erll of levinnox and sir alexander stewart.

Item 1436 the fals erll of athole his son and Robert stewart war put to ded at Edinburgh for tresoun Item the erll of mar Alexander stewart decessit Item 1438 archebald erll of douglas and sister son to king James the first deit at lestalrig Item 1440 Erll willam of douglas archebaldis son beand than 18 zeris of age and his brother david

f. 121v

douglas was put to deid at Edinburgh and malcome flemyng of beggar was put to deid in that samyn place within thre days efter

The zere of god 1449 Sir James auchinlek was slane be richert coluile the 20th day of aprile and within v or vi days cowartlie gaf our the castell and was hedit and iii sum with him and Incontinent efter that he come furth the castell was castin doun be erll william of douglas James son

That samyn zere in the moneth of may sir James stewart the qwenes knycht was tane apon the se be the flemyngis befor the son and thair was put to deid and of thaim that come with him viiixx of ynglismen

That samyn zere the 18th day of Junii qwene mary of Scotland come in Scotland and this qwene was the duke of gillerlandis douchter and sister douchter to the duke of burgone. Thar come with hir xiii gret schippis and ane craike In the quhilk thair was the lord of causere with xvxx of men in harness Master Jhon ralstoun bischope of dunkelden and sir willam of crechtoun chancellere of scotland That tyme was the hame bringaris of the qwene with the counsall of the king of fraunce The duke of sawoy The duke of ostrich the duke of bertane the duke of burgunze and all thire war bundyn In suple and manteinans of king James of scotland and this king forsaid and this qwene war mariit at Edinburgh the thrid day of Julii The zere forsaid

f. 122r

Item in that samyn zere master willam turnbull said his first mass in glasqw the xx day
of september James of Levingstoun was arrestit be the king and Robyn kalendar
capitane of Dunbertane and Jhon of levingstoun capitane of the castell of doun and
David levingstoun of the grene zardis with syndry utheris and sone eftir this sir
alexander levingstoun was arrestit and robyn of levingstoun of lichqw that time
comptroller and James and his brother alexander and Robyne of lithqw war put in the
blakness and thair gudis tane within xl days in all placis and put under arrest and all
thair gudis that pertenit to that party and all officeris that war put in be thaim war
clerlie put out of all officis and all put doun that thai put up and this was a gret ferlie
and in that samyn tyme the forsaid James dochter that was spousit with the lord of the
Isles come till him sodanlie with few personis with hir and thai met in dumbertane sir
duncan persone and led hir with him to kyntyre the xxiii day of the said moneth and it
is to wit that the first arresting was maid at the brig of Inchebelle on kylwyne betuix
glasqw and kirkyntulloch.

That samyn zere the xix day of Januare James the thrid [should be James II] held his
first parliament at Edinburgh In to the quhilk parliament thar was forfaltit Schir
alexander levinstoun lord kalendar and James dundas of that Ilk and Robert brus the
lard of clackman

f. 122v

nannis brother And James of levingstoun sone and air to the said alexander was put to
deid and Robyne of levingstoun of lithqw that tyme comptroller was put to deid baith
togidder on the castellhill thair heidis strikin of
The thrid day of the parliament and that samyn tyme archebald of Dundas brother to
the said James of Dundas stuffit the towre of dundas and said he suld de and It baith
attanis bot gif the king did thaim grace and at the dissolvyne of the said parliament the
king baith send and come him self and askit the said hous and gat it nocht as than and
Incontinent laide ane sege about It that remanit quhill the latter end of aprile and than
It was gevin oure and all that war in It war put in the kingis grace and thai war tane
and sum send till a castell and sum till utheris and the hous was cassyn doune and the
stuf thairof partit betuix the king and the erll of douglas Schir willam of crechtoun and
sir george of crechtoun.

The zere of god 1450 the 19th day of maii qwene mary partit with barne in strivling xii
oulkis befor hir tyme and the barne liffit bot the space of sex houris

Item the said zeire in the moneth of Junii Thar was funding in dunfermling a
merwalous deid cors In the ryping of ane wall for first thair was found

f. 123r

About him a kist of stane and syne ane of tre and syne a cape of leid and syne clathis
of gold and silk als fresche as evir thai ware and the cors hale in hyde and hewe as It
semyte bot of xviii zeris of age and it was xixx zeris sen that wall was maide and men
demyt that It was a barne or cosing of sanct margaretis

The zere of god 1449 The birnyng of Dunbar be young persie and sir robert ogile In the moneth of maii and that samyn zere drumfres was brynt be the erll of Salisbery in the moneth of Junii And that samyn zere erll willam of douglas James son and with him the erll of orknay angus and ormond brynt awnwik in the moneth of Junii the thrid day and come hame wele and did gret scaithe

Item the said erll passit In yngland the xviii day of Julii with xim men and did gret scaith and brynt werkworth And in the hamecummyng tynt iic fut men that war tane and nocht ten men slane bot the lard of glendowyne and the scottis men tuk agane colyne wod for him and ilkane of thire mennis sonnis tuke utheris faderis

   The battel of ~~arbroth~~ brechyne
Item about that samyn tyme the xviii day of maii Thar met and faucht in the feld on the mure besyd brechyne The erll of craufurd callit allexander The

f. 123v

erll of huntlie callit alexander and thair was with the erll of huntlie fer ma than was with the erll of craufurd becaus he displayit the kingis banere and said it was the kingis actioun and he was his luftennend and schortlie the erll of craufurdis brother callit Jhon lyndesay of brechyne and the lard of dundas and uther syndry gentill men wele till iiixx of cotarmouris on that syd and on that uther syd willam of setoun the erllis brother and uthir thre or four of gentill men and v or sex of zemen and the erll of huntlie held the feld and raid in angus with thre or foure thousand with him and the erll of craufurd

Bibliography

A. *Primary MS. Sources*
   Edinburgh
   National Library of Scotland
   Acc. 4233 (Asloan MS. — 'The Auchinleck Chronicle')
   Acc. 5976, Box 6, nos. 10, 11, 13, 14.
   Acc. 6026, Box 4, nos. 15, 16.
   Adv. MS. B 1316/1317.
          34.7.3 (Gray MS.).

Scottish Record Office

Falkland Burgh Records
Inverkeithing Burgh Records.
St Andrews Burgh Records.
Calendar of Charters.
Miscellaneous Accessions.
Cardross Writs.
Crawford Priory Collection.
Ailsa Muniments.
Leven and Melville Muniments.
Dalguise Muniments.
Dalhousie Muniments.
Ross Estate Muniments.
Rossie Priory Muniments.
Lord Forbes Collection.
Gordon Castle Muniments.
Bell-Brander Muniments.
Makgill Charters.
Duntreath Muniments.
Wigtown Charters.
Pitcaple Charters.
Bargany Muniments.
Robertson of Lude.
Morton Papers.
Scott of Harden.
Drummond Castle Muniments.
Henderson of Fordell.
Haldane of Gleneagles.
Ogilvy of Inverquharity MSS.
Dundas and Wilson, C.S., Collection.

Home of Wedderburn.
Comrie Writs.
J. and F. Anderson Collection.
Transcripts.
Register House Charters.
Repertory of State Papers.

West Register House

National Register of Archives (Scotland).
Arbuthnott Writs, Roxburgh, Borthwick, Hopetoun, Irvine of Drum, Stirling of Glorat, Blairs College, Glamis.

Edinburgh University Library

MS Dc.7.63. (Law, 'de Cronicis Scotorum Brevia').

London
British Library

Harleian MSS. 4620, 4134, 4628, 712.
Additional MS. 8878.
Royal MS. 18 B, vi.

Stuttgart
Württembergische Landesbibliothek

Cod. his. 4° 141. (Das Tagesbuch von Georg von Ehingen).

The Vatican

Registra Supplicationum (Vat. Reg. Supp.).
[Microfilms of supplications relating to Scotland, many of them calendared, are now stored in the Dept. of Scottish History, Glasgow University].

B. *Primary Printed Sources and Works of Reference*

Collections for a History of the Shires of Aberdeen and Banff [*A.B. Coll.*], (Spalding Club, 1843).
Illustrations of the Topography and Antiquities of the Shires of Aberdeen and Banff [*A.B. Ill.*], (Spalding Club, 1847–69).
Charters and other Writs illustrating the History of the Royal Burgh of Aberdeen [*Abdn. Chrs.*], ed. P. J. Anderson (Aberdeen, 1890).
Extracts from the Council Register of the Burgh of Aberdeen [*Abdn. Counc.*], (Spalding Club, 1844–48).
Registrum Episcopatus Aberdonensis [*Abdn. Reg.*], (New Spalding Club, 1888–92).
Acts of the Lords of the Isles, 1336–1493, edd. Jean Munro and R. W. Munro (S.H.S., Edinburgh, 1986).
Acts of the Parliaments of Scotland [*A.P.S.*], edd. T. Thomson and C. Innes (Edinburgh, 1814–75), vol. ii (1424–1567).
The Asloan Manuscript, vol. i, ed. W. A. Craigie (S.T.S., Edinburgh, 1923).

Official Correspondence of Thomas Bekynton [*Bekynton Corr.*], ed. G. Williams (Rolls Series, 1872), ii.

Boece, Hector: *Hectoris Boetii Murthlacensium et Aberdonensium Episcoporum Vitae*, ed. J. Moir (New Spalding Club, Aberdeen, 1894).

Boece, Hector, *The History and Chronicles of Scotland*, trans. John Bellenden (STS, 1938–41).

Registrum Episcopatus Brechinensis [*Brechin Reg.*] (Bannatyne Club, 1856).

Buchanan, George, *The History of Scotland*, trans. J. Aikman (Glasgow and Edinburgh, 1827–9).

Calendar of Documents relating to Scotland, vol. iv (1357–1509), ed. J. Bain (Edinburgh, 1888).

Calendar of Entries in the Papal Registers relating to Great Britain and Ireland: Papal Letters, Petitions to the Pope, edd. W. H. Bliss et al. (London, 1896).

Calendar of State Papers existing in the Archives and Collection of Milan, i, ed. A. B. Hinds (London, 1912).

The Book of the Thanes of Cawdor [*Cawdor Book*] (Spalding Club, 1859).

Chalmers of Ormond, D., *Ane Cronikill of the Kingis of Scotland* (Maitland Club, 1830).

The Correspondence, Inventories, Account Rolls and Law Proceedings of the Priory of Coldingham [*Cold. Corr.*], ed. J. Raine (Surtees Society, London, 1841).

Crawfurd, G., *The Lives and Characters of the Officers of the Crown and of the State in Scotland* (Edinburgh, 1726).

Drummond, William, of Hawthornden, *History of Scotland from the year 1423 until the year 1542* (London, 1655).

Royal Letters and other Historical Documents selected from the Family Papers of Dundas of Dundas [*Dundas Papers*], ed. W. Macleod (Edinburgh, 1897).

Charters, Writs and Public Documents of the Royal Burgh of Dundee [*Dundee Chrs.*], ed. W. Hay (Dundee, 1880).

Registrum de Dunfermelyn [*Dunf. Reg.*] (Bannatyne Club, 1842).

Charters and Other Documents relating to the City of Edinburgh [*Edin. Chrs.*] (SBRS, 1871).

The Exchequer Rolls of Scotland [*E.R.*], ed. J. Stuart and others (Edinburgh, 1878–1908).

Extracta e Variis Cronicis Scocie [*Extracta*] (Abbotsford Club, 1842).

Fasti Ecclesiae Scoticanae Medii Aevi ad annum 1638, ed. D. E. R. Watt (St Andrews, 1969).

Ferreri, Giovanni, *Appendix to Hector Boece's Scotorum Historiae*, second edn. (Paris, 1574).

Foedera, Conventiones, Litterae et Cuiuscunque Generis Acta Publica [*Foedera*], ed. T. Rymer (Record Commission, London, 1816–69).

Fraser, William, *The Annandale Family Book* (Edinburgh, 1894).

Fraser, W., *The Scotts of Buccleuch* (Edinburgh, 1878).

Fraser, W., *The Book of Carlaverock* (Edinburgh, 1873).

Fraser, W., *The Chiefs of Colquhoun and their Country* (Edinburgh, 1869).

Fraser, W., *The Douglas Books* (Edinburgh, 1885).

Fraser, W., *Memorials of the Montgomeries, Earls of Eglinton* (Edinburgh, 1859).

Fraser, W., *The Red Book of Grandtully* (Edinburgh, 1868).

Fraser, W., *The Stirlings of Keir* (Edinburgh, 1858).

Fraser, W., *The Melvilles Earls of Melville and the Leslies Earls of Leven* (Edinburgh, 1890).

Fraser, W., *Memoirs of the Maxwells of Pollok* (Edinburgh, 1863).

Fraser, W., *The Sutherland Book* (Edinburgh, 1892).

Fraser, W., *Memorials of the Family of Wemyss of Wemyss* (Edinburgh, 1888).

Registrum Episcopatus Glasguensis [Glasgow Registrum] (Bannatyne and Maitland Clubs, 1843).

Godscroft, David Hume of, *The History of the Houses of Douglas and Angus* (Edinburgh, 1644).

Handbook of British Chronology [H.B.C.], edd. F. M. Powicke and E. B. Fryde (London, 1961).

Highland Papers, ed. J. R. N. Macphail (S.H.S., Edinburgh, 1914–1934).

Historical Manuscripts Commission: Reports of the Royal Commission on Historical Manuscripts [H.M.C.] (London, 1870–).

Hume Brown, P. (ed.), *Early Travellers in Scotland* (Edinburgh, 1891).

Innes, T., *A Critical Essay on the Ancient Inhabitants of the Northern Parts of Britain or Scotland* (Edinburgh, 1879).

Laing Charters: Calendar of the Laing Charters 854–1837, ed. J. Anderson (Edinburgh, 1899).

Lesley, John, *The History of Scotland from the Death of King James I in the Year 1436 to the year 1561* (Bannatyne Club, 1830).

Liber Pluscardensis, ed. F. J. H. Skene (Edinburgh, 1877–80).

Liber Sancte Marie de Lundoris [Lindores Liber] (Abbotsford Club, 1841).

Liber Sancte Marie de Melros [Melrose Liber] (Bannatyne Club, 1837).

Lindsay, Robert of Pitscottie, *The Historie and Cronicles of Scotland* (S.T.S., Edinburgh, 1899).

Major, J., *A History of Greater Britain* (S.H.S., 1892).

Moray Registrum: Registrum Episcopatus Moraviensis (Bannatyne Club, 1837).

Myln, Alexander, *Vitae Dunkeldensis Ecclesiae Episcoporum* (Bannatyne Club, 1831).

Nicolas, H., *Proceedings and Ordinances of the Privy Council of England* (Record Commission, 1837).

Paisley Registrum: Registrum Monasterii de Passelet (Maitland Club, 1832).

Pell Records: From the Original Rolls of the Ancient Pell Office, 1835–37.

Pitcairn, Robert (ed.), *Criminal Trials in Scotland from 1488 to 1624*, vol. i (Edinburgh, 1833).

Proceedings of the Society of Antiquaries of Scotland [P.S.A.S.] (1851–).

Raine, J., *The History and Antiquities of North Durham [N.D.]* (London, 1852).

Registrum Magni Sigilli Regum Scotorum [R.M.S.], ii (1424–1513), ed. J. B. Paul (Edinburgh, 1882).

Rotuli Scotiae in Turri Londinensi et in Domo Capitulari Westmonasteriensi asservati [Rot. Scot.], ii (1399–1516), eds. D. Macpherson et al. (London, 1819).

Scotichronicon, by Walter Bower: vol. 8 (books xv and xvi), ed. D. E. R. Watt (Aberdeen, 1987).

The Scots Peerage, ed. Sir J. Balfour Paul (Edinburgh, 1904–14).

Smit, H. J., *Bronnen Tot de Geschiedenis van den Handel met Ingeland, Schotland en Ierland* (1928), i.

Spalding Miscellany: Miscellany of the Spalding Club (Spalding Club, Aberdeen, 1841–52).

Stevenson, J., *Letters and Papers Illustrative of the Wars of the English in France* (London, 1861).

Stirling Charters: Charters and other Documents relating to the Royal Burgh of Stirling, ed. R. Renwick (Glasgow, 1884).

Treasurer's Accounts: Accounts of the Lord High Treasurer of Scotland [*T.A.*], i, edd. T. Dickson and J. B. Paul (Edinburgh, 1877–1902).

Wigtown Charter Chest: Charter Chest of the Earldom of Wigtown (S.R.S., 1910).

Wigtownshire Charters, ed. R. C. Reid (S.H.S., 1960).

Yester Writs: Calendar of Writs preserved at Yester House 1166–1503, edd. C. C. H. Harvey and J. Macleod (S.R.S., 1930).

C.   *Secondary Sources*

Agnew, Sir A., *The Hereditary Sheriffs of Galloway*, 2nd edition (1893).

Balfour, Sir James of Kinnaird, *Annales of Scotland in Historical Works*, ed. J. Haig (London, 1824–5).

Barbe, L. A., *Margaret of Scotland and the Dauphin Louis* (1917).

Brown, Jennifer M. (ed.), *Scottish Society in the Fifteenth Century* (London, 1977).

Caldwell, David H. (ed.), *Scottish Weapons and Fortifications 1100–1800* (Edinburgh, 1981).

Chrimes, S. B., *Henry VII* (London, 1977).

Cruden, S., *The Scottish Castle* (Edinburgh, 1981).

D'Escouchy, *Cronique: Cronique de Mathieu d'Escouchy*, ed. G. du Fresne de Beaucourt (Paris, 1864–4).

Davidson, J. and Gray, A., *The Scottish Staple at Veere* (1909).

Donaldson, G., *Scottish Kings* (London, 1967).

Duncan, A. A. M., *James I 1424–1437* (University of Glasgow Department of Scottish History Occasional Papers, 1984).

Dunlop, Annie I., *The Life and Times of James Kennedy, Bishop of St. Andrews* (Edinburgh, 1950).

Grant, Alexander, *Independence and Nationhood: Scotland 1306–1469* (London, 1984).

Letts, M., *The Diary of Jörg von Ehingen* (London, 1929).

Lord Lindsay, *Lives of the Lindsays* (London, 1849), i.

Livingston, E. B., *The Livingstons of Callendar and their Principal Cadets* (Edinburgh, 1920).

Macdougall, Norman, *James III: A Political Study* (Edinburgh, 1982).

Macdougall, Norman, *Church, Politics and Society: Scotland 1408–1929* (Edinburgh, 1983).

Nicholson, Ranald, *Scotland: The Later Middle Ages* (Edinburgh History of Scotland, vol. 2: 1974).

Pinkerton, J., *The History of Scotland from the Accession of the House of Stuart to that of Mary, with Appendices of Original Papers* (London, 1797).

Rait, R. S., *The Parliaments of Scotland* (Glasgow, 1924).

Ramsay, Sir J. H., *Lancaster and York* (Oxford, 1892).
Riis, Thomas, *Should Auld Acquaintance Be Forgot . . . Scottish–Danish relations c. 1450-1707*, i (Odense, 1988).
Scott, Sir Walter, *Tales of a Grandfather* (1827).
Stringer, K. J. (ed.), *Essays on the Nobility of Medieval Scotland* (Edinburgh, 1985).
Villon, *Testament: Le Testament Villon*, edd. J. Rychner and A. Henry (Geneva, 1974), i.
Wormald, Jenny, *Lords and Men in Scotland: Bonds of Manrent 1442-1603* (Edinburgh, 1985).

D. *Articles and Book Chapters*

Baxter, J. H., 'The Marriage of James II', *S.H.R.*, xxv (1928), 69–72.
Brown, A. L., 'The Scottish "Establishment" in the Later Fifteenth Century', *Juridical Review*, xxiii (1978).
Burns, J. H., 'New Light on John Major', *Innes Review*, v (1954), 83–100.
Burns, J. H., 'The Conciliarist Tradition in Scotland', *S.H.R.*, XLII (1963), 89–104.
Caldwell, David H., 'Royal Patronage of Arms and Armour Making in Fifteenth and Sixteenth Century Scotland', in David H. Caldwell (ed.), *Scottish Weapons and Fortifications 1100-1800* (Edinburgh, 1981), 73–93.
Crawford, Barbara E., 'William Sinclair, Earl of Orkney and his Family: A Study in the Politics of Survival', in *Essays on the Nobility of Medieval Scotland*, ed. K. J. Stringer (Edinburgh, 1985), 232–253.
Duncan, A. A. M., 'Councils General, 1404-1423', *S.H.R.*, xxxv (1956), 132–143.
Durkan, John, 'William Turnbull, Bishop of Glasgow', *Innes Review*, ii (1951).
Durkan, John, 'St. Andrews in the John Law Chronicle', *Innes Review*, xxv (1974).
Grant, Alexander, 'Earls and Earldoms in Late Medieval Scotland c. 1310-1460', in *Essays Presented to Michael Roberts*, edd. J. Bossy and P. Jupp (Belfast, 1976).
Grant, Alexander, 'The Development of the Scottish Peerage', *S.H.R.*, lvii (1978), 1–27.
Grant, Alexander, 'The Revolt of the Lord of the Isles and the Death of the Earl of Douglas, 1451-1452', *S.H.R.*, lx (Oct. 1981), 169–174.
Grant, Alexander, 'Extinction of Direct Male Lines among Scottish Noble Families in Fourteenth and Fifteenth Centuries', in *Essays on the Nobility of Medieval Scotland*, ed. K. J. Stringer (Edinburgh, 1985), 210–231.
Lyall, R. J., 'Politics and Poetry in Fifteenth and Sixteenth Century Scotland', *Scottish Literary Journal*, 3(2), 1976, 5–29.
Lyall, R. J., 'The Medieval Scottish Coronation Service: some seventeenth century evidence', *Innes Review*, xxviii (1), 1977, 3–21.
Macdougall, Norman, 'Foreign Relations: England and France', in *Scottish Society in the Fifteenth Century*, ed. J. M. Brown (London, 1977).
Macdougall, Norman, 'Bishop James Kennedy of St. Andrews: a reassessment of his political career', in *Church, Politics and Society*, ed. N. Macdougall (Edinburgh, 1983), 1–22.
Mason, Roger, 'Scotching the Brut', *History Today*, 35.
Mason, Roger, 'Kingship, Tyranny and the Right to Resist in Fifteenth Century Scotland', *S.H.R.*, lxvi (2), 1987, 125–151.

Moore, A. W., 'The Connexion Between Scotland and Man', *S.H.R.*, iii (1905–6), 404–406.

Murray, A. L., 'The Comptroller, 1425–1488', *S.H.R.*, lii (1973), 1–29.

Rae, T. I., 'The Historical Writing of Drummond of Hawthornden', *S.H.R.*, liv (1975), 22–62.

Stevenson, R. B. K., 'The Return of Mons Meg from London, 1828–1829' in D. H. Caldwell (ed.), *Scottish Weapons and Fortifications 1100–1800* (Edinburgh, 1981), 419–436.

Stewart, M. M., 'Holland of the Howlat', *Innes Review*, xxiii (1972), 3–15.

Stewart, M. M., 'Holland's "Howlat" and the Fall of the Livingstons', *Innes Review*, xxvi (1975), 67–79.

Wormald, Jenny, 'Bloodfeud, Kindred and Government in Early Modern Scotland', *Past and Present*, no. 87 (May, 1980), 54–97.

Wormald, Jenny, 'Taming the Magnates?', in K. J. Stringer (ed.), *Essays on the Nobility of Medieval Scotland* (Edinburgh, 1985), 270–280.

E.   *Theses*

Borthwick, Alan, 'The Council Under James II: 1437–1460'
   (Ph.D., Edinburgh University, 1989).

Cardew, Anne, 'A Study of Society on the Anglo-Scottish Border, 1455–1502'
   (Ph.D., St Andrews University, 1973).

Chalmers, Trevor M., 'The King's Council, Patronage, and the Governance of Scotland, 1460–1513'
   (Ph.D., Aberdeen University, 1982).

Crawford, Barbara E., 'The Earls of Orkney-Caithness and their Relations with Norway and Scotland: 1158–1470'
   (Ph.D., St Andrews University, 1971).

Kelley, Michael G., 'The Douglas Earls of Angus: A Study in the Social and Political Bases of Power of a Scottish Family from 1389 until 1557'
   (Ph.D., Edinburgh University, 1973).

McGladdery, Christine A., 'Crown-Magnate Relations in the Reign of James II of Scotland, 1437–1460'
   (Ph.D., St Andrews University, 1987).

Mason, Roger, 'Kingship and Commonweal: Political Thought and Ideology in Reformation Scotland'
   (Ph.D., Edinburgh University, 1983).

O'Brien, Irene, 'The Scottish Parliament in the Fifteenth and Sixteenth Centuries'
   (Ph.D., Glasgow University, 1980).

Stevenson, A. W. K., 'Trade between Scotland and the Low Countries in the Later Middle Ages'
   (Ph.D., Aberdeen University, 1982).

Index